Scriptural Answers
for a Spiritual Life

Scriptural Answers for a Spiritual Life

A Collection of Biblical Lessons for Daily Living

DAVID MUSGRAVE

Foreword by Victor Atkisson

RESOURCE *Publications* • Eugene, Oregon

SCRIPTURAL ANSWERS FOR A SPIRITUAL LIFE
A Collection of Biblical Lessons for Daily Living

Copyright © 2024 David Musgrave. All rights reserved. Except for brief quotations in critical publications or reviews, no part of this book may be reproduced in any manner without prior written permission from the publisher. Write: Permissions, Wipf and Stock Publishers, 199 W. 8th Ave., Suite 3, Eugene, OR 97401.

Resource Publications
An Imprint of Wipf and Stock Publishers
199 W. 8th Ave., Suite 3
Eugene, OR 97401

www.wipfandstock.com

PAPERBACK ISBN: 979-8-3852-2146-2
HARDCOVER ISBN: 979-8-3852-2147-9
EBOOK ISBN: 979-8-3852-2148-6

VERSION NUMBER 102824

Unless otherwise noted, all Old Testament translations are those of the author. Scriptures marked ASV are taken from the American Standard Version (ASV), public domain.

All New Testament translations, unless otherwise noted, are from The ESV® Bible (The Holy Bible, English Standard Version®), © 2001 by Crossway, a publishing ministry of Good News Publishers. Used by permission. All rights reserved.

Scripture quotations marked KJV are taken from the King James Version. Public domain.

Scripture quotations marked RSV are from the Revised Standard Version of the Bible, copyright © 1946, 1952, and 1971 National Council of the Churches of Christ in the United States of America. Used by permission. All rights reserved worldwide.

To my wife, Ann, who has daily supported me in everything, and to my loyal readers, for your daily support and encouragement by reading these lessons

Contents

Foreword by Victor Atkisson | ix
Introduction | xi

January | 1
February | 32
March | 61
April | 92
May | 122
June | 153
July | 183
August | 214
September | 245
October | 275
November | 306
December | 336

Afterword | 367
Index of Scripture | 369

Foreword

HAVE YOU EVER WONDERED why you have read every self-help book available, yet your life has not improved? You've hired a "life coach" and taken every recommended supplement to improve your mental and emotional acuity, yet you're still in the same rut as when you started? You even obeyed the "good news" and became a child of God, and were thrilled at the thought, "As a bonus, I can now pray to God and he will fix all of 'my problems'"! The problems we think we have are often performance-related, cosmetic-related, and results-oriented. Unfortunately, our society has conditioned us to believe that if we are not successful in these endeavors, then our efforts are worthless.

David Musgrave has the gift of communicating in short Christian meditations the message that the world's measure of success does not coincide with God's measure of success. In his first book, *The Answer Is Spiritual*, he demonstrated that the answer to most of our struggles and problems in life is not physical but spiritual. God is more concerned with our spiritual growth and maturation in Christ than our own quest for "self-actualization." This second book follows in the same godly outlook on life, with the added emphasis on God's word as that which provides the answers to all of the Christian's problems. Perhaps Jesus said it best in the parable of the rich man and Lazarus (Luke 16:19–31) when the rich man, in torment, asked Abraham to send the deceased Lazarus to his five living brothers to warn them to avoid his fate.

Luke 16:29–31: "But Abraham said, 'They have Moses and the Prophets; let them hear them.' And he said, 'No, father Abraham, but if someone goes to them from the dead, they will repent.' He said to him, 'If they do not hear Moses and the Prophets, neither will they be convinced if someone should rise from the dead.'"

Foreword

I have known the author for almost five years. In this brief span of time, I have been greatly blessed by his extensive knowledge of the Scriptures (including the original languages in which they were written), as well as his magnanimous, humble, and gracious spirit. In this volume of daily devotionals, the author combines his knowledge of the Bible and its languages with a heart of spiritual wisdom, acquired over a lifetime, to present deep and impactful messages in small packages, which will also encourage the reader to return again and again to be encouraged by these spiritual words.

This book picks up, in a sense, where the previous one left off, with the theme that life's problems are not answered by physical means, but by a heart that is fully resigned to the will of God. Such a heart will find the most joy by letting go of attempting to "save itself" and solve all of its own problems. Perhaps a quote from one of the included devotionals will help capture the theme of this second book: "While the answer (solution) to many of life's problems is spiritual, the reply that we need from God has already been given; in this sense, the answer is scriptural."

Aside from being a professor of biblical languages for eighteen years, Dr. Musgrave was a minister of the gospel for twenty-six years, and is presently an elder for the Loveland Heights Church of Christ, where he has served since 2010. It is his combined experience in "feeding the flock" where he serves and "looking out" for them spiritually, as well as his extensive knowledge of the Holy Scriptures (and his experience as a husband and father as well), that uniquely qualify him to provide these "spiritual words" which can daily feed God's children. In this way, the apostle Paul would be pleased with his approach, as he wrote of his own ministry: "And we impart this in words not taught by human wisdom but taught by the Spirit, interpreting spiritual truths to those who are spiritual" (1 Cor 2:13).

Victor Atkisson
Pine Hill Church of Christ
Woodland, Alabama

Introduction

LIFE IS COMPLICATED, IN part because life presents problems. When we have a problem, or in our daily lives we are trying to maximize our efforts toward routinely good results, achieving a positive end often involves more than one factor (for example, good health could depend on both diet and exercise). With regard to our spiritual lives, the answer is both spiritual and scriptural. Both concepts of pursuing life spiritually and living one's life according to Scripture go together because of the common element by which they are united, that is, the truth. In my first book, *The Answer Is Spiritual*, I stated: "I personally believe that there are no easy answers to most of life's problems, and there certainly isn't one answer that can solve all of life's problems." This can again be illustrated by the fact that I now have two books entitled *Answer*. As spiritual beings, it is healthy for us to give attention to our spiritual life, just as we would our physical health. We often know how to tend to our physical health by observation (our body sometimes alerts us when something is wrong), by education (sometimes the body does not alert us, and preventive medicine is applied through knowledge), and by guidance (sometimes we need the advice of a healthcare professional). In the same way, we also need to know how to tend to our spiritual life. It seems inconsistent to believe in a God who would make us as spiritual beings who need to tend to our spiritual life, then leave it up to us to figure out how (anymore than a doctor who would do the same to a patient; see Matt 9:12). Logic tells us that there is a source from which we can know how to keep our spiritual life healthy; and that source is the truth, God's word (John 17:17), the Bible.

By "Scripture" I mean the canonical Bible. Many humans all over the world pursue a type of spiritual life, while the different forms of these pursuits are not uniform. Many also study the Bible, some out of a sincere heart, wanting to learn and live according to its message, some for other,

Introduction

less noble reasons (see Phil 1:15). To pursue a spiritual life and to study are good, but only to the extent that they lead one toward truth. This book is intended to provide a similar type of guidance and instruction as *The Answer Is Spiritual*, in that it is hoped that the reader will hereby receive guidance in their pursuit of truth, for the ultimate purpose of bringing them closer to God.

Scriptural Answers for a Spiritual Life is presented with the same format as *The Answer Is Spiritual*, as it is another collection of the lessons I provided for the congregation where I serve as elder and for other readers. The lessons are again referred to as "Dave's Daily," and about every fifth lesson is likely on the general subject of worship (which I wrote each Friday, in preparation for worship on Sunday). Hopefully these lessons will serve the reader in acquiring more knowledge of God's word, for the ultimate purpose of bringing them closer to God. The answer is spiritual because the answer is scriptural.

    David Musgrave
    Milford, Ohio

January 1

"Be Steadfast"

As Christians, we have a need both to hang in, as well as to press on, in life. Evil is a restless and growing force that is pervasive, regardless of how we think about it. If we do nothing, evil will likely find us (1 Pet 5:8). The Christian has a need both to be active, as well as to be strong (Rom 12:21; Eph 6:10). Paul thus said, "Therefore, my beloved brothers, be steadfast, immovable, always abounding in the work of the Lord, knowing that in the Lord your labor is not in vain" (1 Cor 15:58). The first two words Paul uses ("steadfast, immovable") have to do with not giving up, among other things, so that we can be strong against evil. We have to press on no matter how difficult life is. The harvest fields are white for an evangelistic harvest (John 4:35). Whether it be in this specific area, or in life in general, the one thing we can't do is quit. We can be about the work of the Lord by being steadfast and unmovable. Moving forward is accomplished in part by holding our ground.

January 2

"Every Need"

The phrase "every need" in Phil 4:19 is one word in Greek, and is a form of the same word "all things" in v. 13 (see yesterday's "Daily"). Verse 19 reads, "And my God will supply every need of yours according to his riches in glory in Christ Jesus." Knowing that there may be times in life when we seem to not have what we physically need suggests that, during those times, God is perhaps meeting another, that is, a spiritual need. Such a possibility reminds us both that God's got this, and that, to make sense of life, we must often look at it spiritually. God gives us the ability to face life and to overcome it, whether the physical situation meets our preconceived expectations or not. In this verse Paul also uses the word "in," which is the same word in Greek as the word "through" in v. 13. In Christ and through Christ one has not only ability but also has the meeting of their needs, whether or not it matches what we think. Like a child telling their parent they "need" a cookie when the parent knows better, God knows what we need. The answer is spiritual.

January 3

Not My Problem

HAVING PROBLEMS IN LIFE means we will have situations that must be tended to lest they affect our physical lives or such things as our happiness. The English word "problem" comes from the same Greek word meaning "something thrown in front," like an obstacle. Obstacles are things we must physically deal with in order to keep going forward, but they need not be a spiritual obstacle in our mind or soul. The promises of God include that we are not to worry (Phil 4:6), and we don't need to worry (Matt 6:25–34; 1 Pet 5:7), we can jump over distress with the right attitude (2 Cor 12:10), and we can replace the obstacle of fear with faith. Certainly, we must do what we can physically to fix problems in life; but they need not be an obstacle to our spiritual life or our soul. It can be that these things are not our problem.

January 4

"We Know That We Know Him"

SOMETIMES, IN EDUCATION, A teacher can help a student realize that they know something; that is, that the student had certain knowledge or powers of deduction of which they were unaware. We receive an education to acquire knowledge that we can ultimately put to use to make a living or for other productive means, including our spiritual life (John 13:17). While there naturally are many things we can know, and many things we can't (such as the future), the Bible states that Christians can know of such things as God's providence (Rom 8:28), the promise of heaven (2 Cor 5:1) and their salvation (1 John 5:13), because they follow his word: "And hereby we know that we know him, if we keep his commandments" (1 John 2:3 ASV). To "know God" is to be in a right relationship with him (Jer 31:34). Shakespeare[1] wrote, "Knowledge [is] the wing wherewith we fly to heaven." Following God's word is how we can know we have the promise of this ultimate flight.

---

1. Shakespeare, *Henry VI*, Pt. 2, act, 4 sc. 7, line 73.

January 5

"A Good Conscience"

THE CONSCIENCE HAS TO do with knowledge (the English word "conscience" comes from the Latin word meaning "to know") and belief, or the extent to which knowledge affects the heart. The Bible teaches Christians to follow their conscience (Rom 13:5), but the conscience is not the final court of appeal. It is possible for one to violate God's will even though they follow their conscience (Acts 23:1), and the conscience can be hardened to the point that there is no more feeling therein (1 Tim 4:2). The fact that man has a conscience (and, for example, animals do not) is a reflection of man's spiritual nature, and his need to attend thereto. For this reason we teach children (Prov 22:6), we study to acquire knowledge (2 Pet 3:18), and, by accepting the knowledge we gain, we train our conscience to follow that which is right, the knowledge of God's word which formed our conscience.

January 6

"Why Worship?"

THE NONBELIEVER OR SOMEONE struggling in their faith may raise the question of why they should worship. The psalmist(s) many times say they would "bless the Lord": "Bless the LORD, O my soul, and all that is within me; [bless] his holy name" (Ps 103:1). We today are instructed to worship God (see Rev 19:10), and how to worship God. It seems many don't worship, or stop worshiping, because they see no positive results from their efforts (that is, they think they don't get anything out of it). If we remember that worship is first for God, is to be born of love, and that one of the primary characteristics of love is unselfishness (1 Cor 13:5), we may find that we are blessed for blessing God. This can be true because "it is more blessed to give than to receive" (Acts 20:35). That is, we can get something out of worship.

January 7

"With These Words"

COMFORT CAN BE ACQUIRED in many ways, such as simple things like music or food. Having a friend by one's side is often both one of the best ways to gain comfort, as well as a source of comfort one can acquire in no other way. Paul, writing to the Thessalonians regarding the death of their fellow Christians, ended his teaching there by saying "wherefore comfort one another with these words" (1 Thess 4:18). Words (versus such things as numbers) can comfort or harm the soul (Jas 3:5–12). The word of God can comfort the soul as no other words, because the Holy Spirit, who works through the word, is our "Comforter" (John 16:13; 14:26, the Greek word being the same as in 1 Thess 4:18). When we recall God's word, it is as if we are calling for a friend to stand by our side, to help us through difficult times. We can comfort and be comforted (2 Cor 1:3–4) by looking to our Comforter, which we do by using the word of God.

January 8

Why Did You Do That?

THE REALITY OF EVIL in the world is made clear through an understanding of one of the means by which evil is spread, that is, the human heart. While "evil" can come from other places (in the OT, the word "evil" can mean simply things we don't want, such as God's judgments, see Isa 45:7), it also is something man can control in his heart. When evil is understood as the opposite of good, we can see that it is one of only two ways that man can choose. Thus Jesus asked, "Why do you think evil in your hearts?" (Matt 9:4). The Greek word translated "why" can have a meaning of "for what purpose?" We will give account of our actions (2 Cor 5:10), and action is preceded by the thoughts of the heart. Why would we choose the worse of only two ways, the one from which a bad life begins, and which displeases Jesus? If we do he might ask us at judgment day "why did you do that?

January 9

"Increase Our Faith"

THE DISCIPLES TELLING JESUS "increase our faith" (Luke 17:5) surely reflects a commendable desire on their part. Jesus' answer, "If you had faith like a grain of mustard seed, you could say to this mulberry tree, 'Be uprooted and planted in the sea,' and it would obey you" (Luke 17:6). When Jesus states "if you had faith" it seems to imply several things. It may reflect that the apostles didn't have the faith they needed and, if they had just that little, it would be a sizeable force. As it were, they didn't need bigger and better; and the responsibility of obtaining this faith lay with them rather than with Jesus. Faith comes by hearing the word (Rom 10:17), as it is our faith that works in cooperation with God (Col 2:12). Without faith there is no power (Jas 2:24–26); but perhaps even the tiniest seed of one verse can give us the spiritual strength to overcome whatever physical obstacle seems to be in our way. It is, at the very least, a power within us (Eph 3:20), which can accomplish the best.

January 10

"Not Weaken in Faith"

WHEN GOD PROMISED ABRAHAM that he would have a son, Abraham believed him. He did so in spite of there seeming to be no hope since Abraham was old (Rom 4:20). Romans 4:19 reads, "He did not weaken in faith when he considered his own body, which was as good as dead (since he was about a hundred years old), or when he considered the barrenness of Sarah's womb." By embracing faith, which again comes by hearing the word of God (Rom 10:17), one can not only do great things with a very little (see yesterday's "Daily"), but they can also avoid a weakening of their spiritual life. Though our bodies generally become older and weaker, the Christian can have a spiritual strength like Abraham that can help them overcome hopelessness (Rom 4:18), and can even help them become spiritually stronger (2 Cor 4:16). If one adopts faith and holds onto it, it can give him a strength to conquer hopelessness and perhaps other spiritual obstacles. We can't stop the body getting weaker, but we can see to the spirit getting stronger through faith.

January 11

"I Will Bless Your Name"

In Ps 145:2 the psalmist again promised to worship God using three avenues. He stated, "Every day let me bless you, and praise your name forever and ever." He states (see v. 1) that he will "exalt, bless, and praise" God, using the pattern "exalt . . . bless . . . bless . . . praise" (similar to the guy on the train saying "Next stop Memphis, Memphis next stop"). While the psalm goes on to mention the blessings God offers (vv. 14–20), the psalmist only states here what he is going to do. The reasons one comes to worship are between them and God; but if we come with an attitude of it fulfilling us, or with an expectation of our getting something from God in return for our efforts, we may need to reevaluate our heart. The psalmist states what he is going to do, which includes blessing God (here meaning "praise him"). He doesn't mention here that if he does, perhaps God will bless him.

January 12

"Be Not Displeased"

THE SIGHT OF A sunrise can be more pleasing when seen from a height, such as a ladder, versus the ground. God does not see things the way man does (Isa 55:8–9; 1 Sam 16:7). Since man's vision is limited to this world, and is evidently therefore distorted, we are likely to unnecessarily have a perception of events and circumstances that can affect our soul negatively. An example of this seems to be Gen 21:11–12a, which states that "the thing was very displeasing to Abraham because of his son. But God said to Abraham, 'Be not displeased . . .'" Negative things are part of living in this world and they understandably affect us accordingly; the challenge for us is to overcome them by adopting a different perspective so that we may rise above them. To concentrate on spiritual things such as God's providence for his children (Rom 8:28) and things that are above (Col 3:2) can help us to see a better picture, among other things, because we thereby don't see them according to this world. To do so can help us avoid being displeased or, as Jesus told the apostles, to not let our heart be troubled (John 14:1).

January 13

"We Make It Our Aim"

The purpose behind our actions can determine the course of the action, the outcome, and whether the result is satisfying to us. Ambitions naturally have a selfish component; when goals are entirely for selfish interests, however, the fulfillment thereof can be disappointing. Paul said that their ambition was to bring glory to God: "So whether we are at home or away, we make it our aim to please him" (2 Cor 5:9). The word translated "we make it our aim" is a compound word containing the Greek words for "ambition" and "honor." Yet, Paul states that their ambition for honor is not for themselves but for God. There is not necessarily anything wrong with personal ambitions or desires (like Peter desiring to walk on the water to Jesus, Matt 14:28); yet our actions, including goals, are best satisfied when the ultimate purpose centers around glorifying God (Col 3:17) rather than ourselves.

January 14

"But I Thought"

WHILE WE MAY SOMETIMES be displeased with what we hear, which can produce a misperception which needs to be corrected, it is also possible that we may hold a misunderstanding of how God works that doesn't hurt anything. If we do, God surely knows our thoughts, and evidently lets us temporarily believe our misperceptions. When Abraham was told to sacrifice his son of promise (Gen 22:1–8), the NT tells us that he thought God would let him go through with it, then God would raise the child from the dead (Heb 11:19). While this was a misperception on Abraham's part (God evidently never told him what he was going to do), Abraham's misunderstanding didn't hurt anything. This was true because Abraham believed God (Rom 4:3), thereby following through on God's command. There may be times when we ask God for the resolution to a problem but receive something we had not anticipated. Such can be both exciting and faith-building, as it can serve to reinforce that faith means leaving the outcome up to God regardless of what it might be (Matt 26:39); including whether there is a resolution to our problem.

January 15

Getting on Our Knees

FINDING SOMETHING BEGINS WITH getting on our knees. The saying is that if something is lost, it won't find us. Effort is therefore required on our part. Such effort is, for the Christian, an expression of faith, as he or she puts their belief into action (Jas 2:24–26). Although necessary, effort alone may not be the only element to finding something that is lost. For the Christian, searching combined with faith ensures success, in that, whether we find the lost thing or not, it is a spiritual exercise, and can therefore bring us closer to God (Matt 7:7). In other words, searching begins with "getting on our knees" in prayer (whether we are actually on our knees or not); we then search for the thing that is lost (whether we actually get on our knees to look for it or not). To find something that is lost, therefore, requires us "getting on our knees." To do so can ensure that we will find something, whether we find the physical thing we are looking for or not.

January 16

The Grace of Giving

The biblical concept of grace has to do with favor from God that humans do not deserve, even when they are deserving of punishment. Paul called giving a "grace": "beseeching us with much entreaty in regard of this grace and the fellowship in the ministering to the saints" (2 Cor 8:4 ASV; the Greek word translated "grace" appears seven times in 2 Cor 8). There are many aspects of giving that tell us of the spiritual good we derive therefrom as an act of worship. The fact that God doesn't need our money (Ps 50:12), suggests that giving in worship is not for him, but for us, the worshipers. Since it is more blessed to give than to receive (Acts 20:35), God's requiring this action in worship tells us that he is requiring it not for his sake (as if he's being demanding), but because it is good for us (1 John 4:8). To give is to be blessed, because it is a grace, and therefore something we don't deserve.

January 17

Powerless against Truth

TRUTH IS AGAIN, BY definition, something that does not change. In both science and spiritual matters, our understanding of some things change, but that which we attempt to understand, that is, truth, does not. This means, among other things, that truth cannot be stopped. Like a light shining in darkness, it cannot be overcome (John 1:5). Thus Paul said, "For we can do nothing against the truth, but for the truth" (2 Cor 13:8 ASV). The English word "can" can mean several different things, including one's having freedom, permission, ability, desire, etc. The Greek word in this verse translated "can" means to have the ability. While the Christian might (depending on the political situation) have the freedom to speak against the truth, and it is possible to turn one's ears away from truth (2 Tim 4:4), we do not have the power to stop this unstoppable force. God's word is truth (John 17:17), and Jesus' word, as such, will last forever (Matt 24:35). One might ignore, lie against, and fight against the truth to no avail, as it is a power that will remain. We can't change truth, but it can change us (Rom 1:16; 1 Pet 1:22).

January 18

The Path We Choose

IT HAS BEEN SAID that one reason the young should look to the elderly for guidance is because the elderly have walked a path that the young are going to walk. We are all walking a path that leads to some end, though there are only two eternal outcomes (Matt 7:13–14). On the way to the destination, the type of path we choose is up to us, and the outcome in this life is up to God. It is up to us whether to trust God, thereby accepting his promise of a straight path (Prov 3:5–6), whether to walk in wisdom (Col 4:5), and whether to walk worthily of our calling (Eph 4:1). If we choose a good path, it may be that God will give us physical success while walking this earth (Gen 24:21 speaks of the Lord making Isaac's servant's path prosperous). We don't have a choice whether to walk through this life; we do have a choice what type of path we walk. If we choose the right path before God we can then leave the results up to him, including the promise of where the path will end.

January 19

"Increase Thanksgiving"

WE OFTEN FEEL A sense of gratitude for having a need filled or problem resolved (Luke 17:11–19). Not that this is wrong; yet the Bible encourages us to give thanks for all things (1 Thess 5:18), and for things that we hope to have in the future (Phil 4:6). Paul states that God's grace, in the form of Jesus' death, was extended to many, and this produced an overflow of thanksgiving: "For it is all for your sake, so that as grace extends to more and more people it may increase thanksgiving, to the glory of God" (2 Cor 4:15). God's grace is again defined as mercy when we deserve punishment, and is, therefore, a spiritual blessing (see "Daily" of Jan. 16), rather than a physical abundance that gives us happiness. God's grace can abound not because of sin (Rom 6:1–2), but because of the remedy for sin (2 Cor 4:14), that is, Jesus' death. Whether we have physical abundance (Phil 4:11–12), as Christians, we have reason to be abundantly thankful. Our hearts can therefore overflow with a superabundance of thanksgiving, producing gladness in our heart and glory to God.

January 20

"My Heart Is Established"

As the psalmist contemplated approaching God in worship in Ps 108:1, the first thing he expressed to God was that his heart was right: "My heart is established, Oh God; let me sing, and let me sing praises, indeed [with] my glory." The Hebrew word translated "established" has a meaning of "being properly set." The attitude reflected by the psalmist likewise tells us of our need to have our heart spiritually set right when we approach God in worship today. This, in turn, suggests that it is possible for one's heart not to be properly set when coming to God in worship. The possibilities of what an improperly set heart consists of could include selfishness (1 Cor 11:17–21), a desire to be elsewhere, or having a rift with one's brother in the Lord (Matt 5:23–24). Getting our heart right is a responsibility Christians bear in order to be able to worship God properly (among other things it is not dependent, for example, on the "quality" of worship offered by those serving). Other things can affect the condition of our heart; but only we can spiritually establish our heart properly before God. To do so in preparation for worshiping God can help establish a proper relationship with God.

January 21

"Why Think Evil?"

Evil can reside in the heart of humans as well as elsewhere, such as in the spiritual world (Eph 6:12). God stated that he makes good and evil (Isa 45:7, a general statement that God is responsible for everything). We overcome some forms of evil by not letting it overcome us, and, rather, overcoming it with good (Rom 12:21). When Jesus did something good, the scribes interpreted his actions to be evil. He responded by asking why they thought his good action was evil: "But Jesus, knowing their thoughts, said, 'Why do you think evil in your hearts?'" (Matt 9:4; see also Isa 5:20). There is evil in the world, and there can be evil in the hearts of humans, whether spontaneous, planned (Prov 1:10–19), or a seemingly intentional misinterpretation of something good, as in Matt 9:4. The Christian can overcome evil, including that which might arise in their heart, with good, beginning with implanting good in their heart (Phil 4:8). We can thereby form a correct perception of the One who went about doing good (Acts 10:38) as good, not evil.

January 22

"Overcome Evil"

Paul's teaching "do not be overcome by evil, but overcome evil with good" (Rom 12:21) tells us several things about evil and about victory. This verse tells us that there is going to be a victor, and that who the victor is depends on us. The first part of the verse states "do not be overcome" (passive), while the second is "overcome" (active). The word so translated is again the Greek word *nike*, and means "to have victory." As Christians, we are assured that the war will end with our victory (Rev 2:10); in the meantime, we need to be active to win as many battles as possible. Often in life to not be active is to allow another force to fill the void left thereby. Evil is an active force (1 Pet 5:8); thus, if we aren't active, our passivity could ensure at least a temporary victory for evil. The best way for us to not let evil have the victory over us is for us to achieve victory over evil by being spiritually active, not passive.

January 23

"The Goodness of God"

GOOD IS GOOD NO matter what we think of it or call it. Paul's teaching that "the goodness of God leadeth thee to repentance" (Rom 2:4 ASV) tells us that to understand an act of goodness or kindness as coming from God depends on the person's heart. That is, it is again possible for one to call evil good and good evil (Isa 5:20). It may be difficult to prove that something good came from God (Esth 4:14; Phlm 16); yet one can choose to believe that all good gifts come from God (Jas 1:17), and thereby let goodness affect them in a positive way. Goodness is goodness no matter what we think of it. Whether it softens our heart to lead us to repentance is up to us.

January 24

"More Blessed to Give"

It can brighten our spirits, or be a blessing, to receive something as a gift. Paul said to the elders of Ephesus, "In all things I have shown you that by working hard in this way we must help the weak and remember the words of the Lord Jesus, how he himself said, 'It is more blessed to give than to receive'" (Acts 20:35). To give can be an exercise in spirituality. That is, while the action of giving can be done mechanically (without any thought of how it might affect giver or receiver), it can also be carried out with a spiritual element such as love. Paul said this is the only way for giving to do any spiritual good (1 Cor 13:3). As a spiritual experiment, watch for a change in demeanor when, for example, giving a server in a restaurant a tip in cash. If their countenance brightens, it suggests you have blessed them. Then observe the effect this can have on your heart. Such an experiment can reinforce to the Christian the need to look at life spiritually (in this example, the money is secondary to one's being spiritually blessed) by observing the effect of such actions on the soul. Giving is, again, a grace (2 Cor 8:7) that benefits the soul of the giver. No doubt it blesses the recipient; by looking at giving spiritually, it, perhaps, blesses more the giver.

January 25

"Pray in Every Place"

Paul's teaching in 1 Tim 2:8 reminds us today of the importance of public prayer: "I desire therefore that the men pray in every place, lifting up holy hands, without wrath and disputing" (ASV). While there are several spiritual lessons to be learned from this verse, the takeaway for this lesson is the phrase "in every place." This phrase here teaches the importance of prayer offered when the church is gathered together (other verses, as well as logic, support this understanding [1 Cor 1:2; 1 Thess 1:8]). This being the case reminds us that prayers offered by a gathering of Christians is a special occurrence. Our prayers at home alone are meaningful and necessary (1 Thess 5:17). When one rises to utter a prayer while the congregation listens with their eyes closed serves a purpose as well. Among other things, it is a time when many hearts join their thoughts in accord, which then surely rouses the attention of the One listening (Matt 18:20), and can also draw those hearts closer together.

January 26

From Darkness to Light

Physical darkness can have an appeal, such as when we need sleep. Even spiritual darkness can appeal to the dark realms of the human heart. Perhaps this is one reason the Bible admonishes to avoid darkness (Eph 5:11) and to walk in light (1 John 1:7). Having light shine on us when we are in darkness can be refreshing (cf. Matt 4:16) or it can be painful (as a blinding light shining in the eyes). Jesus told Paul of those who would "turn from darkness to light and from the power of Satan to God, that they may receive forgiveness of sins and a place among those who are sanctified by faith in me" (Acts 26:18). Light is more powerful than darkness (John 1:5), but it requires individual effort to choose one over the other. One can turn from darkness or turn from the truth that sets free (2 Tim 4:4; John 8:32), but they must choose one. To not choose light is to choose darkness; and trying to get around in darkness can affect our happiness and well-being or, more importantly, it will affect our eternal state.

January 27

From Evil to Good

EVIL AND DARKNESS ARE both forces which can be overcome. Turning from them (see yesterday's "Daily") is but a first step. Further effort is necessary, since darkness will not go away on its own, and evil will not turn away from us (see 1 Pet 5:8). Thus Peter said that if one desires to love life and see good days, "let him turn away from evil and do good; let him seek peace and pursue it" (1 Pet 3:11). Inasmuch as nature abhors a vacuum, turning from darkness and evil must be followed by positive action, that is, doing good. By doing good we won't eliminate evil, but we can thereby overcome it (Rom 12:21), and, in the process, love life and see good days.

January 28

"Understanding and the Knowledge"

PAUL TOLD THE COLOSSIANS (Col 2:1) that he was striving for them and others for a reason: "That their hearts may be encouraged, being knit together in love, to reach all the riches of full assurance of understanding and the knowledge of God's mystery, which is Christ" (Col 2:2). Paul's goal, as stated in this verse, was the encouragement of their hearts and their unity in love. But two other purposes, perhaps in accord with these things, are their "assurance of understanding and the knowledge of God's mystery." For a group to be encouraged and to be knit together are wonderful things. One reason the church is different from other groups is because her goal includes having these blessings based on spiritual substance; that is, the knowledge of God's word, that which gives true spiritual encouragement (the Greek word translated "encourage" is directly related to the word "Comforter" in John 14:26) and is the proper basis for unity before God (John 17:20–21). God's word is ultimately the reason a church is acceptable or not, in God's sight (Rev 1–2). The basis of all other efforts, however noble, may result in striving after the wind (Eccl 1:14).

January 29

Putting It Together

WHEN PAUL SPOKE OF the Colossians being encouraged and knit together (see yesterday's "Daily"), he used the phrase "full assurance of understanding." A very picturesque phrase in the original Greek (this word translated "understanding" meaning "a coming together," as of two rivers merging), it has to do with our certainty of comprehending. Paul states this in reference to "God's mystery," that which had been concealed but has now been revealed (Rom 16:25). This reminds us that God's word can be understood, but that it might take time and mental energy to reach that point. If we apply ourselves to growth, which includes making the effort to know God's word (2 Pet 3:18), we have assurance that our understanding thereof will eventually come together. We, therefore, can't give up, even if doesn't seem to make sense in the meantime. If it seems to take too long, it doesn't mean it is going to fall apart; it could mean that more effort and patience is required on our part. Until then, we can be certain that, one day, it will come together–one day the rivers will join—whether we see it now or not.

January 30

"Praise the Lord, All Nations"

THE PSALMIST CALLED UPON others to praise God (Ps 117:1) because of God's devotion to his people. Psalm 117:2 gives the reason: "For his covenant loyalty has been mighty over us, and the truth of the LORD is eternal." The psalmist here praises God because his loyalty has been strong (the Hebrew verb is in the past tense), and because of God's quality of faithfulness that always is (the Hebrew word translated "faithfulness" is related to the Hebrew word meaning "truth"). Christians today, likewise, can possibly influence others as they praise God for the relationship they have with him, and, by so praising him, help to keep this relationship strong. Relationships can change. God's faithfulness means that he will do his part to keep the relationship strong. Through the Lord's Supper (1 Cor 11:23–29) we thus, likewise, look back to what God has done, upward to what God is and does, outward to others, and inward as we reflect on our need to praise him; and hopefully thereby influence others to do likewise.

January 31

"Rejoice with Those Who Rejoice"

THERE ARE SOME (MANY?) who, when learning of others' good news, immediately reply with something negative (possibly reflecting what we call "sour grapes"). The counterpart of this is to take delight in another's misfortune (often called by the German word *Schadenfreude*). This may be a natural inclination. Yet, as in many other realms, the biblical reaction to someone else's good or bad news should be the opposite of that which seems natural; that is, the biblical response is spiritual. Thus, the Bible teaches, "Rejoice with those who rejoice, weep with those who weep" (Rom 12:15). Paul doesn't give a reason in this verse for our so responding, and it seems we cannot know whether such a response will do any noticeable good. Rather, we follow this teaching in order to have the mind of Christ (Phil 2:5), which was, in part, characterized by obedience (Phil 2:8). Rather than follow our possibly natural inclination, the mind of Christ dictates that we follow God's word, which tells us to rejoice with those who rejoice.

February 1

Awakening to Truth

WHEN ONE HAS A pleasant dream they may wake up disappointed when they realize that it was only a dream (contrariwise with having an unpleasant dream). Either way, we don't choose either what we dream or to what we wake up. Imagine being told that when you awake in the morning all of your troubles will be over, only to find that, on awakening, it wasn't true. The Bible speaks of the need to spiritually awaken (Eph 5:14), including Paul's admonition on what we awaken to: "Awake to soberness righteously, and sin not; for some have no knowledge of God" (1 Cor 15:34a ASV). Among other things, this verse tells us that, spiritually, we can choose to what we awaken. One of the biggest problems with myths is that they aren't true. They may help one to dream, but one day they will have to awaken to the truth. Though we can't choose either what we dream about or to what we waken, to turn to God's righteousness and truth (Eph 6:14–15) would be a great awakening for the soul, and could spiritually be too good to be true; or cause one to be "like those who dream" (Ps 126:1).

February 2

"Hidden in God"

THE LIGHT OF THE Christian's life is, again, not to be hidden (Matt 5:16). This is true, in part, because the Christian's life is not their own (1 Cor 6:19). One can, however, have a solitary place to gain spiritual respite away from evil and the material world, a place with Christ in God. Paul stated that the Christian is to set their mind on things that are above (Col 3:2) because they have spiritually died, and "your life is hidden with Christ in God" (Col 3:3). We are hidden in God because we have spiritually given up our life (Gal 2:20). Yet being hidden also means we have protection (John 10:28) and a place where we can be alone with Christ (Mark 6:31). Giving up our life to become a Christian is how one has a new light that they let shine for Christ, which they are not afraid to do because they are hidden with Christ in God.

February 3

"Unreasonable and Evil"

PAUL SPOKE TO THE Thessalonians of their being delivered from "unreasonable and evil men": "And that we may be delivered from unreasonable and evil men; for all have not faith" (2 Thess 3:2 ASV). In language, two words are often coupled when they go together, such as when they have a similar meaning ("good and ready") or when they form a unit (like "cup and saucer"). The Greek word translated "unreasonable" (also translated "wicked, perverse") literally means "out of place." When one is not right with God, he or she is spiritually out of place, and is, therefore, in an evil condition. There is no in-between one place and another, or between good and evil, in the sight of God. Just as Adam and Eve were expelled from the garden, and Judas went "to his own place" (Acts 1:25), so humans left their place with God by their sin (Rom 3:23). By reasoning with God through faith (that is, God's word, Rom 10:17), we can put our soul right with him (Isa 1:18; Acts 24:25), by returning to our proper place. Sin is unreasonable and evil; to be right with God is the opposite of this, that is, it is reasonable and good. By being restored to our proper place, we'll be good and ready to go to heaven.

February 4

"It Is No Evil"

ONE OF THE PROBLEMS Malachi faced was that Israel had been home from captivity long enough that they had gotten careless in their worship, and were offering anything (or sub-standard sacrifices) to God. Malachi therefore rebukes them by showing them that they seemed to not care whether their worship was acceptable to God: "And when you bring near [the] blind to sacrifice, it is no evil! And when you bring near [the] lame or [the] sick, it is no evil!" (Mal 1:8; every translation consulted except the ASV translates the one phrase as a question ["is that not evil?," ESV]). Today we partake of the Lord's Supper, which includes unleavened bread. Leaven in the Bible is a symbol of evil (Exod 12:15; Gal 5:9). To remember Jesus' death with this spiritually pure element thus serves as a reminder that there is no evil when we remember the pure life and holy sacrifice of the unblemished Lamb of God, who died to make our lives pure with regard to sin (1 Pet 1:18–19). When we approach God in the proper way, with the proper elements, it is not evil, but good.

February 5

Just Imagine

MANY TIMES IN LIFE when we anticipate something good, like a new place to live, a new job, etc. we imagine that it is going to be the greatest experience we've ever had, perhaps only to be disappointed. It has been said that reality is often somewhere in-between our imagination and what we are told to expect—except when it comes to what God has in store for those who love him. Paul said, "But, as it is written, 'What no eye has seen, nor ear heard, nor the heart of man imagined, what God has prepared for those who love him'" (1 Cor 2:9). We can try to imagine what heaven will be like, and we are told what heaven will be like or not like. But the "reality" of this spiritual place is beyond comprehension. This is perhaps why the closest God could come to helping us understand it is to tell us that it is not like it is here (1 Pet 1:4), and to compare it to things we know (Rev 21:10–21). We can try and mentally prepare for some event, but the reality often doesn't match our expectations. We can spiritually prepare for heaven, and the "reality" is going to be far better than what we imagine.

February 6

Form or Power?

WHICH IS REAL, AN invention such as the automobile, or the idea which gave birth to the invention? Paul taught that it is possible to live a life that has an outward appearance of godliness, but is not based on truth: "Holding a form of godliness, but having denied the power thereof: from these also turn away" (2 Tim 3:5 ASV, referring to the ungodly of vv. 2–4). True godliness comes from a heart that directs one to live their life according to God's word (Rom 6:17). God's word is elsewhere referred to as "power" (Rom 1:16; see Eph 3:20). Not that it is always wrong to give proper attention to outward things (Jesus took upon himself the "form" of a servant, Phil 2:5). But to give all of one's attention to only appearing godly without truly following God's word is to be like a look-alike entertainer with no talent, or an imitation product of lesser quality in a store. By adopting the spiritual principles of God's word, we can be autumn trees with outward fruit (Jude 12; Gal 5:22–23), rather than just looking like trees without bearing fruit (Mark 11:13–14). While such things as an impression can be important (1 Tim 3:7), the appearance is not the ultimate determining factor (John 7:24). That which makes one godly is not the form, but the power of godliness, that is, the power of God's word, the truth.

February 7

Power and Responsibility

Power is, for many, a desirable quality, while responsibility is, to many, burdensome. For the Christian, to be blessed with talent or substance carries great responsibility, and to take on responsibility in life is usually the means of acquiring power. Power and responsibility thus go together. Christians have been given power in the form of the gospel (Rom 1:16; see also yesterday's "Daily") and of talent (Matt 25:14–30), and Christians are to be good stewards of that which they have been given (1 Cor 4:2; 16:2). We utilize this power by taking the responsibility of keeping it in our lives (Eph 3:20). By taking responsibility, it may be that God will give us more (Matt 25:28; 2 Cor 9:10). If God has given to us, we have a need to be responsible with that which he has given. A power (something for which many in general long) has thus already been given to the Christian. That which many avoid (responsibility) is the means to possibly acquiring more talent, and, certainly, the way to glorify God.

February 8

"Have You Not Read?"

THE LEVEL OF KNOWLEDGE God expects of each of us may be difficult to say, and surely depends upon one's individual level of maturity (see John 3:10; Heb 5:12–14). Yet the Bible again teaches of our need, as Christians, to study in order that we might spiritually grow (2 Pet 3:18); surely God expects us to have read his word. Thus, Jesus asked the Pharisees, "Have you not read?" (Matt 19:4). In asking this question Jesus is simultaneously giving them a rebuke. Reading does not guarantee understanding (Matt 12:7; Acts 8:30). But the mental development resulting from knowledge and understanding begins with the action of reading. When Jesus returns he hopes to find faith on earth (Luke 18:8), faith that comes by hearing the word (Rom 10:17). How much better that he find faith in us, rather than to hear him say, "Have you not read?"

February 9

"How Do You Read It?"

TRUTH, AGAIN, IS NOT changeable. When Jesus asked the man, "What is written in the Law? How do you read it?" (Luke 10:26) He was surely not asking him what the passage meant to him. That is, truth, again, does not depend on what we think. While the gospel can have a different effect depending upon the ears upon which it lands (Luke 8:4–15; Acts 17:32–34), there is only one gospel by which people are saved (Gal 1:6–10). Jesus was, therefore, surely using this question as a teaching device. The answer the man gave was not his understanding (that is, it was not "his truth"), but rather the truth (v. 27). Scripture is to be interpreted (Matt 12:7; 1 Cor 5:9–10; 2 Pet 3:16) but the right answer begins with what Scripture says. This is why Jesus could therefore commend him in v. 28 by saying, "You have answered rightly."

February 10

Keeping Our Feet on the Ground

LOOKING AT LIFE SPIRITUALLY has to do not with the Christian walking around with their head in the clouds but with how we estimate and react to life (there was a play in ancient Greece making fun of philosophers entitled *The Clouds*). This mindset can be appreciated by observing Jesus' reacting to Satan's temptations with Scripture (Matt 4:1–11), to his teaching to "consider" the lilies of the field (Matt 6:28–30), to Paul's teaching to "take account" of the spiritual things he mentions (Phil 4:8), to such things as our estimation of someone's improper behavior (2 Thess 3:15, counting him as a brother rather than as an enemy). To do these things requires not only a proper application of our thoughts but also that which ultimately shapes our heart and mind (see Acts 28:26–27), that is, truth, or Scripture. The best way to not have our head "in the clouds," but, rather, to keep our feet on the ground, is by concentrating on the words of heaven.

February 11

What Good Does It Do?

THE BIBLE TEACHES THAT evil is influential (Gal 5:9; 1 Cor 15:33), and of the Christian's need to do good (Gal 6:9). Doing good is necessary in order to overcome evil (Rom 12:21), which tells us that not doing good may contribute to the persistence of evil. We may wonder, however, whether our doing good does any good; for example, whether our efforts may change someone's heart. While Jesus did good (Acts 10:38), his efforts were not always appreciated (Luke 17:11–19), including the final benevolent act of his death on the cross. Perhaps the influence of our efforts for good depends on the heart upon which they fall (see Rom 2:4). If so, our need, as Christians, is to remember the importance of doing good regardless of whether there is some practical good that we can see or a personal reward for which we might hope. Whether people appreciate our efforts, or whether our efforts change someone's heart, etc. we may never know; but we can know that by doing good we have made an effort to counter evil, possibly affected someone's spirit, and contributed toward our ultimate end of bringing glory to God (Eph 1:12); which are all good things.

February 12

"Knowledge and Understanding"

JEREMIAH WAS CALLED TO tell Israel that she had betrayed God by going after false ways. Yet God wanted to help his nation, so he said, "And thus I will give to you shepherds according to my heart, and they will shepherd you with knowledge and understanding" (Jer 3:15). Knowledge and understanding are important, but do not always go together (one may have knowledge, for example, of one of the sciences, but not understand why it is the way it is). Truth that comes from the heart of God is meant to influence our heart and our mind (Acts 28:26–27). We today, therefore, can know (1 John 5:13) and understand Scripture (Matt 12:7), especially with someone to help us (Acts 8:30–31; not shepherds who "feed themselves," Jude 12). By thus being fed we can thereby avoid a famine of the word (Amos 8:11) and, equally important, be brought closer to the heart of God, which is surely the purpose of a knowledge and an understanding of the word that comes from his heart.

February 13

God Is Watching over His Word

WHEN GOD GAVE JEREMIAH the charge to preach his word, he said that he would keep watch over his word: "Then the LORD said to me, 'You have seen well, for I am watching over my word to perform it'" (Jer 1:12). Christians today have a need to keep God's word, which includes keeping it in one's heart (Ps 119:11), in their life (1 John 2:5), and in the face of persecution (1 Pet 1:3–14). If we keep his word, his grace will establish us (Heb 13:9), inasmuch as one is saved by grace through faith (Eph 2:8–9), and faith comes by hearing the word (Rom 10:17). God's word is set (Rev 22:18–19), and he will see to its preservation (God stating that he will keep watch over his word is, perhaps, a reflection of how we came to have our English Bible). It is up to us to keep it, lest we disappoint God and fellow believers, like the psalmist who said, "Streams of water flow down my eyes, because they do not keep your instruction" (Ps 119:136).

February 14

How to Know We're in Love

WE AGAIN OFTEN SPEAK of love as a feeling that unpredictably comes and goes. In the Bible, however, love is more of a mental process that we choose, rather than a feeling of the heart (not that affection is not an important element). John not only spoke of love as a commandment but he also gave indication of how we can know that we love: "And this commandment we have from him: whoever loves God must also love his brother" (1 John 4:21), and "by this we know that we love the children of God, when we love God and obey his commandments" (1 John 5:2). Inasmuch as the church consists of all kinds of people, with different backgrounds, etc. it seems the only way for such a group to spiritually survive and thrive together is by utilizing a bond that ties us together as a people, that is, the bond of love. With this tie that binds, one can overcome negative elements such as differences in personality, perception, etc. If we choose to love God and obey his commandments, we can know that we have the kind of relationship with his people of which he approves; we can know we are in love.

February 15

"To Him"

To receive extraordinary blessings can thrill the soul, which is perhaps a reason we often seek those things. Yet, in Eph 3:20–21, Paul's emphasis is not on us, but on God: "Now to him who is able to do far more abundantly than all that we ask or think, according to the power at work within us, to him be glory in the church and in Christ Jesus throughout all generations, forever and ever. Amen." We can do our part to see to it that the power of which Paul speaks is "at work within us"; but the extent to which God blesses us is up to him (Jas 4:15), and to believe that God is the cause of such blessings is up to the individual believer (that is, we may not be able to prove it to the nonbeliever). Paul's wording, however, reminds us that great things are, nevertheless, not something we (alone) accomplished, but, rather, something that should cause us to look to God. The purpose of God's doing "far more abundantly than all that we ask or think" is to glorify him, not us.

February 16

"Established by Grace"

A GIFT CAN LIFT the spirits, thereby, in a sense, making one feel free (Hos 13:6). Receiving the unmerited favor of God's grace sets the spirit of the sinner free (John 8:32). Grace is also a concept that makes the soul stable before God. The writer of Hebrews spoke of our being "established" by grace, or by God's unmerited favor: "Be not carried away by divers and strange teachings: for it is good that the heart be established by grace; not by meats" (Heb 13:9a ASV). The wording of this verse reminds us of the power of God's word to give us strength and stability in life (the Greek word translated "establish" means "to make sure or stable," often in contexts involving the word of God). The sinner being saved by grace through faith (Eph 2:8; faith coming through the word, Rom 10:17) tells us that not having faith means that one is not established, and they, therefore, are subject to being tossed about on a sea of doubt (Jas 1:6). Rather, the acceptance of the free gift of salvation (Rom 6:23), which comes to man through the intangible medium of the word, is that which establishes our heart before God, because we have been set free by God's grace.

February 17

"Let Me Bow"

WHEN THE PSALMIST DESCRIBES his worship to God in Ps 138:2, he emphasizes not only God (in the form of "your name"), and God's word ("your truth"), but also qualities of God which have to do with his efforts to reach the hearts of humans. In v. 2 the psalmist states, "Let me bow toward your holy temple, and give thanks [to] your name for your covenant loyalty and your truth." Two qualities the psalmist mentions are God's "covenant loyalty" and his "faithfulness." In the OT, both of these have to do with God's dedication to his nation (the Hebrew word translated "faithfulness" is related to both Hebrew words translated "truth" and "amen"). The fact that one can count on God to always be there (Deut 4:7) is something unique to God; that is, we can't say this of humans (Mal 3:6; Heb 13:5–6, 8). When the psalmist states, "I will," he thereby determines to engage in the temporary act of worship in order to maintain an ongoing relationship with the One who will never leave his children. Is not our one hour of worship (in addition to the rest of our spiritual life) worth a relationship that will last for all eternity?

February 18

"Stand Firm in Grace"

THE RECEIPT OF A gift often means one is imposed upon with certain obligations. Political freedom (being able to choose where to live and work, how many children to have, how much money to make) can be taken away. Freedom therefore imposes on the free the obligation of holding it firm. Being established by God's unmerited favor means the recipient has certain obligations, including maintaining the relationship brought about by that grace. Thus, Peter said one has the obligation of standing firm in God's grace: "By Silvanus, a faithful brother as I regard him, I have written briefly to you, exhorting and declaring that this is the true grace of God. Stand firm in it" (1 Pet 5:12). The Greek word translated "stand firm" means "to hold to one's commitment," or "to hold one's ground." Whether it be the wiles of the devil (Eph 6:11—which contains the same word in Greek), or our own deluded attitude (that is, thinking we are right when we aren't, 1 Cor 10:12), Christians have a spiritual freedom that requires us to hold onto that freedom. Jesus will never let us go (John 10:29); yet the gift of God's grace requires that we be firm to never leave it or let it be taken away.

February 19

Answered Prayer

GOOD THINGS ARE GOOD for us especially when they affect our spiritual life. It may be difficult to prove, for example to a nonbeliever, that a positive outcome is the result of a prayer request. Yet the Christian can put two and two together and realize, or, perhaps more properly, believe, that such is the result of God working in their life. In such a case, the benefit of good things should be spiritual, that is, to strengthen our spiritual life or our relationship with God. Job's response to loss was to bless God (Job 1:21). The one leper who returned to thank Jesus thereby reflected the appreciation in his heart for what Jesus had done for him (Luke 17:15). Paul, reflecting on his suffering and persecution, said God delivered him from them (2 Tim 3:11). For good things to do us any good, we need to look at them spiritually. This includes remembering them as time goes on, as well as recalling our belief that this was something God did. Otherwise, we might be guilty of the destructive approach of thinking only of ourselves, or satisfying our own desires (Jas 4:3); and that doesn't do any good.

February 20

"His Delight"

Though it may be difficult to imagine, some people do not like coffee. Similarly, it seems that spiritual things appeal to some and not to others (see 1 Cor 2:14–15; this is not to equate coffee with spiritual things), and some things can be an acquired taste. To delight in things pertaining to God basically has to do with one's attitude; unlike coffee, this delight is spiritual rather than physical. Thus Ps 1:2 states that the one is blessed whose "delight is in the Lord's instruction; so he meditates on his instruction day and night." The delight of the blessed one is set in juxtaposition to the actions of not associating with the ungodly (v. 1). Perhaps he chooses God's word of life because logic has forced him to conclude that there is no where else to go (John 6:68). Perhaps he delights in having guidance, like one accepting advice after attempting and failing at a project. Attitude can be changed; to be blessed, it is important to choose to take delight in the teaching of God. Otherwise, where else would we go?

February 21

In Peace and Safety

THE PROBLEM OF INSOMNIA can evidently be caused by different things, both physical and spiritual. For part of his life, David was a refugee from Saul (1 Sam 21:10–15). Yet, in Ps 4:8 he states, "In peace I will both lie down and sleep; for you alone, O LORD, you have me dwell in safety." David uses two phrases ("in peace" and "in safety") that paint a picture of a security only God can provide. David was able to sleep because he had a physical security based on a spiritual tranquility. While the ways of the flesh are contrary to the Spirit (Gal 5:17), a healthy spiritual life can affect one's physical life, and our physical surroundings (such as persecution [Matt 5:11] or poverty [Luke 6:20]) can affect our spirit. Like David, the Christian is at peace with God (Rom 5:1), and, therefore, can rest easy, knowing that he or she has a security that only God can provide.

February 22

May the Hearts Rejoice

THE BIBLE SPEAKS OF both seeking for (Acts 17:27) and of finding the Lord (Jer 29:13). It is good to have goals; but, again, having an unfulfilled goal may provide blessings that reaching a goal may not. The hole in the heart created by desire can produce emotions such as dissatisfaction, anticipation, and, therefore, a motivation to fill the hole. Once we find what we are looking for (that is, once we reach our goal), these motivating emotions can be more difficult to maintain. The psalmist reflected, in a context of worship, "May the hearts of those who seek the LORD rejoice!" (Ps 105:3b). Seeking the Lord, whether in worship or in our everyday spiritual life, is a pursuit that can stimulate our soul to greater spirituality (Isa 55:6; Matt 7:8). To not seek the Lord suggests we are not engaged in such spiritual efforts, in which case we might be subject to the same chastisement of Jer 2:8, where the Lord rebuked the priests for not asking, "Where is the Lord?"

February 23

What's the Hurry?

When encouraging Christians to add the "Christian graces" of 2 Pet 1, Peter said, "For this very reason, make every effort to supplement your faith with virtue, and virtue with knowledge" (2 Pet 1:5). Every translation consulted rendered the one word either "make every effort" or "give diligence." The Greek word so translated bears a connotation of eager persistence. It is used in other contexts of serving the Lord (Rom 12:11), as well as of giving (2 Cor 8:7), and of holding onto one's hope (Heb 6:11). Peter also said that the result of adding these spiritual qualities is that "they keep you from being ineffective or unfruitful in the knowledge of our Lord Jesus Christ" (2 Pet 1:8). To strive for an active spiritual life includes the Christian's need to be eagerly persistent in the present, and leave the future growth up to God (1 Cor 3:6). We may not be able to hurry spiritual growth; yet we can eagerly tend to it now, and look forward to effective fruitfulness in due course. While the fruit may not appear for a while, Jesus knows we are making this effort, and he is looking forward as much as we to seeing the fruit (Matt 21:19).

February 24

"The Word of the Lord Has Become"

THE WORD OF GOD does not change (Matt 24:35), and it can change the heart of the hearer (Luke 8:4–15). This, of course, depends on the hearer (Acts 17:32–34). Jeremiah was called to preach to Judah regarding her departure from the Lord (Jer 3:11), which included (was caused by) her not following his word: "To whom would I speak and warn, that they may hear? Here, the word of the LORD became a reproach to them; they would not delight therein" (Jer 6:10). While the lessons in this verse are many, one of the keys to understanding what God's people had become is the word "become" (an accurate translation of the Hebrew). Since the word of God does not change, yet Jeremiah states the word had "become" a reproach, was it really the word that changed? What it becomes depends on what we become.

February 25

Happiness or Joy?

Upon retiring from his stressful job, a man said he had mixed emotions—joy and happiness. While there is nothing necessarily wrong with happiness (depending on the source thereof) it is a temporary condition, inasmuch as it depends on things that happen to us. There might be times in life when the temporary quality of happiness is found to be incompatible with the enduring spiritual quality of joy. Though these two may not always be mutually exclusive, life is fleeting (Jas 4:13–15), one's life does not consist in the abundance of possessions (Luke 12:15), and the ways of the flesh are incompatible with the Spirit (Gal 5:17). The Bible promises things that may produce happiness, such as God caring for our needs (Phil 4:19) and God's providential care (Rom 8:28). Yet, being temporary, happiness is therefore, perhaps, better left up to God. Christians rather do well to concentrate instead on the spiritual quality of joy, by pursuing the fruit of the Spirit (Gal 5:22–23), which results therein. This will certainly please God (Ps 1:6), and could even make us happy; I mean, joyful.

February 26

"Reading, Exhortation, and Teaching"

One of the few acts of worship Paul mentions in the books of Timothy and Titus is, "Until I come, devote yourself to the public reading of Scripture, to exhortation, to teaching" (1 Tim 4:13). The one Greek word is correctly translated "the public reading of Scripture" (as opposed to private reading), as reflected in its only two other appearances in the NT (Acts 13:15; and 2 Cor 3:14). "Exhortation" and "teaching" are clearly public, versus private, activities. Paul's specifying these things should not be surprising, as these letters are written to preachers. Perhaps he emphasized them because Timothy was shy (1 Cor 16:10; though it may be difficult to imagine a shy preacher). This verse nevertheless reminds us that the Scripture reading and/or the sermon are no less important acts of worship than singing, the Lord's Supper, giving, and prayers, and therefore must be given full devotion by the listener as well as the preacher. A saying I heard years ago was that "good preaching is made by good listening." Just as it's possible to engage in the Lord's Supper in an "unworthy manner" (1 Cor 11:27), so, perhaps, it is possible for us to mistreat the Scripture reading and sermon by not devoting ourselves thereto.

February 27

"Faithfulness Has Perished"

PART OF THE MESSAGE God gave to Jeremiah included that "faithfulness has perished, and has been cut off from their mouth" (Jer 7:28; the Hebrew word translated "faithfulness" is related to the Hebrew word translated "truth"). The word can fall (1 Sam 3:19) be thrown to the ground (Dan 8:12), or become a reproach in the mind of the hearer (Jer 6:10), but truth will live (Matt 24:35). Faithfulness, however, can die, especially if one does not hold to the truth. The existence of truth, therefore, in the heart of the believer, depends on their keeping it, or their faithfulness (Ps 37:3). Just as we can count on God to be faithful (1 Cor 10:13; 1 John 1:9), so we are to hold onto the truth as part of our life of faithfulness by nurturing the seed of the word of God (Luke 8:11). Truth can't be killed, but it can die if it is not kept in the fertile ground of the believer's heart.

February 28

What to Do with Good Things

WHAT DO WE DO with good things we receive or when good things happen to us (such as in answer to prayer)? Whether intentional or not, gifts seem to impose some kind of obligation on the recipient. What God ultimately intends for us surely is our spiritual good. Not that he doesn't delight in our happiness over good things; but positive responses to prayer are not for the purpose of satisfying our selfish desires. James said, "You ask and do not receive, because you ask wrongly, to spend it on your passions" (4:3). To "spend" suggests that we have used up that which has been given to us. If God intends us to do something with answered prayers, how much better to concentrate on these good things for spiritual good (Phil 4:8)? To do so could result in a better appreciation for the gift, a brighter outlook on life (less worry), and a deeper glorification of God (Job 1:21). Isn't this the purpose of the Christian life (Eph 1:12)?

February 29

"He Meditates"

Some of the thoughts we hold in our mind are negative or otherwise counterproductive to our spiritual life. Such thoughts, though they occupy a place in our mind, may nevertheless be described as "vain" or empty with regard to any benefit to our soul. My understanding is that the brain is always active. The mind, however, seems to be different (such as someone who is still alive but, sadly, has lost their mental capabilities). While we all learn in different ways, Christians all share the common necessity of gaining a knowledge of Scripture (2 Pet 3:18), which requires that we apply our mind. Thus the Bible speaks of meditating on Scripture (Ps 1:4) and of storing up good thoughts (Phil 4:8). A good way, though certainly not the only way, of accomplishing this is to repeat Scripture to oneself in the course of the day. The Greek word translated "think" in Phil 4:8 has a sense of "doing repeatedly." The psalmist said that the one who is blessed meditates on God's law "day and night," meaning "always" (Ps 1:2). To repeat Scripture to oneself serves the purpose of crowding out other thoughts, of lifting our heart with good thoughts from God, and of strengthening our soul in the process (Acts 20:32). God is thinking about us (Jer 29:11). Though we also have to think on other things, to concentrate on Scripture is beneficial for a healthier spiritual life. We certainly can't create better thoughts than Scripture; to concentrate on anything else could be to meditate on a "vain thing" (Ps 2:1).

March 1

The Christian's Default Mode

THE MEANING BEHIND THE word "default" has to do with failure (the word "default" contains the word "fault"). The English word "default" is defined as "to make a selection automatically in the absence of a choice made by the user" or "due to lack of a viable alternative."[2] It, therefore, can have a negative (such as defaulting on a loan) or a more-or-less positive (such as a default mode on a computer) connotation. The will is part of the make-up of humans, as given to them by God. It seems that God would have man to freely exercise his will, but that the will of humans is to be used for spiritual good, ultimately to lead us to God's will (Ps 37:4). Human will is, therefore, not to be the default mode. Since we don't know what is best for ourselves (Prov 14:12; Jer 1:6; 10:23), we don't know that everything will turn out the way we want, and, even if we were able to solve all of our problems, all things are going to come to an end one day (Heb 9:27; 2 Pet 3:11), and failures remind us that God's will is to be the ultimate mode (Matt 26:42), especially when our mode has failed (Acts 21:14). Though one's will can get him or her into trouble (Gen 3:1–8), it need not be something bad (Matt 14:28). God's will should be our default mode when our will has proven faulty.

---

2. Merriam-Webster Dictionary, "Default."

March 2

The Acts of Worship

MOST CHURCHES OF CHRIST today engage in five "acts of worship," and many other fellowships (probably) have a similar format when they worship as well. The acts of worship (singing, prayer, Lord's Supper, giving, and preaching) are not listed together in any one place in the NT. Deducing that these things are to be fulfilled is a matter of the authority of God's word combined with logic. We can know today that these things are to be carried out, but that there may be variables (such as their order of execution). From Cain (1 John 3:12) to Solomon (1 Kgs 11:4) to Judah in Jeremiah's day (Jer 5:19) to the misuse of the Lord's Supper today (1 Cor 11:27), it is possible to engage in false or unacceptable worship. To remember that worship is a spiritual exercise should point us to God's word for our authority, and thereby help us ensure its acceptability. Scripture, not ourselves (Matt 15:9), tells us how to worship.

March 3

Especially God's Household

LOOKING AT LIFE SPIRITUALLY can include where we decide to apply all types of effort for good. Paul taught "so then, as we have opportunity, let us do good to everyone, and especially to those who are of the household of faith" (Gal 6:10). We hear advertisements from time to time encouraging us to support certain types of businesses. A key in Paul's teaching is the word "especially," which means "to the highest extent." Christians can and should do good to all (Eph 2:10), yet we are to do good especially to God's house, the church (1 Tim 3:15). There may be many reasons to support (for example, local) businesses. Yet, like Jesus when he was younger (Luke 2:49), a spiritual focus to our life and efforts can change the way we do good, including in business, by helping us to do good to all; and especially to God's household.

March 4

"Whatever You Do"

A POPULAR SAYING IS "if you're going to do something, do it well" (or similarly). We can look at our motivation for work from different perspectives, such as making something look nice, making it work well, saving money, etc. all of which are good reasons (1 Thess 4:12). Yet knowing that the opinions of others should be secondary (Gal 1:10), that physical things will one day be gone (2 Pet 3:10), and that the Christian's heart is not to be geared toward money (see 1 Tim 6:10), should cause us to wonder whether there is a higher reason for the motivation behind our actions. The Bible tells us to do our physical work diligently (Eccl 9:10; 1 Thess 4:11), yet the Christian has a greater motivation, that goes beyond physical reasons. Paul said, "Whatever you do, work heartily, as for the Lord and not for men" (Col 3:23; see also v. 17). The Christian works because they are first working for God. Doing something half-heartedly may save such physical expenses as time, energy, and/or effort; the Christian gives their best effort not for physical reasons, but for reasons that go beyond this life. The Christian works, knowing that their motivation produces actions that bring glory to God, and that promise us an eternal reward in return (Col 3:24). If you're going to do something, look at it spiritually.

March 5

By Way of Reminder

MANY THINGS CAN PROMPT us to action, such as fear, the prospect of success, or even our own memories. Memories can be good or bad (that is, trauma), and can even lie dormant unless they are revived. Peter said that he used remembrance to help his readers to be motivated, or "stir them up": "I think it right, as long as I am in this body, to stir you up by way of reminder" (2 Pet 1:13). Peter's readers evidently needed to be stirred up, though not because they didn't have knowledge (v. 12). While it is good to forget the things that are behind (Phil 3:13), we can also choose to use our memories for positive spiritual good. Even bad memories, such as being enslaved (Deut 15:15), can be used for a closer relationship with God. If memories lie dormant, we might need to be "stirred up." Otherwise we might lie as dormant as the memories.

March 6

If Nothing Else

EVANGELISM IS FOR THE purpose of saving souls. Before engaging in this spiritually vital endeavor, however, it might be beneficial to remember the stark reality that our chances of "success," of getting the hearer to believe the gospel, are not very good. In the parable of the sower, the sower's "success" rate was only 25 percent (Luke 8:4–15). Yet whether our efforts end in baptism, or if the hearer turns their ear from the truth, by engaging in evangelism we have succeeded. Paul told Timothy to be diligent in his duties, "Keep a close watch on yourself and on the teaching. Persist in this, for by so doing you will save both yourself and your hearers" (1 Tim 4:16). While much of Paul's teaching in Timothy and Titus has its first application to Timothy and Titus as preachers, his words nevertheless remind us that such things as evangelism do good. Among other things, evangelism reinforces that, just as when we first obeyed, we thereby "save ourselves" (Acts 2:40), and that our labor is not vain in the Lord (1 Cor 15:58). Without being evangelistic we certainly won't save the hearer, and it won't do us much good either. By being evangelistic we, as Christians, save somebody, even if nobody listens.

March 7

"With My Voice"

For some, talking is as natural as breathing, while for others (introverts) it takes a great deal of effort. The use of our voice can nevertheless be an ultimate expression, as it were, of the fruit of our soul (though we are not told so, perhaps this is why both the plan of salvation [Rom 10:10] and worship today [Eph 5:19] include the use of our voice). The psalmist said, "With my voice I cry out to the Lord; with my voice I implore the Lord's favor" (Ps 142:1). Two other times in the psalm he makes reference to pouring out his complaint (v. 2), to his cry (vv. 5–6), and to God attending to his cry (v. 6). In several avenues of worship it is proper to be silent. Yet, whether it be a cry of anguish like Jesus' at his death (Matt 27:50), our crying out to God in prayer, or our singing to him in song, we can know that when we do, he hears such expressions (see Jer 33:3). As fruit is the ultimate expression of a fruit-bearing tree, so Christians today express themselves in part with the fruit of their lips (Heb 13:15), a cry which God hears, and which is pleasing to his ears.

March 8

Knowledge Is Potential Power

The saying that "knowledge is power" (credited to Francis Bacon) is true in many ways. For example, if one knows what to do in the event of a medical emergency, that knowledge can give them confidence in knowing that they are possibly better equipped to handle the emergency. Knowledge is also, however, seemingly only power in potential. This is because, according to Scripture, knowledge is to be built upon and used for spiritual good. While we are thus to grow in knowledge (2 Pet 3:18), knowledge is but a block upon which to build toward spiritual growth (2 Pet 1:5–9), without which it could remain power in potential only. Jesus said, "If you know these things, blessed are you if you do them" (John 13:17). Therefore the power and/or confidence brought by the knowledge Jesus offers can help us to face and even defeat the ultimate enemy of death. After that there is no more potential for either (Ps 6:5; 2 Pet 1:13).

March 9

Darkness and Time

Two of the many things that affect us but do not affect God are darkness and time. The psalmist said, "And should I say, 'Surely the darkness will sweep over me, and the light about me be night; even the darkness will not come about from you—the night will lighten—as is the darkness, so is the light" (Ps 139:11–12). We stumble in darkness, and our physical health, and life itself, is affected by the "wrackful siege" of time.[3] God is outside of both of these realms, inasmuch as he had created them (Gen 1; Isa 45:7); he, therefore, is affected by neither (see also 2 Pet 3:8). If we hold to and grow in him, we can spiritually rise above both of these even though we remain bound to a world affected by both. We rise above spiritual darkness (1 Thess 5:7–8) and spiritual death (Eph 2:1) by rising to become more like the One who is above darkness and time (1 John 3:2–3).

---

3. Shakespeare, Sonnet 65.

March 10

A Lying Computer

WORDS ARE POWERFUL BECAUSE they convey ideas. The individual word may not be evil (in other words, there's no power in saying "open sesame"), but may be used alone or in context with other words to convey a message of false ideas. An instrument that conveys words is also only a mechanical tool; it is the words and, more importantly, the ideas behind the words, that contain the power. Such expressions as a "false pen" (Jer 8:8), an "iron stylus and . . . an adamant point" (Jer 17:1), and the pen of the tongue (Ps 45:1) are figures of speech to point the hearer to the true source of the ideas, the heart and hands that formed the words. Allowing for the occasional annoyance of autocorrect, a message on a computer today depends on what we type (and even alerts us to the possibility of our having used the wrong word); thus the pleasantness or bitterness of our message ultimately lies with us. God conveyed his will to us by means of words that are the message of truth (John 17:17). Words and ideas can change the world; God's word is powerful to change our lives (Rom 1:16). Even a false pen, or a lying computer, can't change that.

March 11

Belief Is Power

GUNPOWDER HAD BEEN INVENTED by the fourteenth century but offered little or no power, as no use (that is, the gun) had been invented for it. Again (see yesterday's "Daily"), words and ideas can change the world. Words, including the word of God, are powerful to the extent that we let them find a place in, and thus change, our heart. Not all seeds fall into good ground and germinate (Luke 8:15). It is, therefore, our acceptance or belief of the word that, in effect, gives it its power; as stated by Paul in Rom 1:16: "For I am not ashamed of the gospel, for it is the power of God for salvation to everyone who believes, to the Jew first and also to the Greek" (likewise for the one who already believes, Eph 3:20). Just as with the twin actions of faith and works (Jas 2:24–26), and works and love (1 Cor 13:2), so the gospel, when believed, is thereby given a function and becomes as powerful as dynamite.

March 12

"With My Whole Heart"

WHILE THE VOICE IS an instrument with which we are to, and should, give glory to God in worship (see "Daily" of Mar. 9), that which directs, or should direct, the voice is the heart. The psalmist said, "Let me give thanks to the LORD with all my heart; let me recount all of your wonderful acts" (Ps 9:1). A lying tongue (Prov 6:17) may fool humans, but not the One who knows the deceitful heart from where such words spring. The dispensing of similar words in worship is, therefore, likewise in vain (Matt 15:9), and surely sounds to God like a clanging cymbal (1 Cor 13:1; 14:15). The way to avoid this is to determine to worship God with a right heart, one that will more likely dispense true words, to offer up a sound that is pleasing to God (Ps 19:14).

March 13

Walking a Straight Path

WALKING A STRAIGHT PATH in life is generally preferable to walking a crooked path (unless one is a hiker). As we walk through this life, we choose which path we take (Ps 1:1), and we can control such things as our physical speed and our spiritual outlook (Eph 4:1); yet we don't determine the path itself. The wise man thus said, "Know him in all your ways and he for his part will make your paths straight" (Prov 3:6; the language is very emphatic, that is, "he for his part will make your paths straight"). The word "know" in this verse tells us of the need to apply our mind to thoughts of God as we walk. We usually fret over mundane things, over which Jesus told us not to worry (Matt 6:25–34). A way to know God on our walk is to concentrate on such spiritual things as God's word (Ps 119:105), his will (1 John 5:14), and his providence (Rom 8:28). In other words, a straight physical path is provided if we concentrate on the spiritual.

March 14

Falsehood and Not Truth

A FOUNDATION OF TRUTH is necessary to build a building that is strong, and that, therefore, will last (Matt 7:24–27). Without truth as a foundation, one might have to do such things as twist parts of the building to make it fit. Even if the building is strong, without a foundation of truth it will eventually crumble. Jeremiah pointed out these same erroneous ways of his countrymen to show that the bottom line of their spiritual troubles was that they failed to follow God. In Jer 9:3 he stated, "And they bend their tongue [like] a bow; they are strong in the land with regard to falsehood and not faithfulness; for they proceed from evil to evil, and they do not know me, says the LORD." Their not knowing God and not building upon a foundation of truth meant their building would not last. Knowing God, or being in a right relationship with him (1 John 5:13), means one will build upon truth. This would then mean that everything proceeding therefrom is not bent but properly built, and is built from truth to truth. Such a building is sure to last.

March 15

"A Sustained Mindset"

IN A WORLD WHERE we sometimes have to bear heavy burdens, we all need support. This is seemingly especially true when it comes to the mind, as mental burdens can often be more difficult to bear than physical. Christians can, of course, help each other with their burdens (Gal 6:2), as well as bear their own (Gal 6:5). The promise given in Isa 26:3 is that by placing faith in God the believer has support: "A sustained mindset you will protect with a perfect peace, because he is trusting in you." While the world does, and would like to continue to, dump unpleasant things on our mind, God offers us a way to have our mind sustained. The result of having a sustained mindset is that one is thereby protected with a "perfect peace." Our mind is upheld, or sustained, with the burdens of this life by placing our faith in God.

March 16

Lean on God

TO BE SUSTAINED BY God (see yesterday's "Daily") means that we are not (entirely) supported by other things. If in life we have several things propping us up, it is often no great tragedy if we lose one of them. Spiritually, however, we are required to place our whole trust in God. Perhaps it is possible to have such props in life as friends, hobbies, etc. as long as those things are also supported by our trust in God. Trusting in God means such things as delighting in him (Ps 37:4, the first Hebrew verb therein meaning to "roll upon"), and not leaning upon others (Jer 17:5 states that one who leans on men is cursed), likely because leaning on people is like leaning on a reed that shakes (Ezek 29:6–7). Proverbs 3:5 again states, "Trust in the LORD with all your heart and do not lean upon your understanding." Not that it is wrong to use our own understanding; but to trust in God with all of our heart suggests he is the only one upon whom we can lean.

March 17

"My Praise"

JEREMIAH REFERRED TO GOD as "my praise": "Heal me, O LORD, so that I may be healed; save me, so that I may be saved, for you are my praise" (Jer 17:14). While God is not the object of praise for everyone in the world, he is the object of praise for those who worship him. This means that when we do praise him it is a personal matter. Some aspects of worship are corporate (such as "speaking one [to] another in psalms . . ." [Eph 5:19] and communion as a participation in common); yet all worship is personal. When we pray, sing, and offer our offerings ("each of you is to put something aside," 1 Cor 16:2), such acts flow from our heart to God, the father of the one "who loved me, and gave himself up for me" (Gal 2:20b ASV). This tells us that we can know that when we engage in worship, God knows the condition of our heart for good or bad (Matt 5:23–24; 1 Cor 11:27). Hopefully he will be pleased with my praise. At least I know that when I engage in worship, Someone is listening to me.

March 18

Doing What We Hate

THERE ARE TIMES IN life when it may be good to do something we hate. Jeremiah preached God's word, but said he would rather not: "And if I should say, 'I will not mention him, nor speak again in his name,' then it becomes in my heart as a burning fire contained in my bones, and I am weary of holding [it] in, and I can't" (Jer 20:9). My favorite author, who published over forty books, didn't like to write; and a friend of mine, who has run in over twenty-five marathons, doesn't like to run. Not that one has to be a writer or a runner. But these illustrate that, in life, we may dislike a physical action from which good can be done; or that often, in life, we must endure physical pain or discomfort in order to attain some higher good. Whether it be temptation (1 Cor 10:13), a person we dislike (1 Cor 13:4–5; 2 Thess 3:15), or the general pains of having to endure this life (Rev 21:4), we can do good by looking beyond the physical (pain) to the spiritual (pleasure) that could result.

March 19

I'd Rather Not

JUST AS IT MIGHT at times be necessary to do something unpleasant (see yesterday's "Daily"), so the reverse of this may also be true; that is, there are times we need to avoid doing something we hate. The Christian is to hate evil (Rom 12:9), though we often succumb to the seduction of sin (Heb 11:25). Paul spoke of himself in this regard in Rom 7:15: "For I do not understand my own actions. For I do not do what I want, but I do the very thing I hate." Paul is here expressing that he hates sin, but he sometimes gives in to it. As with doing things we would rather not for a good purpose, so we avoid doing bad things we would like to do by concentrating on the good that results from resisting. Since it is often true that "the harder course is the better course," so it is necessary for the Christian to endure the occasional pain of foregoing sin for the good of pleasing God and for the purity of their soul. We do that which we hate, and avoid that which we hate, by concentrating on the One we love and on spiritual reasons for doing the right thing.

March 20

"According to Your Faith"

THE POWER OF GOD to help is limited to us, not to him. God may act independently of our actions, such as doing good to lead us to repentance (Rom 2:4), and seeing to it that all things work together for the good of his children (Rom 8:28). Yet some biblical promises are conditional, in that God would have us do our part first. Matthew said of Jesus, when he healed two blind men, "Then he touched their eyes, saying, 'According to your faith be it done to you'" (Matt 9:29). We get the impression from this passage that Jesus exercising his power to help the men is conditioned upon their faith (in v. 28 he asked them if they believed he was able to do it). This suggests that the help God offers is more about spiritual than about physical good (that is, it is not necessarily always about fixing a physical problem). Just as God would have us call to him so that he can answer (Jer 33:3), and give to him before he gives to us (Luke 6:38), so God would see a faith and a power (Eph 3:20) in us, so that he can respond accordingly. What are we waiting for?

March 21

Early Detection

MOST PROBLEMS IN LIFE do not fix themselves. A health problem, a leaky roof, or a corrupt heart often only become worse over time. The Bible teaches that sin (evil) is powerful and pervasive, insomuch that, when left alone, "a little leaven leavens the whole lump" (Gal 5:9). When left alone sin can lead to a further hardening of the heart, contributing to the next generation having grown further in evil (Jer 16:12). Evil is looking for a residence (Luke 11:24), and, given the chance, will put down roots and grow (Luke 11:25). Evil can be stopped with good (Rom 12:21), ultimately the good news of the gospel. If we wait until tomorrow, hoping that the problem will go away (Exod 8:10), it is likely not only to be there, but to have grown (Luke 11:26). Evil grows, but it can be overcome with good; if we act now (2 Cor 6:2).

March 22

"Praise Is Suitable"

THERE'S ONLY SO MUCH one can do to change their physical appearance. Many desire the attention, pride, etc. that goes with being physically attractive. Even if one were the most physically attractive person in the world, there is no guarantee that they would be considered attractive by everybody (for example, by a particular person in whom they were interested). Fortunately, God does not see as man sees. While man is impressed by such outer things as physical stature (1 Sam 16:7) and physical beauty (Song 2:14), God is impressed by inner things such as the heart, proper worship (Ps 96:9), and righteous living (Isa 64:6, to the contrary). The psalmist stated, "Praise the LORD! Because it is good to praise our God in song; because it is pleasant, and praise is suitable" (Ps 147:1). Just as putting on Christ upon conversion (Gal 3:27) makes one spiritually attractive to God (Rev 22:14), so proper worship is attractive to God; and that's something we can change.

March 23

The Unanswered Question

A QUESTION WE OFTEN ask when we don't understand something, seemingly especially when it impacts us negatively, is "why?" Why is my life the way it is, why do bad things happen to good people, etc.? For philosophers, this is the start of a journey. For one trying to follow the Bible, it can be a perplexing question that leaves many discouraged (in other words, for many, it signals the end of a journey). It seems that the Bible does not provide an answer to many of these questions. For example—though the readers of the book of Job are told what happened behind the scenes (Job 1–2), Job himself never was, and was never told why his experiences occurred. Habakkuk, likewise, didn't understand why his country was being punished by means of the evil Babylonians, yet concluded in the end, "But as for me, I will exult in the LORD, I will shout in exultation in the God of my salvation" (Hab 3:18). We may never know why there are negative things like pain and suffering in life any more than we can know why there are positive things, such as why God loved the world (John 3:16). Maybe it is not an accident that such questions are left unanswered? While we do need to find truth (2 Tim 3:7), the journey of searching for answers serves a purpose as well (Acts 17:11). Could it be that this is why God left some questions unanswered?

March 24

With God It Is Easy

IF IN LIFE IT requires more energy and effort to do the right thing, as it seems to, and if, again, "the harder course is the better course," as it seems to be, how can Jesus' yoke be "easy" and his "burden . . . light" (Matt 11:30)? When Paul taught Christians to "be strong in the Lord" (Eph 6:10), his wording suggests that the Christian use a strength they already have. The Christian is also to grow (2 Pet 3:18), which suggests increasing in spiritual strength. Isaiah 40:31 again shows that concentrating on things spiritual can give us strength to meet the challenges we face in the physical realm: "But those who wait for the LORD will renew [their] strength; they will raise their pinions like the eagles; they will run and not grow weary; they will walk and not become faint." "Waiting on the Lord" surely includes several things, such as the knowledge that a day of rest awaits when our running comes to an end. That is, knowing that rest awaits can give energy now (2 Thess 1:7; the opposite of which is the lack of energy when one realizes they have a difficult task ahead). Whatever physical strength we have is going to end one day. God offers a spiritual strength that can help us to both overcome physical weakness and to continue in spite thereof. With God the better course is easy.

March 25

Weak in Faith

WHILE EVERYONE'S PHYSICAL STRENGTH diminishes over time, their spiritual strength can again become stronger (2 Cor 4:16). Paul referred to Abraham in this regard: "In hope he believed against hope, that he should become the father of many nations. . . . He did not weaken in faith" (Rom 4:18–19). Both physical and spiritual strength can be controlled. Physical strength will inevitably decline, in spite of the amount of attention we bestow thereupon (1 Tim 4:8). Weakness in faith is, likewise, within our control yet, unlike physical strength, need not become weaker (if it does, it seems we ultimately have only one person to blame). If we apply ourselves to a strong spiritual life, especially with regard to the fountain of faith (God's word; Rom 10:17), we can maintain our strength of faith. Imagine if our faith were as "weak" as a mustard seed (Matt 17:20).

March 26

Growing Strong in Faithfulness

IN THE SECULAR WORLD it is possible for one to become a success based on who they are, rather than on what they've done. With God "success," including spiritual strength, is not earned (Eph 2:8–9), but is based on how we apply ourselves to spiritual things. Thus Jeremiah said, "It is of falsehood and not faithfulness that they have grown strong in the land" (Jer 9:2). "The land" is the land promised to God's people of old, and where they were to remain planted so that they might grow (Ps 37:3). To grow strong in money, power, prestige (3 John 9), or even self-accomplishment without God's approval (Ps 127:1) is an artificial growth, and will likely mean some kind of adversity for the person or those around them (Matt 7:24–27). A life of faithfulness is one built on trust in God (Prov 3:5–6) . . . by following his word. If we are faithful to God, true spiritual strength will be the result (Gal 5:22–23).

March 27

Giving as a Spiritual Act

ATTITUDE IS A LARGE part of what determines acceptable worship before God. While some acts of worship can only be defined as acts of worship (such as prayer or the Lord's Supper), all acts of worship are conveyed with either an acceptable or unacceptable attitude (1 Cor 11:27). Jesus' words "you cannot serve God and mammon" (Matt 6:24) remind us of the incompatibility between flesh and spirit, in this case between God and substance (so the word "mammon" means). Not that money is always wrong; but our attitude can determine how important money is to our heart. Parting with our money in worship can therefore be a pivotal moment when our heart is put to such a test (it would be easy to think of money only in physical terms [as we do in the secular world] when offering the same to God). Hence one reason for emphasizing that this is an act of worship. Unless we think of the offering as spiritual rather than physical, it becomes simply "mammon," rather than part of a spiritual act of devotion with which we hope to touch the heart of God.

March 28

The Fall of Blame

LOOKING FOR SOMEONE TO blame, rather than letting blame fall where it should, is nothing new. Adam, Eve, and the serpent were all to blame for sin (Gen 3), and could not escape when the light of truth eventually shined on them. Trying to avoid a blinding light, or any light that exposes something we wish to keep hidden, is understandable. Spiritually, trying to avoid the light is an attempt to avoid the truth (John 3:20–21), and therefore, in effect, to continue to live in darkness (see Matt 4:16, to the contrary). We can deflect, but we can't avoid the light or what it exposes. It is therefore best for our soul to admit when we are wrong, in part, because to do so is to admit the truth, which is often as easy as looking into a blinding light.

March 29

Putting Fruit to Use

A POINT WE OFTEN make with regard to the "fruit of the Spirit" (Gal 5:22–23) is that fruit is the result, rather than the reward, of being a fruit tree. This result stems from maturity rather than the tree's concentrating on producing. For the Christian this means that by concentrating on their spiritual life, the "fruit of the Spirit" ("love, joy, peace, patience, kindness, goodness, faithfulness, gentleness, self-control," Gal 5:22–23) will result. Without going through each of the nine qualities, we can also see elsewhere in Scripture that the Christian is told to apply these qualities in their life (for example, "love one another" 1 Pet 1:22; "rejoice in the Lord always," Phil 4:4, etc.). Both concentrating on and not concentrating on producing fruit can be good. We concentrate on maturing spiritually toward the end of producing fruit; we concentrate on using fruit to perpetuate more fruit (for example, if we rejoice it will make us joyful). We are thereby twice blessed, and the fruit with which we have been blessed does not go to waste.

March 30

Jesus' Expectations

THE DEFINITION OF "HOPE" as desire combined with expectation tells us that hope has to do with the will. Sometimes one becomes discouraged, even to the point of leaving Christianity, because their expectations were not met (that is, life didn't go the way they wanted or expected). Jesus, likewise, has expectations, including that his hearers know Scripture (Matt 19:4; 21:16), that a mature tree should bear fruit (Matt 21:18–22), for a teacher of Israel to be able to understand basic spiritual concepts (John 3:10), and for his disciples, likewise, to understand (Mark 8:21). All of these have to do with spiritual things, and, therefore, ultimately derive from God's word. It is not necessarily wrong to have expectations for life; but perhaps a way to avoid discouragement is to conform our will to God's (Ps 37:4; Jas 4:3, 15), including changing our perspective from physical to spiritual (Col 3:2). To change our will is to revise our expectations, which could mean less discouragement and more hope. This is what Jesus is expecting—I mean, hoping for (Luke 18:8).

March 31

"Prepared for the Time to Come"

BEING PREPARED FOR WHATEVER may fall in life is a good thing. Yet, we can't anticipate every possible event, inasmuch as we don't know the future. Sometimes it seems we prepare for one thing, only to get hit by another unexpected tragedy. While it is good to do all we can to make our physical lives go as smoothly as possible, it is also not a guarantee for physical success. To prepare spiritually gives one a strong foundation that is both necessary and practical. We can be prepared spiritually by following such teachings as arming ourselves with the right attitude (1 Pet 1:13; 4:1), and laying a good foundation (Matt 7:24–27; 1 Tim 6:19), including being ready for Jesus' return (Matt 25:1–13). We may still have to endure physical pain; but a strong spiritual life with God means he can turn something bad into something good (Gen 50:20), we can at least survive the storm inside (in our soul; Heb 6:19) if not on the outside and, as a result of our being prepared, Jesus will be prepared for us (John 14:3). The best preparations are made not on the outside but on the inside.

April 1

The Fool

THE PSALMIST STATED, "THE fool has said in his heart 'there is no God'" (Ps 14:1). It seems that this can mean either that one believes there is no God and that makes him or her a fool, or that their being a fool led them to conclude that there is no God. Again, one's being an atheist will likely eventually be seen in one's actions (Ps 14:1 goes on to say "they have acted corruptly, they have done abhorrent acts; there is none who does good"), including the lack of any spiritual activity, such as worship (see 1 Cor 11:20). Years ago a famous atheist took a poll by calling people at home in a particular city on Sunday morning, when most churches were conducting worship services. When a respondent replied that they believed in God, the atheist concluded that this person was a "practical atheist." If we live as if there is no God, including our presence at worship when Jesus is there (Matt 18:20), we may or may not be an atheist, but we could be a fool.

April 2

Why Does God Want Us to Worship Him?

SCRIPTURE TEACHES US TO worship God (John 4:24; Rev 19:10). The problem with a human wanting constant adulation is that it is a desire born of selfishness, and, therefore, can likely never be satisfied. Though I wouldn't be surprised if there is one, I don't know of a verse of Scripture that tells us why God wants us to worship him. I have heard people criticize God for his wanting us to worship him; thus we might raise the question of why we are taught to (also knowing, from such books as Habakkuk, that God does not mind the sincere questioner). The fact that God is love (1 John 4:8), and love is unselfish (1 Cor 13:5), leads us to conclude that worshiping God is good for us rather than God. God doesn't need our physical help (Ps 50:11–13), and God's ways toward man are for man's good (Jer 29:11). Knowing these things can help us both to properly engage in worship (that is, unselfishly), as well as to avoid changing it into something else, such as something that satisfies us. What is best for us is to offer to God what he wants, which is unselfish worship to the One who doesn't need our worship.

April 3

Putting the Physical First?

THE STRUGGLE IN THE Christian life is overcoming the physical with the spiritual (Gal 5:17; Eph 6:12), or the struggle between the "natural man" and the "spiritual man" (1 Cor 2:14–15). The incompatibility of flesh and spirit reinforces to Christians the need to concentrate on putting the kingdom of God first (Matt 6:33). Jesus often saw to peoples' physical needs (such as healing them) first. By doing so the person was then able to listen to Jesus' teaching (they could concentrate on the spiritual), since they were no longer in physical pain. We certainly need to take care of physical things such as ailments and hunger. Perhaps, though, we can strike a balance in our struggle by where we place our emphasis. Our need is to concentrate on putting spiritual things first, thereby making physical things secondary (that is, in the emphasis of our heart). Jesus doesn't heal miraculously today as he did in the first century, and we should not ignore such things as physical ailments (Jas 2:24–26). Yet, by concentrating on the spiritual we can leave the physical for him to take care of first if he chooses. By putting him first he may take care of us first, so that we can concentrate on that which is most important, our spiritual life.

April 4

"Uncircumcised Ears"

MEMBERS OF THE SAME family often hear each other in a unique way (for example, a couple that has been married for thirty-nine years sharing an inside joke from when they were first married). Anyone can understand the Bible. But when God spoke of Israel as having "uncircumcised ears" (Jer 6:10), it surely struck a chord with his hearers as it put them in the same category as one outside of God's covenant people (see David referring to "this uncircumcised Philistine," 1 Sam 17:26). The Bible speaks of having an ear, or a mindset, that is conditioned (or not) toward receiving God, as the ears stood for one's attitude (most people in the ancient world could not read). It thus speaks of being "dull of hearing" (Heb 5:11), of one turning their ears from the truth (2 Tim 4:4), and of taking heed what or how we hear (Mark 4:24; Luke 8:18). Having the right kind of ears means we have the right mindset. Christianity being a way of life that begins in the mind and the mind being something we can, to a large extent, control, we can, therefore, have the right kind of ears to hear what God wants, rather than what we want. We can have ears that are right with God, a mind that is right with God, and, thus, a life that is right with God. It depends, not on the message that is sent (Jer 1:12), but on what kind of ears receive it.

April 5

That's Reasonable

WE WANT THINGS IN life to make sense; but humans can't be left to reason with themselves and expect to arrive at truth (to illustrate, something that makes sense to one person may not make sense to another). God is reasonable, and wants to reason with us. Isaiah 1:18 reads, "Please come, so that we may resolve [this], [ESV, "reason together"], says the LORD; even though your sins are as crimson, they will be [made] white as snow. Even though they be red as scarlet, they will be as wool." The NT speaks of those who "reasoned with themselves," which is often spoken of negatively (Matt 21:25; Luke 5:21) or is questioned by Jesus (Matt 16:8; Mark 2:8). There are also verses that speak of reasoning with Scripture (Acts 17:2) and reasoning with regard to spiritual things (Acts 19:8). To work through something in our mind can be good, but the reasoning process with God must be toward a spiritual end, that is, to bring us to an understanding of Scripture so that we can be right with God. Without the Bible to guide our reasoning process, we might reason through something, but still end up in the wrong spiritual place. That is, after all of our own reasoning, we might find ourselves as one of the "unreasonable and evil" (2 Thess 3:2).

April 6

Worn Out

Though he doesn't give one, Paul evidently had a reason for teaching that Christians to "pray without ceasing" (1 Thess 5:17). We surely need to be encouraged to keep up our prayer life. Again, it is generally harder in life to do the right thing. If we keep trying with seemingly no results for our efforts, we might become discouraged or "worn out." In Jesus' parable in Luke 18, the judge in the parable decided to grant the lady her request "lest she wear me out by her continual coming" (18:5 ASV). In other words, with regard to a consistent prayer life, somebody is going to be worn out. Either we continually pray and, as in the parable, "wear out" the Lord, or we become worn out, and possibly give up due to discouragement. Since one of us is going to be "worn out," it might as well be the One who invites us to lay our petitions at his throne (Heb 4:16), in the hope of receiving our requests according to his will (1 John 5:14). Knowing that the Lord in reality does not actually become weary of sincere requests (Isa 59:1) can give us the strength we need to "pray without ceasing"; or not get worn out.

April 7

Storing Up

PAUL'S TEACHING ON GIVING in 1 Cor 16:2 is that Christians are to plan their giving by storing up in view of worship on the first day of the week: "On the first day of every week, each of you is to put something aside and store it up, as he may prosper, so that there will be no collecting when I come." What Paul describes is a deliberate storing up of our money in order to express our love and devotion to God. In the NT storing up can be intentional, as with good things (Matt 6:19–20), unintentional, such as storing up God's wrath by living a sinful life (Rom 2:5), or both, by storing up money for ourselves rather than for God (thereby incurring his displeasure, Jas 5:3). Certainly it is not wrong to save, such as in view of emergencies. But what determines whether our storing up is acceptable includes both the amount and, perhaps more importantly, the heart that decided the amount. How and the extent to which we store up our physical things will determine what we have stored up in eternity.

April 8

"Where Shall I Go?"

THE PSALMIST EXPRESSED THAT there is nowhere he can go where God is not: "To where would I go from your Spirit? And to where would I flee from your presence?" (Ps 139:7). This type of question (rhetorical) is one that everybody knows the answer to (just like God asking Adam and Eve, "Have you eaten from the tree?" Gen 3:11), and is asked to emphasize a truth. The psalmist does not want to go anywhere that God is not (v. 10), and anywhere he finds himself he knows that God is there. This fact is a fearful truth for the sinner, but is a comfort to the child of God (John 3:20–21). This is true because of the nature of God (omnipresent), and because of our nature (as children we need our Father). Even the best parent can't always be there for their child; God can, God is, and God always will be (Matt 28:20; Heb 13:5)—no matter where we go.

April 9

"My Sleep Was Pleasant"

AFTER RECEIVING A MESSAGE from God, Jeremiah said, "At this I awoke and looked, and my sleep was pleasant darkness to me" (Jer 31:26). The message Jeremiah received had to do with the restoration of God's people from slavery (v. 23), and of God satisfying and replenishing their soul (v. 25). God does not give new revelations today (Jude 3; Rev 22:18–19). Yet the restoration of his people then included the type of speech they would utter (v. 23). For Jeremiah, having received a message from God made his sleep sweet. Imagine if we went to sleep with thoughts of God and his word (Ps 4:8). Imagine then how we would awaken.

April 10

"This Is a Holy Man of God"

WHETHER THROUGH SPEECH, ACTION, or demeanor, a holy life can be seen. The light of the gospel certainly is not to be purposely dimmed (Matt 5:16), but is to shine for the purpose of bringing glory to God (Eph 1:12). If we live the Christian life, people should be able to tell (though impressing others is not our primary goal, John 12:43). The woman in 2 Kgs 4:9 could recognize that Elisha was a holy man: "And she said to her husband, 'Here [please], I know that he is a holy man of God, passing by us continually.'" As Christians, there is a light within us that cannot and should not be hidden (1 Tim 5:25), and which is painful for some to see (John 3:20). When others recognize this spiritual character of our lives, it is a good thing, in part, because it suggests a character of life that God will recognize in the end (Rev 14:1).

April 11

I'll Make It Up

Part of living in a temporal world is the reality that we are going to suffer loss. Whether it be money, time, or the pain of hurt relationships, we often want to make up that which has been lost. The sad truth is that many things in life can't be recouped, especially illustrated by the loss of the abstract and fleeting quality of time. The wise man said, "A brother offended is harder [to breach] than a strong city; strife is like the bars of a fortress" (Prov 18:19). Even if a brother offended is won back, there is often irreversible damage to the relationship. The Christian today is blessed in knowing that forgiveness with God means we don't need to make up such offenses as sin, inasmuch as salvation is not earned (Eph 2:8–9), and God forgets when he forgives (Heb 8:12). Forgiveness also carries the promise of heaven, where we do not need to make anything up, because we no longer lose anything (1 Pet 1:4; Rev 21:4).

April 12

But This Is Mine

ANANIAS AND SAPPHIRA WERE punished for keeping back part of the proceeds from a sale of land, then lying about the amount they gave (Acts 5:1–11). How much we give is between us and God, and this is not to say that we would suffer a similar fate as they. With regard to worship in general, the psalmist said, "Let me praise the Lord with all my heart" (Ps 9:1). Worship is to be with our spirit (John 4:24), and, therefore, with our heart (see 1 Cor 14:15). Worship being a devotional act we offer to God, it is, therefore again, by definition unselfish. Whether we promise to worship God with all of our heart is up to us; if we do, let us be careful not to keep back a part for ourselves.

April 13

Eating God's Word

EZEKIEL WAS TOLD TO "eat this scroll" of God's word (Ezek 3:1), with the result that it was "in my mouth as sweet as honey" (v. 3; see also Rev 9:9–10). Some things in life, such as the different elements of a meal, are enjoyable because of the way they compliment each other. There is nothing wrong with having a favorite verse or book of the Bible; but since God said he is "watching over my word to perform it" (Jer 1:12), it is surely no accident that the Bible consists of sixty-six books which, either directly or indirectly, compliment each other. For example, the book of Exodus begins with information on Joseph's family which, in order to understand it, one needs the book of Genesis. The OT itself was written for our learning (Rom 15:4), and is necessary to understanding the NT. Keeping in mind the entirety of God's word can thereby help us to handle "aright the word of truth" (2 Tim 2:15), and sweeten the eating thereof.

April 14

No More Need of Pain

Two benefits we can glean from pain are the knowledge that pain is usually part of growing, and that pain can cause one to turn to God when they might not have otherwise. In other words, we can, again, gain spiritual benefit from physical pain. Pain is part of living in this temporal world, seemingly made worse by the reality of sin (Gen 3:16). John said that, in heaven, God will have removed all pain: "He will wipe away every tear from their eyes, and death shall be no more, neither shall there be mourning, nor crying, nor pain anymore, for the former things have passed away" (Rev 21:4). This fits the idea that in heaven we won't need to grow or turn to God, and that the pain accompanying these things will have been resolved. While living in this world knowing these things can change our perspective regarding the pain we endure, and help us use it as a motivator to look toward that time when we won't "need" pain anymore.

April 15

Slave or Free

THE DISTINCTION BETWEEN THE physical and the spiritual can be illustrated by the paradox of servitude in the Christian life. That is, while sin promises freedom, but actually enslaves (John 8:34), the Christian life offers spiritual freedom by one's becoming a servant of the Lord (1 Pet 2:16). The way to appreciate and to distinguish between both is to adopt a spiritual mindset (Col 3:2). By so doing we can thereby see life with its pains, limitations, and obligations as a necessary part of enjoying the blessings of spiritual freedom (as the saying goes, "freedom is not free"). While we are bound to this temporal world, our spirit is, and can only be, free in Christ (John 8:32). The spiritual mindset we adopt will help us to bear joyfully the yoke of servitude for Jesus (Matt 11:28–30), and avoid the enslavement of the freedom promised by sin.

April 16

Think It Through

WE LIKE FOR OUR plans in life to work. No plan is guaranteed to work, but every plan will likely work better with enough thought behind it. Whether it be counting the number of calories in a diet or planning the number of times a runner runs during the week, a plan is more likely to be successful with proper thought. Inasmuch as the mind, again, governs the heart and the heart prompts action, our actions then, ultimately, come from our thoughts. The biblical Greek word translated "repentance" literally means an "after-mind"; and spiritual growth is conditioned by thinking on certain spiritual things. Thus, Paul again said: "Finally, brothers, whatever is true, whatever is honorable, whatever is just, whatever is pure, whatever is lovely, whatever is commendable, if there is any excellence, if there is anything worthy of praise, think about these things" (Phil 4:8). To engage in such mental activity is not the end but rather the beginning, as reflected in Paul's next thought, "practice these things, and the God of peace will be with you" (v. 9). We have the God of peace, and thus the peace of God (v. 7) not by doing only nor by thinking only but by fulfilling the thoughts in our mind that have been fostered by God's word. There is hereby no guarantee of success as a physical plan, but we are guaranteed success by the spiritual quality of peace.

April 17

"Rend Your Hearts"

How one reacts to truth is likely a reflection of the condition of their heart. A light shining in one's eyes can be painful; but for one living in darkness, who longs for light, even though it may require painful adjustment, it is likely refreshing (Matt 4:16). When King Jehoiakim heard the word of God through Jeremiah, his reaction was to cut up the physical copy and burn it (Jer 36:23). The Bible laments that the word did not cause the king nor others to fear nor tear their garments in repentance (Jer 36:24). Naturally, there can be different reactions to the word, including neutral (Acts 24:25), violent (Acts 7:54–59), or penitent (Acts 2:37). The word of God is not bound (2 Tim 2:9), nor can it be burned (including that Jeremiah reproduced his book, Jer 36:32). When we hear the word of God, our need is to tear our heart, not our garments (Joel 2:13)—and certainly not the Bible.

April 18

Wait and Pray

PAUL'S ADMONITION TO "PRAY without ceasing" (1 Thess 5:17), combined with Jesus' teaching to not give up on unanswered prayer requests (Luke 18:1–8), can seemingly add another dimension to our prayer life, which is the suggestion of not rushing our requests. That is, knowing that the action of prayer can strengthen our spiritual life, and that prayer can be spiritually more beneficial than simply receiving a request born of selfishness (Jas 4:3), tells us that there is a spiritual benefit to purposely delaying. For example, if a decision lies before us, but the decision does not have to be made today, to delay action would allow one more time to pray about it, and would help focus their mind away from themselves and perhaps only having their desires fulfilled. This is only a suggestion (I don't know of any Scripture which specifically teaches this idea). But who knows?—we may get what we ask for. Of course, that would mean an end to our praying about it.

April 19

Twisting the Scriptures

ARGUING WITH GOD IS not a good idea. Peter evidently learned his lesson when, after resisting God in Acts 10, he later taught (referring to Paul's writings), "There are some things in them that are hard to understand, which the ignorant and unstable twist to their own destruction, as they do the other Scriptures" (2 Pet 3:16). Not knowing God's word, combined with being spiritual unstable, can cause one to twist the Scriptures. The means by which we overcome this dilemma includes a knowledge of God's word combined with, and for the purpose of, spiritual growth. Unlike Peter (Acts 10:15), we won't be told directly by the Lord that we are misguided in our understanding. We do have the last thing Peter wrote: "Grow in the grace and knowledge of our Lord and Savior Jesus Christ" (2 Pet 3:18). When Peter argued with God, he was coming from a place of his knowledge of the former teaching of God's word. I wonder whether Peter ever thought back on the time he argued with God, and said to himself, "I wish I had had someone tell me to grow in grace and knowledge"?

April 20

Whether Good or Evil

THE MEN IN JER 42:6 stated that they would obey God no matter what: "Whether it is good or evil, we will obey the LORD our God to whom we are sending you, in order that it may be well with us when we obey the LORD our God." In the Bible "good" is, again, a concept defined by God (Gen 1:4), and "evil" is basically stuff we don't want (for example, the word "evil" is used to refer to God's judgments, Jer 35:17). God brings about both (see Isa 45:6), and they are not to be confused (Isa 5:20). The motivation of the men in Jeremiah was "that it may be well with us." Simply doing "good" does not make one right with God (Matt 7:22–23); and, while it is good to sacrifice (Ps 54:6), to obey is better (1 Sam 15:22) because it will mean good things for us, whether in this life or the next. But we obey no matter what.

April 21

"I Was Glad"

O<small>FTEN IN LIFE</small> A feeling of anticipation brings more delight than the fulfillment of a desire. For example, we likely get more excited at the suggestion, rather than the receiving, of ice cream. If so, this could be because we like ice cream, we don't have ice cream, and it looks like we are going to get ice cream. The psalmist said, "I was glad when they said to me, 'Let us go to the house of the L<small>ORD</small>'" (Ps 122:1; also ESV). The psalmist rejoiced simply at the suggestion that he and his neighbors go to worship, for seemingly the same reasons as our getting ice cream. We today don't worship in a specific location (John 4:21). Yet our attitude toward worship, and toward going to worship, is conditioned by the spiritual condition of our heart, including whether we want to go and be with Jesus and his people (Matt 18:20). The angels in heaven rejoice at the turning of one sinner (Luke 15:7); could it be because of the excitement of knowing they will see them in heaven?

April 22

Which Verse Do I Use?

ONE OF THE BEST ways to overcome temptation is to use the "sword of the Spirit," as Jesus did when he was tempted (Matt 4:1). Whether it be a temptation to sin, or the trial of a difficulty in everyday life, God's word is the necessary power to be spiritually successful (Rom 1:16). While the Bible speaks of only one sword of the Spirit (Eph 6:17), there are many verses in the Bible (it would be difficult to quote the entire Bible every time we are tempted). We might wonder, therefore, which verse do we use?—a question to which there may not be one answer. In time of need, the action of searching through our Bible, or searching our own database (that is, our mind), can be a profitable exercise, and one with which we will surely be successful (Prov 2:4-6; Matt 7:7). Like a miner having to sift through tons of dirt to find a single ounce of gold, to so search is a profitable spiritual exercise that reinforces our determination of heart. Not that there is any "dirt" in God's word; but searching strengthens our resolve to find the gold, and can thereby bring us closer to God—especially if we don't stop searching.

April 23

Think on the Negative

As Christians, we are taught to concentrate on the positive: "Finally, brothers, whatever is true, whatever is honorable, whatever is just, whatever is pure, whatever is lovely, whatever is commendable, if there is any excellence, if there is anything worthy of praise, think about these things" (Phil 4:8), again meaning that we are to add these things to "the account of our mind." Doing this provides us with a spiritual reserve to prepare us for challenging times. To consider the negative, however, can also provide the benefit of spiritual preparation, for the purpose of overcoming whatever might happen. Thus Shadrach, Meshach, and Abed-Nego said that even if God did not deliver them from the furnace, they still wouldn't worship Nebuchadnezzar's image (Dan 3:18); Paul said he was ready to be bound and to die for Jesus (Acts 21:13); and the psalmist said he would not fear "even though I should walk through the valley of the shadow of death" (Ps 23:4). We dwell on the positive to overcome the negative; we consider the negative in order to overcome it beforehand, lest negative circumstances overcome us. Both the positive and the negative can provide us with strength to be victorious in the Christian life. When looked at spiritually, both positive and negative can be positive.

April 24

Consistency and Truth

IT IS A TERRIBLE feeling to know that we have disappointed someone we look up to. Jesus seemed disappointed in the disciples after he had calmed the storm, when he said to them, "Where is your faith?" (Luke 8:25). Whether it be one's health, occupation, or personal relationships, consistency is important in many realms of life (not that there is anything necessarily wrong with being spontaneous). It is difficult for fallible humans to be 100 percent dependable, simply because we are fallible humans (Rom 3:23). Being consistent seems to depend on such things as determination of heart and steadfastness of soul. It also depends on holding to an unchanging standard. Being consistent does not mean we will always be right, or that we will never sin. Yet, the results of being inconsistent may include not improving in some endeavors, and that others, including the Lord, will not be able to depend on us. We develop the quality of consistency not by relying on how we feel, which can change, but by determining to follow a standard, something that does not change. That unchanging standard is truth, and the personal embodiment thereof is Jesus, who is truth (John 14:6). By following him we are more likely to be consistent, or to not disappoint him.

April 25

Unselfish Prayer

T̲h̲e̲ ̲a̲c̲t̲s̲ ̲o̲f̲ ̲w̲o̲r̲s̲h̲i̲p̲ in which the Christian engages should first be to praise God, yet also to benefit the participant by his or her so engaging therein. Most of the acts (communion, giving, preaching, singing) can seemingly more easily be understood as primarily unselfish. Prayer is one of the few acts of worship that might be looked at as selfish, that is, a time for us to ask God for things we want. It seems important, therefore, to emphasize that prayer is also an act of worship, and is therefore intended first for God. While, certainly, God wants us to ask him for the things we desire (Heb 4:16), and we might receive what we want through persistent prayer (Luke 18:1–8), this avenue of worship is no different than giving; it is something we offer to God in order to bring glory to him. By keeping such things in mind as Jesus' teaching that we begin our prayer with words of praise to God ("hallowed be your name," Matt 6:9), we can thereby reinforce that we are engaging in something designed to please the One to whom it is directed; and also be reminded that he is listening to us.

April 26

"I Am Not Worthy"

WE SOMETIMES SPEAK OF being worthy of such things in life as praise from others or holding a certain position (such as a job). In so doing we probably mean that we haven't earned it (even if we may not even realize it). In the Bible worthiness has to do with balance. The Greek word translated "worthy" is *axios*, from which comes the English word "axis" (and the related word "axle"). An axle balances two tires. Thus several Scriptures using this word reflect the idea of balance, or something that corresponds to something else, including John the baptizer (Mark 1:7), the Christian and the Lord's Supper (1 Cor 11:27), and one's life after repenting (Matt 3:8). Rather than looking at such actions as a measuring up to, perhaps we should think of them rather as actions that correspond, or balance, like a corresponding tire. Rather than spending time and effort doing things that we think will earn us a place (Matt 7:21), a spiritual life based on truth keeps us stable (Col 1:23) because it corresponds to truth, thereby keeping us in balance, or "worthy."

April 27

Unbelief

WE MAY THINK OF unbelief only as a mindset that has concluded that God does not exist. While this is certainly one manifestation of a lack of faith, unbelief can be observed in other ways as well. Hebrews 3:19 tells us, "So we see that [Israel was] unable to enter because of unbelief." Throughout their history Israel evidently believed that God existed, yet continually lapsed into idolatry (1 Kgs 11:4–5), adultery (Jer 5:8), and other sins. Believing that God exists will do our soul good when it is translated into action, specifically that of doing God's will (Matt 7:21; Jas 2:26). This is one way to know that one is a believer—or an unbeliever.

April 28

"Your Truth"

To take possession of something does not change what the thing is. For example, when one buys a house, it is now their house, even though the house has not changed. Many today refer to "my truth," in a seeming effort to redefine something that cannot be changed. The psalmist, however, referred to God's truth: "Let me bow toward your holy temple, and give thanks [to] your name for your covenant loyalty and your truth: For you have magnified your word over all your name" (Ps 138:2). Truth is from God, as reflected in such things as Jesus' (John 14:6) and God's word (John 17:17) being referred to as "the truth." Truth is God's because he has defined it; and truth is truth because it can't be changed. There is, therefore, no such thing as "my truth," unless we take possession of God's truth and make it ours. When we do, it will change us (1 Pet 1:22), but our doing so does not change truth. "Let me bow toward your holy temple, and give thanks [to] your name for your covenant loyalty and your truth."

April 29

"Turn from Evil"

THERE CAN BE DIFFERENT responses to evil, including facing it down with Scripture (Matt 4:1–11), resisting it (Jas 4:7), and fleeing from it (2 Tim 2:22). The psalmist gave three directions in this regard: "Turn away from evil and do good, and stay indefinitely" (Ps 37:27). We turn from evil, among other things, because it is not going away, and because the turning from it (such as with regard to sexual abstinence) works every time. We do good because one likely cannot do good and evil at the same time (Ps 1), and because doing good is part of overcoming evil (Rom 12:21). Once we do these things, we then stay with that which made us right with God (Col 2:6), or never turn back to evil.

April 30

Providence and the Word

THE PROMISE OF GOD's providence (Rom 8:28) is qualified by two things. Paul said in this verse, "And we know that for those who love God all things work together for good, for those who are called according to his purpose." God promises to care for everyone in a general way (Matt 5:45). Romans 8:28 offers God's promise of special providence for those "who love God," for those who are "called according to his purpose." Both of these can be connected with God's word, inasmuch as Jesus said if one loves God they will keep his commandments (John 14:15), and also because one is called "through the gospel" (2 Thess 2:14), which is according to God's purpose (2 Tim 1:9). God's word doesn't tell us what the future holds for our lives, nor whether events will work in our favor. Yet through God's word, one can know that whatever does happen can be for spiritual good (perhaps to meet our spiritual need, Phil 4:19), and can ultimately bring glory to God (Eph 1:12). Even if these things don't conform to our purposes, by conforming to his purposes in love, it works together for good

May 1

"That I Might Learn"

WE CAN LOOK AT troubles through different lenses, depending on the motivation of our heart. Like Paul (2 Cor 12:10), the psalmist looked at a humble state as a motivator, in that it caused him to learn God's word: "It is good for me to have been afflicted, in order that I may learn your statutes" (Ps 119:71). The Hebrew word translated "afflicted" has a sense of being bowed down. Like a flower borne down by weather, sometimes life or evil causes us to be afflicted or bowed down. Whether the psalmist had let God's word fall to the ground (1 Sam 3:19), it was cast to the ground (Dan 8:12); or being bowed down was the only time the psalmist looked up, he considered being bowed down a good thing, as it caused him to learn God's word. And learning God's word surely lifted him up.

May 2

Advice for Life

WHAT ADVICE WOULD YOU give someone on the best way to live their life? While the Bible is not a manual on how to get life to physically work, it does contain advice on how to live one's life before God (such as Peter's admonition for those who would "see good days," 1 Pet 3:10). Three biblical admonitions that I would offer as advice for life include the following: "Trust in the LORD with all your heart" (with the result that he will "make your paths straight" (Prov 3:5a–6b); work hard (Eccl 9:10, inasmuch as rest is a good thing [Mark 6:31], but time is fleeting [Jas 4:14]); and don't give up (1 Cor 15:58; Rev 2:10, inasmuch as quitting is final). Advice is plentiful; but we are only given one life, and getting it to "work" is not easy. How we define a "good" life also depends on our own perceptions, and should, for the Christian, be defined according to what God calls "good." Following any biblical advice is always good, as the Bible offers us a good, and even a more abundant, life (John 10:10).

May 3

One or the Other

WE SOMETIMES SPEAK OF "grey areas," or questions, the answers to which are not clear to us. While it may seem naïve to say that there are no such things as grey areas, the concept of truth suggests that most (all?) realities are either one way or the other. That is, the Bible speaks of "good," as well as its opposite, "evil" (Isa 45:6). If one is not a friend of Jesus (John 15:14) they are his enemy (Matt 12:30; Rom 5:10). The existence of truth means there is such a thing as its opposite, that is, error. We may struggle in life to know which is which, and some go so far as to call something by its opposite (that is, calling "evil" "good" and "good" "evil," Isa 5:20). It may be that a "grey area" is a reflection not of the truth but of our lack of understanding thereof. A light in our home can't be on and not on at the same time; how much more is this true with regard to truth?

May 4

Lifting God's Name

TO WORSHIP IS TO offer or lift to God in order to please him. The Bible speaks of the worshiper lifting his soul (Ps 25:1), lifting his heart (Lam 3:41), and lifting holy hands (1 Tim 2:8). In the Ten Commandments, God states that the worshiper was not to "take up the name of the LORD your God in vain" (Exod 20:7). The word "take" is literally in Hebrew "lift" (or "bear"), and appears just after a commandment against worshiping other gods (v. 6). Certainly, speaking God's name in a profane way (that is, cursing) is unacceptable to God (Eph 4:29), and the Christian today is not strictly bound by the Ten Commandments. Yet purity requires that when we lift God's name in worship we do so with a pure heart, out of pure motives, and in a pure manner; in other words, not in vain.

May 5

No Harm in Asking

To make request of someone is often an imposition on the one being asked, and thus requires that we do so in a proper way (such as following certain social customs). The man in Luke 11 who came to his friend at midnight is described as doing so in an improper fashion: "I tell you, though he will not get up and give him anything because he is his friend, yet because of his impudence he will rise and give him whatever he needs" (Luke 11:8). The Greek word translated "impudence" appears only here in the NT, and bears a negative sense, of one not caring about what is proper. The widow in Luke 18:5 likewise came to the judge so often that he feared she would "wear [him] out" (ASV) by her continual coming. The fact that God encourages us to come to him in "confidence" (Heb 4:16) suggests that making a request of him is not an imposition; it does not bother God that we ask, unless we ask for the wrong reason (Jas 4:3).

May 6

"Heal Me"

HEALING IS SOMETHING ONLY God can do. This means, among other things, that God should also receive the praise for healing. Today our bodies heal naturally (non-miraculously, the way God made them) with the help of doctors and medicine. In the first century the apostles and others had the ability to heal miraculously (something we don't have today). One can still pray for healing today, to ask God to assist our body in the natural healing process. Jeremiah prayed for healing, for the purpose of his being healed: "Heal me O Lord, so that I may be healed" (Jer 17:14). Jeremiah followed this with a request for salvation ("save me, so that I might be saved"), and finally expressed praise to God: "Because you are my praise." Even if "only" through natural processes today, only God can heal, only God can save from sin (Isa 53:5), and only God is our praise.

May 7

"Healed Slightly"

HEALING SOMETHING ONLY SLIGHTLY can do more harm than good because of the negative effect it can have on one's attitude, that is, the realization that they aren't really healed. Error can satisfy in the short run, often because it is easier both to offer and to accept than truth is (for example, it satisfies "itching ears," 2 Tim 4:3). Thus, a temporary fix based on error can be more harmful, in that it offers one a false hope, since it is not based on truth. The false prophets of Jeremiah's day may have made people feel better with a promise of peace, but their message thereby did more harm than good. "And they healed the fracture of the daughter of my people superficially, saying, 'Peace, peace'; when there is no peace" (Jer 8:11; see also yesterday's "Daily"). God offers true peace to the one whose mind is sustained by him (Isa 26:3). While the sword of truth may initially cut (Matt 10:34), any wound sustained thereby is likely to heal better in the long run than a false treatment, or a "slight healing," based on a lie.

May 8

Treasure and the Heart

OUR REASONS FOR PLACING a value on certain things and not on others can be mysterious, evidently because of the mysterious nature of the human heart (why, for example, does not everybody value cuneiform tablets?). Jesus said, "For where your treasure is, there will your heart be also" (Matt 6:21). Our life will follow the direction of our heart, and our heart is governed, at least in part, by the emphasis we place on that which is important to us. We may think that something made of gold or a family heirloom is valuable, but not want to put forth the effort to take care of it. On the other hand, if we put forth effort into preserving something (such as our lawn), our heart will be conditioned accordingly because of the effort we have made. Saving money is not necessarily wrong. But Jesus' words tell us that the effort we make, or where we place our treasure, is where we can expect our heart to settle; and, with that, our life will surely follow.

May 9

"Their Heart Is Far from Me"

WHILE IT IS NECESSARY to draw near to God (Ps 73:28; Jas 4:8), it is possible to worship him though our heart is centered on another treasure (see yesterday's "Daily"). Jesus said that the Pharisees and scribes drew near to God, yet worshiped him "in vain": "This people honors me with their lips, but their heart is far from me; in vain do they worship me, teaching as doctrines the commandments of men'" (Matt 15: 8–9). What made their worship vain was that, in their worship, they taught the commandments of men. The choice between God's commandments and the commandments of men is a choice between truth and error, or God's will and man's. To properly draw near to God begins in the heart, and is made acceptable by following through thereon according to God's will or his teaching. Otherwise our drawing near to him leaves us afar off.

May 10

Standing Afar Off

WHILE IMPROPER TEACHING CAN cause one's heart to be far off from God (see yesterday's "Daily"), one can properly draw near to God by standing afar off. In Luke 18 Jesus told about the Pharisee, who tried to draw near by telling God how great he was (vv. 9–12), and the publican, who stood "afar off" in humility (vv. 13–14). Jesus said the publican was justified rather than the Pharisee. In both this passage and Matt 15:8–9, the one who was displeasing to God was so because of the improper placement of their heart, and both tried to get past God with false or improper words. The publican in Luke 18, however, was justified before God because the humility in his heart caused him to stand afar off—and this drew him near to God.

May 11

Command and Condition

COMMANDS ARE EVIDENTLY GIVEN due to the importance of what needs to be done, perhaps combined with the commander either being reluctant or not knowing their need to take action. God's commands are for our good, whether we realize it or not. There are seemingly some who don't realize they are in a less than desirable state. Perhaps this is why God commands the sinner to come so that he might reason with him (and thus receive forgiveness; Isa 1:18), to come so that they might receive rest from the labor of sin (Matt 11:28–30), and to "come so that we might walk in the light of the Lord" (Isa 2:5). God also offers us, from this, a result that we can enjoy and appreciate; and it begins with something that is good for us—the command to "come."

May 12

True Power

TO BE TRULY EMPOWERED comes not from without, but from within. A politician who wins an election, or a nation that acquires strength to defend itself has a type of power, yet it is not lasting, in that such power is temporal (see John 19:11). Jesus said that a power that can do physical harm need not be feared, compared to the Power that can destroy our soul (Matt 10:28). True power resides in such actions as accepting responsibility (versus, for example, having a position of power dropped on one), having an inner strength that helps us endure persecution (Rom 5:3–4), and a belief that not only saves our soul (Rom 1:16) but grants us access to a power that can do beyond what we can comprehend (Eph 3:20). True power is spiritual.

May 13

No Room for Doubt

James taught that having faith means there is no room for doubt: "But let him ask in faith, with no doubting, for the one who doubts is like a wave of the sea that is driven and tossed by the wind" (Jas 1:6). Like computer memory, we choose whether to save positive or negative thoughts. And, like our home or other space, if we want to accommodate someone, we will "make room" for them. It seems unclear (to me) whether the mind has a capacity for unlimited memory storage; and we usually do in life what we want to do. When it comes to the use of our mind, Christians are instructed to add good thoughts (Phil 4:8), and to remember things that contribute to their spiritual life (2 Pet 1:12; Jude 17). When it comes to doubt, the Christian may or may not have the room; but we certainly choose whether to make room.

May 14

Decrease to Increase

IN MANY AREAS OF life (such as money [Luke 12:18], or a child's growth [Luke 2:52]), we like to see an increase; for other things, such as an undesirable medical condition, we naturally want to observe a decrease. While the Christian life promises abundance (John 10:10), whatever the Christian is or becomes is best left up to God's will. As John the baptizer was beginning his ministry he made the statement, "He must increase, but I must decrease" (John 3:30). This simple statement puts into perspective the ingredient necessary for our exaltation (that is, humility; Luke 14:11; 1 Pet 5:6), as well as the need to bring glory to God. As the forerunner who prepared the way for the Messiah (Matt 3:3), John evidently did not want to increase along with Jesus. For the Christian, by "increasing" the Lord (Col 3:17), and "decreasing" ourselves (humbly submitting our will to his), we will thereby bring glory to him, and receive an increase (we will be exalted) in return (Matt 23:12). Decreasing his will is what Jesus did (Phil 2:7–8), and being exalted is what he received (Phil 2:9).

May 15

"If You Will Not Believe"

LIKE ANY GOOD THING, belief (like unbelief) is a choice. Among other things, to believe in truth provides a stability that anchors the soul (Heb 6:19). While some prefer to not stay in one place, it is good to be stable (as it shows that one has "horse sense"). Isaiah 7:9b, to the contrary, reads, "If you will not believe, you will indeed not be established." The words translated "believe" and "be established" are from the same Hebrew word, having to do with confirmation or support (the word "amen" comes from this word). Faith is necessary to being established, and being established is necessary to avoiding being tossed about by the swells of life (Jas 1:6). If we believe, God offers us support (Isa 26:3) and a place in which not only to be planted, but to grow and flourish to his glory (Ps 1:3).

May 16

"What This Means"

When things happen to us, especially "bad" things (such as a delayed flight or bad medical news), we often look for meaning therein; that is, we want to know why such things happened. It may, at times, be difficult to find meaning in such things as another person's speech, what an author is trying to say, or why certain events befall. At the same time, many seem either not to look for, or not be able to find, meaning in Scripture. Jesus (quoting Hos 6:6) said we have a need to find the meaning in Scripture: "Go and learn what this means: 'I desire mercy, and not sacrifice'" (Matt 9:13; the Greek word translated "learn" is related to the Greek word meaning "disciple"). There may or may not be a meaning in the thing that happened to you yesterday at the grocery store (Paul said he wasn't sure why something happened, Phlm 15). Yet, as truth (John 17:17), Scripture contains meaning for which we have a need to look, to find, and to learn.

May 17

"If You Had Known"

IF WE DO THE right thing because the right thing (truth) is in our heart, it follows that we do the wrong thing because truth is not in our heart. A lack of truth will lead to negative things both in this life and in the life to come. Jesus' rebuke in Matt 12 tells us again of the importance of knowing truth, or the meaning of Scripture: "And if you had known what this means, 'I desire mercy, and not sacrifice,' you would not have condemned the guiltless" (Matt 12:7). That which he states tells us that the listener didn't know the meaning of Scripture, that it is possible to know the meaning of Scripture, and that it is necessary to know the meaning of Scripture. Jesus' listeners not having knowledge led to their condemning the guiltless. When Israel was devoid of knowledge of Scripture, it led to physical distresses, such as hunger and thirst and the spiritual calamity of their rejection by God (or exile; Hos 6:6; Isa 5:13). Study, knowledge, and learning God's word toward the goal of truth will change our heart, may change our lives, and is certainly the basis for doing the right thing.

May 18

"Let Them Grow"

THOSE WHO DESIRE GOOD likely do not like evil. We often therefore wish evil weren't here, or wish God would do something about it. Jesus said that God is going to do something about evil: "Let both grow together until the harvest, and at harvest time I will tell the reapers, 'Gather the weeds first and bind them in bundles to be burned, but gather the wheat into my barn'" (Matt 13:30). A gardener doesn't like weeds growing alongside the desirable plants, and, therefore, pulls them up. When "bad" things happen in life that we don't understand, we often look for someone to blame (people often blame God). Yet God's ways are not the same as humans' (Isa 55:8–9), and he has assured us that evil will one day be dealt with. Until then God has told us that (not necessarily why) evil coexists with good. Both are to grow together until one day when one will live on and the other will not.

May 19

"I Will Not Delight"

ONE MIGHT LOOK FORWARD to going to worship for some reason other than spiritual (such as only to see other people). The abuse of worship comes from an improper life, and causes the rejection thereof by God. Christians assemble to encourage one another (Heb 10:24–25), and we come together to eat the Lord's Supper (1 Cor 11:20). An abuse of the Lord's Supper (1 Cor 11:21–22) can cause God to reject our worship. This is what happened to Israel in Amos 5:21: "I hate, I despise your feasts, and I take no delight in your sacred assemblies." God uses both words "hate" and "despise" together, both in the past tense, to warn them that their assembling (future tense) will bring him no pleasure. In like manner, a hypocritical or otherwise improper spiritual life today will cause our worship to be unacceptable to God. If we live an improper life and God has rejected our worship (Matt 5:23–24), our looking forward to assembling with other Christians may be in vain. Under such spiritual conditions, God certainly does not look forward to it.

May 20

The Easy Yoke

WHEN JESUS SAID, "MY yoke is easy and my burden is light" (Matt 11:30), he didn't give a reason therefor. Jesus' yoke could be easy because even something normally difficult can be easy with a different attitude (that is, when we want to do it). It is also true that a life without Jesus is more burdensome because sin carries a wage one must pay (Rom 3:23; Heb 12:1–2), versus one's being rewarded for being a Christian (Matt 20:1–16); and sin is a life of servitude (John 8:34), versus a life of freedom (John 8:32). Again, it is generally harder to do that which is right or good (such as working, losing weight, etc.), as reflected in the proverb "the harder course is the better course." We are going to bear a burden. To not choose Jesus' yoke is to have chosen the yoke that is much more burdensome due, in part, to the price tag it carries. The "harder course" of Jesus' burden is not only better, but is also easy and easier.

May 21

Truth Is Humbling

IT IS USUALLY DIFFICULT for one to admit that their thoughts need to be replaced with truth. That is, truth is humbling. The arrogant think their thoughts don't need an adjustment. Yet God's thoughts are not man's thoughts (Isa 55:8), and it is dangerous for us to rely on our thoughts (Prov 3:5–6; Jer 10:23). While truth sets free (John 8:32), it also is a sharp sword that can cut through the devices we create in our mind (Rev 1:16). To rely only on ourselves, to the point that we don't think we need to change, is to imprison ourselves within ourselves. Not that our ideas are always wrong; but the acceptance of truth sets free when we discard false ideas, even our own, and replace them therewith. To do this requires humility, or admitting we are wrong. Truth is therefore humbling; except to the humble (Luke 14:11).

May 22

"So Shall It Be"

Is GOD'S WILL ALWAYS fulfilled? Isaiah 14:24 reads, "The LORD of hosts has sworn as follows: 'Surely as I have imagined, so it was; and as I have taken [my own] counsel, it will be fulfilled.'" The answer to this question can be difficult, especially when we look at such things as the pervasiveness of evil in our world and throughout time. It seems that while humans can resist the will of God (Acts 5:38–39), ultimately, God's will is going to be done (the Hebrew word in Isa 14:24, translated "so it was," is in the past tense; of the translations consulted, only the NASB translates it as past tense). Thus we are taught to (Jas 4:15) and given the example of (Matt 26:42) relinquishing our will to his. If God's will is going to be done, is this not in our own best spiritual interest?

May 23

A Satisfactory Alternative

OFTEN IN LIFE WE think that the solution to our problem is either Plan A or Plan B (nothing else). The wise man again said, "Trust in the LORD with all your heart and do not lean on your understanding. Know him in all your ways, and he for his part will make your paths straight" (Prov 3:5–6). At one point in their history Israel had a serious problem. Assyria, one of the most vicious empires that ever existed, was coming to get Israel. God's prophets had warned his people that their sins would mean punishment (Jer 25:9). Israel's leaders naturally looked for a physical solution. They thought they had to choose between either paying Assyria the taxes they demanded, or hire Egypt to help them fight against Assyria. The prophets, however, also warned them that Egypt may not be the savior they had hoped for, since they were only human (Isa 31:3). The prophets tried to point them not in the direction of east or west but rather upward, to a spiritual solution. God could have given Israel a straight path through their crisis; but instead of looking upward (spiritually), they chose to lean on the natural solutions of Egypt (2 Kgs 18:21) and their own understanding; and they suffered physically for it.

May 24

"The Lord's Memorial"

THOUGH DEATH IS A reality (Heb 9:27), the impact of one's death seems to depend upon several things (including the life that they lived, the circumstances of the person's death, and the interpretation of that life by those left behind). A military person who gives their life touches the hearts of those who believe in America. The death of a loved one with whom we spent many years, or the death of a child with whom we were not able to spend time, touches our heart in another way. To spend such mental energy is not only for the positive purpose of reminiscing but can also provide a positive influence toward our present spiritual life. The action of the Lord's Supper (1 Cor 11:24), the meaning thereof that we apply (1 Cor 11:25), and how it affects our heart for spiritual good (1 Cor 11:28), are all purposes of remembering the death of Jesus. The reality of death need not paralyze us now; but can rather teach us "thus to ruminate,"[4] especially on the reality, the meaning, and the spiritual good of the memorial of Jesus' death.

---

4. Shakespeare, Sonnet 64.

May 25

"Diligent to Enter Rest"

LIKE ANY GOOD THING that brings a reward, belief requires effort. Israel was not able to enter into the promised land of rest due to unbelief (Heb 3:19); that is, they were disobedient (Heb 4:6). Based on this fact, the Hebrews writer encourages Christians today to avoid a similar end by giving diligence to do what is right: "Let us therefore give diligence to enter into that rest, that no man fall after the same example of disobedience" (Heb 4:11 ASV). The promise of rest as a result of living the Christian life is based on the fact that we labor now for the Lord (1 Cor 15:58). The Christian is then encouraged to give diligence, or make every effort, to secure his or her calling and election (2 Pet 1:10), to ensure their spiritual purity (2 Pet 3:14), and to promote the unity of God's people (Eph 4:3). Such efforts, though perhaps difficult as we labor through this life, will result in a rest that is made sweeter by the effort we expend. It is borne along by our belief, and given application by our diligence—or our making every effort to enter that rest.

May 26

Getting What We Want

DESIRE CAN BE A strong emotion that impels us to fulfill our will, whether the result thereof be good or not. It seems, from Scripture, that God wants his children to have what they want, within the confines of his will (1 John 5:14). It also seems that one of the main things God wants from us is our will (Matt 26:42). The psalmist again said, "And take pleasure in the LORD, so that he would give you your heartfelt requests" (Ps 37:4). We want our desire (that which we want) to be satisfied; what God wants is our will. Based on the psalmist's wording, one of the main things we can do to fulfill that which we want is to give up that which fuels our wants, that is, our will. We do this by conforming our will to God's will (Jas 4:15). Whether our desire is satisfied is ultimately up to God. We can get what we want if we give up not necessarily our want but, rather, our will. In so doing we thereby give God what he wants.

May 27

"There—I Said It"

SPEECH IS SPIRITUAL. ANIMALS communicate, but even nonbelieving experts say that humans possess a language intuition, which animals do not (watch how quickly children pick up speech). Words can be used for good or evil (Jas 3:9), and God hears the words we use (Matt 12:36). Several verses remind us that our speech can and should be used to bring glory to God, including Jesus' words at the raising of Lazarus: "I knew that you always hear me, but I said this on account of the people standing around, that they may believe that you sent me" (John 11:42). Good works by themselves can bring glory to God (Matt 5:16). If we combine "spiritual things with spiritual words" (1 Cor 2:13), our good works can serve a spiritual as well as a physical purpose. Just as the Word (Jesus, John 1:1) came to us to cause us to behold his glory as one from God (John 1:14), so our speech can point others to God (see Col 4:6). In the words of Paul, "We believe, and thus we speak" (2 Cor 4:13). When we follow Jesus' example, we speak so that others will believe.

May 28

How Much Is Enough?

How much is enough? Naturally, Paul wanted relief from his "thorn in the flesh" (2 Cor 12:7), and, toward this end, he prayed for its removal (v. 8). Part of God's answer included his reassurance that "my grace is sufficient for you" (v. 9). Paul thus decided instead to boast in his weaknesses, so that the power of Christ might rest upon him. In Paul's case, God's grace is seen to be something that allowed the negative element of his thorn in the flesh. The Greek word translated "sufficient" often appears in contexts having to do with the physical (such as enough wages [Luke 3:14], enough oil [Matt 25:9], or enough food [John 6:7]), or of our being sufficed spiritually with what we have (1 Tim 6:8; Heb 13:5). Even when life seems deficient—that is, it seems we don't have enough or we have to tolerate something unpleasant—God fills our needs (see Phil 4:19) with sufficient grace.

May 29

The Center of Worship

THERE IS (OR SHOULD be) a reason Christians gather together to worship God. While, surely, there are different motivations for one's coming to worship, the Bible speaks of a "center of gravity," that draws us together, that is, the Lord's Supper. The importance of the communion as a participation in common is illustrated by Scripture teaching (Luke 22:14–23; 1 Cor 11:23–29), as well as by the example of Paul and his companions, who, while travelling, waited seven days in a certain place specifically so they could observe the Lord's Supper (Acts 20:6–7). All of the "acts of worship" are equally important. That which draws us together is the resurrection of Jesus, the act he said would "draw all people" to himself (John 12:32). The center of worship, the commemoration of his death and resurrection, draws us to Jesus and to each other.

May 30

Destructive Criticism

CRITICISM LIKELY REFLECTS THAT something is wrong. In some situations (such as the military) accuracy and diligence are vital to success, and, thus, criticism is likely inevitable. To be critical, however, could reflect a type of heart the Christian should be careful to avoid. Jesus said, "Judge not, that you be not judged" (Matt 7:1). While it is necessary to "reprove, rebuke, and exhort" (2 Tim 4:2), it is also necessary to not take account of evil (1 Cor 13:5), but instead to exhort and build up fellow Christians (1 Thess 5:11). To avoid being critical doesn't mean one ignores what is wrong; but the spirit which endures is surely more important than the physical that is temporary, and the proper use of our tongue is an important part of preserving that spirit (Jas 3:6–12). If a criticism arises, it may indicate that something is wrong. On the other hand, if one is critical, it may indicate that something else is wrong. Not that we're judging.

May 31

Learning to Be Obedient

LEARNING OFTEN GIVES ONE a sense of accomplishment or power. Obedience can be thought of as giving up our will. Combining these two concepts, learning in the Bible is for our spiritual good (2 Pet 3:18); one ultimate manifestation of which is our obedience to God's will (John 13:17). Rather than being mechanical (or like a trained animal), scriptural obedience is intended for our good and growth (spiritual), and is, therefore, connected with learning. The Hebrews writer said of Jesus, "Although he was a son, he learned obedience through what he suffered" (Heb 5:8). Submitting to God's will is necessary; not only because it results in our carrying out actions which please God but also because our heart is thereby directed away from what we want, toward what God wants (Ps 37:4). Jesus learned obedience through suffering; we learn the gospel of his suffering, which gives us power (Rom 1:16) to be obedient.

June 1

More Than Enough

Physical excesses are often not good for one's physical life, and certainly are not good for the soul. Thus the Bible warns, for example, of the dangers of being rich (1 Tim 6:17). God has promised in his word to take care of his children (Ps 37:25). This promise carries many blessings, among them that it removes the need for worry (Phil 4:6). The Christian is also told that God will "fill up" every need of theirs (Phil 4:19). In addition to our needs, Jesus said that he offers a spiritually rich life: "The thief comes only to steal and kill and destroy. I came that they may have life and have it abundantly" (John 10:10). The Greek word translated "abundantly" has a meaning of "that which is beyond what one needs." God will thus fill up what we do need, and give us an abundant life that goes beyond what we need. Not that every Christian is going to be physically rich; but, in Christ, the Christian has a life that is spiritually rich, whether their physical life reflects it or not. Physical riches can be a thief; Jesus offers a spiritual life to excess, and that's good for us.

June 2

"Supply Virtue"

IF IT IS GOOD to be good, we might say it is better to be excellent. The Bible speaks of "virtue," or a moral excellence based on God's word. Faith being the basis of the Christian life, the Christian is told to supplement their faith with this quality: "Yea, and for this very cause adding on your part all diligence, in your faith supply virtue; and in your virtue knowledge" (2 Pet 1:5). Excellence, such as in sports, is attained by one's consistent application of principles, such as those that make the athlete so. Virtue in the Christian life begins with what they think ("if there be any virtue, and if there be any praise, think on these things," Phil 4:8), and is manifested by what the Christian does (Phil 4:9, "these things do"). Unbelief, or a lack of faith, can be seen in the life one lives (Heb 3:19). A lack of virtue can also be manifested in a life that is spiritually lacking excellence, hence the need to add this quality. If we supply this quality to our faith, Peter said an entrance into the kingdom will be supplied to us (2 Pet 1:11); and that's excellent.

June 3

"While I Live"

WHAT TIME WE HAVE been given is going to be spent. The Christian should determine to use their life to bring glory to God, which includes praising him in worship (Eph 1:12). The psalmist similarly determined, and so declared, that he would praise the Lord his whole life: "So I will bless you while I live" (Ps 63:4). The psalmist may be thinking that he would praise God now because he won't be able to praise him in the afterlife (Ps 115:17 states "the dead do not praise the LORD"; also ESV). Having more knowledge of the afterlife (2 Tim 1:10), the Christian has the promise of being with and worshiping God in eternity (Rev 5:13), if we utilize our time accordingly. Similarly to the psalmist, our life, which is temporal anyway, can then be looked upon as something we can use to prepare us for the time when we have life no more. If the psalmist thought that this life was all there is, and he determined to use his one life (with evidently nothing after) to praise God, is it not fitting for us to use our life both to bring glory to him now, as well as to prepare us for praising him for all of eternity?

June 4

The Most Important People in Town

It is painful to watch one's nation in decline, especially when one may feel as if they can do nothing to save her. Individuals will be judged in eternity (Rev 20:11–15); based on observing history, it seems that God judges nations in time. A nation or a group is viewed differently by God when that group is given to righteousness (Prov 14:34). Abraham negotiated with God to spare Sodom, to which God replied he would, if finally only ten righteous people were found therein (Gen 18:22–33; even though the inhabitants of the town are earlier described as "evil and sinners very much with regard to the Lord," Gen 13:13b). Such truths remind Christians today that God considers the righteous to be the most important spiritual element in a nation. In a world which seems to be less and less concerned about spiritual things, Christians are the salt that, perhaps, is preserving what was once a God-fearing nation (Matt 5:13), and can be the light that helps her to safety (Matt 5:14). Preaching the gospel can save a soul (Rom 1:16). Being a righteous person contributes to the salvation of our nation. One person can't save a nation; or can they?

June 5

Is Prayer Practical?

BOTH JESUS (MARK 11:24) and James (Jas 5:17–18) used practical examples in their teaching on the power of prayer. Christians are to pray and ask God for help (Heb 4:16), and we naturally want to see our requests realized. We are also to leave the results of our requests up to God's will (Matt 26:42; 1 John 5:14). It seems that we can observe whether our requests have been granted, while determining whether God's will has been done is a matter of faith (see Acts 21:14). James taught on prayer, saying, "Elijah was a man with a nature like ours, and he prayed fervently that it might not rain, and for three years and six months it did not rain on the earth" (Jas 5:17; see also Jesus in John 16:24). Since we may not always receive what we ask for, we conclude that the primary benefit of prayer is spiritual rather than physical. Yet God appeals to us to pray based on the practical benefit we may receive. To see such a blessing is to be blessed; to believe in prayer, whether we see our requests realized or not, may mean a greater blessing (John 20:29).

June 6

"Dull of Hearing"

WORDS ARE IMPORTANT BECAUSE words have meaning that can affect the soul. This is one reason the Bible encourages us to watch the words we use (Jas 3:2–12; Matt 12:37), to take heed how (Luke 8:18) and what (Mark 4:24) we hear, and to give attention to the meaning of words (Matt 12:7; 2 Pet 3:16). Is it possible for words to lose their meaning? Or could it be, when we say they have lost their meaning, that the problem in this regard is not the words, but our hearing? The Hebrews writer said, "About this we have much to say, and it is hard to explain, since you have become dull of hearing" (Heb 5:11). The Greek word translated "dull of hearing" appears in the NT only here and in Heb 6:12. It has a meaning of "being stupid," not because of natural ability, but because one has not applied themselves to understanding. We may say that words do not lose meaning, though we, through our own inattentiveness, might lose the ability to grasp their meaning. If we do, it could mean we lose something more important—what that meaning means for our soul.

June 7

Who's to Blame?

ADMITTING GUILT IS SURELY one of the most difficult things for most of us to do. After he had killed Abel, Cain said, "My punishment is greater than [I can] bear" (Gen 4:13. This can also be translated "my iniquity is too great to be forgiven"). When we have, or think we have, done something wrong, we sometimes look for someone else to blame (especially, it seems, in politics). Adam and Eve kept trying to pass their guilt, evidently not stopping to think that God already knew who was to blame (Gen 3:9–12). Of course, it is unjust for one to inappropriately take or be assigned blame; yet the solution to true guilt is, after realizing one's wrong, to admit their guilt (2 Sam 12:13; Acts 2:36–37), then give it to the One who promised he would bear our guilt by bearing our sin away (1 Pet 2:24). The world might try to falsely assign blame to the innocent or to excuse the guilty (though their sin will find them out, Num 32:23). By coming to God on his terms, the truly guilty are forgiven because of the innocent One who bears our guilt.

June 8

Good Preaching

MANY YEARS AGO I heard a saying, "Good preaching is made by good listening." As much as preachers enjoy being told that they had a good lesson, Scripture places emphasis on us as listeners for the sermon to be "good." Among other things, what we consider a good sermon can surely vary from person to person. Preachers have the obligation of preaching the truth in love (Eph 4:15), and to be faithful to the word of truth (2 Tim 2:15), among other things. They also surely have the obligation of being a good employee (that is, to do their best, Col 3:22–23). After this, what we consider a "good" sermon depends largely on how we, as listeners, respond. Someone who is starving would likely consider a piece of plain bread the most delicious food they've ever eaten. We, as listeners, are to hunger and thirst after righteousness (Matt 5:6), and therefore to consider the feet of the preacher to be beautiful (Rom 10:15). We can do this in part by being careful not to be "dull of hearing" (Heb 5:11; see "Daily" of June 10). The preacher is to make effort, for his part, and offer "good preaching"; if it's not a good sermon, perhaps a reason is because we didn't engage in "good listening."

June 9

There's More to It

MANY TIMES WE SEE others become a success in life due to one talent they possess (such as in athletics, finance, or entertainment). While this sometimes causes us to marvel at that person's achievements, the sad reality is that, since there is more to life than just one thing, the other aspects of this person's life sometimes reflect unsuccess. In other words, "success" is not simply based on one thing. Humans are physical, mental, and spiritual (see 1 Thess 5:23); and the saying is that if one is hurting anywhere, he or she is going to be hurting everywhere. The intersection of different aspects of life is reflected in such Scripture teaching as works being necessary to faith (Jas 2:24–26), the need for the Christian to love one's neighbor as themselves (Mark 12:31), giving proper attention to all of one's household (Eph 5:22–6:4; Col 3:18–4:1) and several other aspects of the Christian life (Eph 6:10–20). We are to use whatever talent with which we have been blessed, even if it's just one (Matt 25:14–30). But a "successful" spiritual life, like success in the physical aspects of life, does not depend on just one thing.

June 10

"To Whom Shall We Go?"

WE ARE OBLIGATED TO look for truth (though truth often shows itself, generally speaking, it won't find us). Truth is unchanging (Matt 24:35), and God's word, as truth (John 17:17), has already been given (Jude 3). These things would seem to make truth easier to find, since it means that it isn't going anywhere. More than once in the book of Hebrews the writer states that God has spoken, whereupon he cites a passage of the written word. After beginning the book by stating that God has spoken through his Son (1:2; see John 14:6), he then states what the Holy Spirit has said (3:7, which is a quotation of the written word), and what God had said (Heb 4:4, citing Gen 2:2, which is not a quote of God speaking). The medium through which God has spoken today is the written word. We might go here and there looking for answers in life (Isa 30:1), until we realize that there is one place to look for a message from the Father (John 6:68). It is the message that has already been given, and that isn't going anywhere. It is therefore up to us to look for it, knowing it can be found.

June 11

"God Has Hidden Us"

BEING IN A DARK place is not as bad if we are with someone (Ps 23:4). Being in a tomb can surely be an unpleasant thing for the living. While we have no control over the fact that we will physically die (Heb 9:27), we do have a choice in our spiritual death (Rom 6:2; Eph 2:1). We also do not have any control over our physical remains, though our spirit will be directed according to the life we have lived (John 5:28–29). When we die spiritually in this life, God hides us (as if in a tomb) with Christ: "For you have died, and your life is hidden with Christ in God" (Col 3:3). Paul teaches that we, therefore, are to set our mind on things that are above (Col 3:2) since we, among other things, can look forward to being raised and leaving this world behind (1 Cor 15:20). Dying spiritually means we need fear neither the world, dying physically, being put in a tomb, nor what comes after the tomb because we have been hidden with Christ.

June 12

"I Will Be Still"

THE IDEA OF BEING still is spoken of both with regard to God's people (Ps 46:10) as well as of God. The psalmist was evidently afraid (Ps 46:2), but took comfort in God, his refuge and help (v. 1). Isaiah 18:4 is a description of God waiting before acting on behalf of his people: "For thus the LORD has said to me, 'let me be quiet so that I may gaze in my setting, as the dazzling heat in daylight, as the cloud of dew in the heat of harvest.'" Isaiah goes on to describe God pruning the nations (v. 5), and the sprigs being left to the animals (v. 6). It is good for Christians to be active, such as doing good to overcome evil (Rom 12:21), which is also active (1 Pet 5:8). We can't fix everything, there may be times when our best efforts are to no avail, and there are surely times when we must stop forcing our will against God's (Jas 4:15). In other words, there will be times when we must "be still" and leave everything up to God (not that we give up, 1 Cor 15:58). Our being still can mean good things, as it suggests our leaving events up to him. God being still is another matter.

June 13

Given or Received (or Both)?

WORSHIP IS OR SHOULD be something given. The Bible speaks of things given and things received, which are naturally two different things. The word "give" is, of course, used to describe God's benevolent actions toward humans (John 3:16; 2 Cor 9:15); the word "receive" is used of man's responsibility to receive those gifts, including such things as the gospel (1 Cor 15:1) and Jesus' teaching (1 Cor 11:23). To receive implies acceptance; and something may be given but not received (to illustrate, a doctor may prescribe, or "give" a medicine that is not received, but is rather rejected, by the patient's body). Thus, God gave his Son (John 3:16), but he was not received: "He came to his own, and his own people did not receive him" (John 1:11). Our need is to receive the gifts of God, and to offer in return our gift of worship, trusting in faith that it will be received.

June 14

Going to the Lord

IT SEEMS THAT MANY like the idea of turning to God, without knowing exactly how to turn to God. That is (without trying to judge what is in one's heart), many seem to want to turn to the Lord only for the help they may receive, or because it provides them with a good feeling. In John 6 most people left the Lord because they could no longer tolerate what he was saying. When Jesus asked whether the disciples would leave, Peter's answer was framed in terms of the words Jesus offered: "Lord, to whom shall we go? You have the words of eternal life" (John 6:68). While there may be many proper reasons to turn to the Lord, we ultimately come to him today by accepting his word. Doing good works, attending worship, and praying (Acts 10:4) may be good things in and of themselves; but until we look to the word, we have not truly looked to the Author and Perfecter of our faith (Heb 12:2).

June 15

"To Him Who Is Able"

WHEN WE SPEAK OF ability, we are speaking of some talent with which we were born, a skill we have acquired or, the reverse thereof, a skill we have lost. An ability is a physical talent that could come and go. When the Bible describes God as "able," this seems to be a figure of speech, inasmuch as God is not a physical being (John 4:24), and, therefore, need not be spoken of as possessing something that he can't acquire or lose (not that this quality is, for him, not real). The Bible speaks of God being able to save (Heb 5:7), to guard his children (Jude 24), and to do far beyond what we can imagine: "Now to him who is able to do far more abundantly than all that we ask or think, according to the power at work within us" (Eph 3:20). This verse speaks of God being "able" to do far beyond what we could conceive. This quality in this verse, we have elsewhere noted, is dependent upon the power of God working in us. In other words, God is not defined as possessing or not possessing an ability that can come and go, and is, therefore, not limited thereby; rather, it is us who are either limited or blessed by God's "ability."

June 16

"Without God"

WE ALL LIKELY ENJOY moments of solitude (Mark 6:31), some, naturally, more than others. Being completely alone, however, is not good (Gen 2:18). There may be times that the Christian is physically alone, but he or she is never spiritually alone. The atheist may never be physically alone, but they, sadly, are spiritually alone, and will be when their spirit departs this life. The word "atheist" comes from the Greek word meaning "no God"; to live according to this belief is thus to live without God. The Christian has assurance that by walking in the light (1 John 1:7), and obeying Jesus' commands (Matt 28:18–20), including worshiping with other Christians (Matt 18:20), Jesus is with him. Jesus is an eternal being (Heb 13:8), and, therefore, is not going anywhere. Whether God is with or without a person, however, is up to them, not God (he would be with them if they would; see 2 Pet 3:9). Living with others, one may never be lonely; living, and especially dying, without God, one is alone.

June 17

Smarter with Jesus

INTELLIGENCE IS EVIDENTLY A talent with which one is born (nature) as well as a skill which can be developed (nurture). A formal education, therefore, can change one for the better (depending on what one learns) because of the development of intellectual skills and of increased knowledge. Spending time with Jesus, today through studying his word, makes us better. Especially in comparison to the negative things that go into our head each day, to spend time with God's word is to open a fountain of light (Ps 119:130) that lightens our way (Ps 119:105). Thus the psalmist said, "I have more insight than all my teachers, because your testimonies are my contemplation" (Ps 119:99), that he has more wisdom than his enemies (v. 98), and more understanding than the aged (v. 100). Is this because he has more knowledge than they? Or is it because he learned spiritual principles that changed his soul for good? One might be "unlearned and ignorant" (Acts 4:13) but can be "smarter" because of increased knowledge of Jesus and his word.

June 18

The Blessedness of Worship

NATURALLY, WHEN WE ENGAGE in an activity or project, we would like to know what benefit, if any, we receive therefrom. To worship is to bless God (Ps 34:1), and through worship we are blessed. Proper worship is an act of giving (including [1 Cor 16:2], but not limited to [Heb 13:6] giving money), and is, therefore, to be unselfish (1 Cor 13:5). While Paul said that improper giving profits us nothing (1 Cor 13:3), Jesus said that "it is more blessed to give than to receive" (Acts 20:35). A way, therefore, for the Christian to be blessed is to give of themselves unselfishly in worship, or to bless God.

June 19

Unfolding God's Word

GOD'S WORD IS A spiritual power (Rom 1:16) waiting to be tapped. Like any resource, it only does us good when we make use thereof. To leave God's word hidden, or unexposed to the light, is to leave it in a state in which it will provide no light for us. The psalmist said, "The opening of your words enlightens; it gives understanding to the simple" (Ps 119:130). To appreciate the word "unfolding," picture a scroll that has to be unrolled, such as those used by the Jews both in ancient times and today. To expose God's word, as it were, to the light of day is the beginning of understanding it and of being sustained by it. Exposing God's word to the light gives us light (Ps 119:105), thereby enabling us to walk in the light (1 John 1:7). To not do so is to leave it as a treasure hidden (Matt 13:44), or unexposed to the light, therefore offering us no light.

June 20

Upheld by God's Word

WE ARE WEAK (SOME more than others), and, therefore, sometimes need power to support us. The Hebrews writer said that God upholds the world with his word: "He is the radiance of the glory of God and the exact imprint of his nature, and he upholds the universe by the word of his power" (Heb 1:3). The phrase "the word of his power" can also mean "his powerful word." Any words can be powerful to change one's life for good or for bad; how much more the power of God's powerful word (Rom 1:16)? The Christian today can be sustained by God's word. Unlike the world, the Christian chooses to be so supported, which he does by spending time with God's word. The world is also going to pass away, while God's truth is eternal (Matt 24:35). By being sustained with God's truth, Christians have an eternal support to guard their minds (Isa 26:3; Phil 4:7); and, while our physical life will also pass away (Heb 9:27), unlike the world, we will live on thereafter. Being too weak to stand on our own, Jesus, the Word (John 1:1, 14) holds us in his hand (John 10:28–29), thereby sustaining us with power.

June 21

Settled in Heaven

NOT ONLY DOES GOD uphold the world with his word (see yesterday's "Daily") but, similarly, the psalmist said that "forever, O LORD, is your word positioned in heaven" (Ps 119:89). The Hebrew word translated "positioned" contains a notion of being set up or established, such as a person being put in charge (Ruth 2:5), or something inanimate being piled up, like the waters of the Red Sea (Ps 78:13). God's word is truth (John 17:17), and truth, by definition, does not change. It has therefore been determined, or set up, in heaven, and is at the same time holding up the world (Heb 1:3). God's word is also many other things, including powerful (Rom 1:16) and effectual (it will not return to him void, Isa 55:11). To look to heaven for God's truth, which has been established therein, is to look for the spiritual substance that is (or can be) that which, again, sustains both the world and our lives as we live in this world.

June 22

"I Will Sing with the Spirit"

Paul said, "I will sing with the spirit" as well as with the mind or understanding (1 Cor 14:15). To sing with the mind suggests singing that involves the thoughts. To sing with the spirit reminds us that singing is an act of worship that is (or can be) for the purpose of bringing us closer to God, who is a Spirit (John 4:24). Understanding affects the spirit (Philip asking the eunuch, "Do you understand what you are reading?" Acts 8:30). Paul's assertion also suggests that the opposite can be true; that is, that it is possible to sing without the spirit or understanding. Singing a spiritual song (as opposed to a secular song) is surely part of what it means to sing with the spirit. Paul's words also suggest that this is something he purposed to do (like Daniel, Dan 1:8). Though it may be difficult for one to know exactly when they are following Paul's teaching, Paul's description suggests that proper singing engages our spirit. We do so as an act of worship, to glorify our spiritual Father. To do otherwise might suggest that we are not worshiping.

June 23

Spiritual or Spiritually Minded?

HUMANS ARE DIFFERENT FROM animals, because humans are spiritual beings (Gen 1:26). This truth is reflected in such things as man's ability to contemplate the future, to marry (things animals don't do), as well as the fact that none of the animals were suitable as a mate for Adam (Gen 2:18–20). The fact that humans are spiritual beings is a truth that does not change (regardless of how the world tries). Humans can also be spiritually minded, or use their mind to pursue spiritual things—something that can change him or her. Paul said, "Have this mind among yourselves, which is yours in Christ Jesus" (Phil 2:5). We can use our mind to pursue truth, to grow spiritually (2 Pet 3:18), and, thereby, to be spiritually free (John 8:32). The fact that we have a spirit is a truth that does not change; using our mind to pursue spiritual things based on truth is an attitude in which we have a choice, and which can change our spirit forever. The difference is in our mind.

June 24

Grin and Bear It

THERE IS AN INTERSECTION near my home with the two street names "Grin" and "Barrett." The real phrase, "grin and bear it," has to do with those times in life when one endures painful hardship by forcing a smile on their face. While the Christian life offers joy (Gal 5:22), and grinning during times of pain may help to change our attitude and impress others with our evident spiritual strength, the Christian is not required to always be happy; that is, there's nothing wrong with crying (John 11:35; Rom 12:15). As Christians, we are, however, required to bear up under life's hardships, which includes such things as not giving up our faith in God because we have suffered (or are suffering) in this life. Thus Paul said, "Not only that, but we rejoice in our sufferings, knowing that suffering produces endurance, and endurance produces character, and character produces hope" (Rom 5:4). There will surely be times in life that are so painful that we don't feel like grinning; and in life we can't take two streets at once. But, spiritually speaking, during those times when life intersects with difficulty, it is up to us whether to take Grin; but we do have to take Barrett. I mean, we must bear it.

June 25

Solace and Salvation

PAUL TOLD THE ELDERS of Ephesus that the word of God "is able to build you up and to give you the inheritance among all those who are sanctified" (Acts 20:32). This tells us that the Bible is the source we need for two of the most important aspects of our lives, namely, getting through this life and the condition of our spirit after our life ends. Peter said that God has given us "all things that pertain to life and godliness" (2 Pet 1:3). The Bible is not necessarily a manual to which we can refer to in order to fix a particular problem in life. Yet the Bible should be where we turn for such things as a burden that weighs upon our mind (and we therefore need solace, 2 Cor 1:3–4), or when we are concerned about what the future holds with regard to the afterlife (salvation). The Bible is all we need for such questions, and, therefore, it is the source to which we should turn. Or, implied in Peter's words in John 6:68 when he asked Jesus "to whom shall we go," the Bible is the source from which we should never turn in the first place.

June 26

What's Right

It seems that the emotion of anger can be complex to understand; that is, it seems that there can be many reasons one gets angry. Jesus' evident display of anger in John 2 was seemingly based on what we call a "righteous indignation"; that is, it was based on what was right: "And making a whip of cords, he drove them all out of the temple, with the sheep and oxen. And he poured out the coins of the money-changers and overturned their tables" (John 2:15). We may say that Jesus ultimately got angry because they contradicted the truth, compared to our anger, which is often when someone contradicts us. The natural emotion of anger can be overcome (for the purpose of avoiding sin, Eph 4:26) with a strong spiritual life, that helps one be angry for the right reason (hence the phrase "righteous indignation"). To become angry for the right reason is spiritual rather than natural, and suggests that we are more concerned about "what's right" than "who's right."

June 27

Why Should I Care?

We should care about our worship, both with regard to what we offer, as well as the way in which we offer it. That is, the fact that the Bible teaches us to worship God in spirit (John 4:24), to sing with the spirit and understanding (1 Cor 14:15), and to give cheerfully (2 Cor 9:7), suggests that the mentality of our worship is as important as the mode. The worshipers in Mal 1 evidently didn't care about the quality of the offering they made to God: "And when you bring near [the] blind near to sacrifice, it is no evil! And when you bring near [the] lame or [the] sick, it is no evil!" (Mal 1:8). Since God knows all, and, therefore, doesn't need to remember that his Son died for our sins (1 Cor 11:24), doesn't need our money (Ps 50:12), and that he already has people singing to him (Rev 4:8), why should he care? God cares because this is what's best for us. If God cares about our worship for our sake, should not we care about our worship for his sake?

June 28

Restrained or Constrained?

To be "restrained" is to be held back from doing something one wants to do (like a prisoner in chains). To be "constrained" is to be compelled to do something they perhaps would rather not (Jer 20:9). The Bible describes Paul on one occasion as constrained to speak the word: "But when Silas and Timothy came down from Macedonia, Paul was constrained by the word, testifying to the Jews that Jesus was the Christ" (Acts 18:5 ASV). We are physically restrained by the limitations of this physical life, such as by time and by gravity. We are spiritually restrained by the limitations God has placed upon us (Gen 2:16–17, limits which are given for our spiritual freedom; see John 8:32). Being constrained to do God's will, surely, is dependent upon a heart that has been properly conditioned through a knowledge of his word. Perhaps, if we restrain our thoughts to more of God's word (see Rom 12:2), it will constrain us to fulfilling his will.

June 29

Reasoning and Persuading

IN SELLING, FOR A prospect to buy a product involves both their mind (being convinced by the information regarding what the product has to offer), as well as their heart (being persuaded to take action). Without the first, they may buy the product but be unhappy with it afterward; without the second, they may be convinced of the merits of the product but not make the decision to buy. What prompts a person to follow God is surely complicated, yet seems to involve both the mind (see Isa 1:18 ASV) and the heart (being persuaded, Acts 2:37; 26:28). Thus, the Bible states that Paul's evangelistic efforts included both: "And he entered the synagogue and for three months spoke boldly, reasoning and persuading them about the kingdom of God" (Acts 19:8). Just as with conversion (Acts 2:38), worship (John 4:24), and our daily lives as Christians, our need is to continue to develop our mind through learning (2 Pet 3:18), and to keep our heart conditioned to following God's will (Eph 5:17). Beginning with these two things, one is more likely to "buy" what God is "selling"; and be happy with it.

June 30

"Provoke One Another"

IN THE CONTEXT OF Christians' need to assemble (Heb 10:25), the writer of Hebrews also taught, "And let us consider one another to provoke unto love and good works" (Heb 10:24 ASV). While that which he calls "love and good works" are surely positive things, the word he uses to describe how we initiate them ("provoke") can have a negative connotation. The Greek word so translated appears only here and in Acts 15:39, where Paul and Barnabas had to part ways over a sharp disagreement (it is also translated differently in almost every translation I observed). Like most good things, love and good works usually require initiation and effort; that is, they usually don't happen on their own, and are often, relatively, not easy. Something, therefore, is often required to prompt us to do the right thing. Evil is persistent (1 Pet 5:8) and pervasive (Gal 5:9), yet good will ultimately win (Rev 2:10b; 20:14). In the meantime, something is usually necessary to prompt us to do positive things; even if that something is negative.

July 1

Taking Blame and Taking Wrong

THERE IS A DIFFERENCE between taking blame and taking wrong. The Bible teaches not to take vengeance (Rom 12:19), but rather to take wrong: "To have lawsuits at all with one another is already a defeat for you. Why not rather suffer wrong? Why not rather be defrauded?" (1 Cor 6:7). We are to take blame when we did something wrong; to take blame when we are not wrong amounts to an injustice. To take wrong means that we accept the fact that evil has been done against us, but we have no desire to take vengeance or otherwise spread evil, and we may rather even do good in response (Rom 12:21). As Christians, we know that we can take wrong and unjust blame because God will one day make all wrongs right; and we can take blame when we are wrong, because Jesus will take the blame for us (Isa 53:6), even though he didn't do anything wrong.

July 2

Giving Is Spiritual

OF THE ACTS OF worship in which we, as Christians, engage (singing, praying, giving, the Lord's Supper, preaching), giving could be the only one that we think of as physical or secular. Money is a physical commodity that allows us to provide for physical means, is something we more or less depend on, and the act of giving (or paying) is common to many secular activities. It is good, therefore, for us to be reminded to look at giving, and all of worship, as spiritual, so that we engage therein for such purposes as pleasing God. Paul said, "Each one must give as he has decided in his heart, not reluctantly or under compulsion, for God loves a cheerful giver" (2 Cor 9:7). To contemplate Scripture teaching in this regard can help us to treat giving as a spiritual rather than a physical exercise. This can then help our attitude, our amount, and, more importantly, be for the purpose of pleasing the One to whom the physical should be directed, the spiritual being Whom we worship in spirit (John 4:24).

July 3

Freedom and Prosperity

FREEDOM AND PROSPERITY GO together. The Bible warns us of the danger of riches (1 Tim 6:17), and of a mindset of desiring to be rich (1 Tim 6:9); yet political freedom is necessary both for prosperity, and for such things as being allowed to go worship and to live and work where we choose. The Christian has spiritual freedom (Gal 5:1), which includes spiritual prosperity (that is, the child of God has access to spiritual riches, Eph 1:3; 3:8). Physical prosperity can be, but need not be, detrimental to our spiritual life, yet a strong spiritual life contributes to a good physical life (1 Cor 3:16), including our physical needs (Phil 4:19). Inasmuch as we are imprisoned in this life (the ancient Greeks called the body the "prison house of the soul"), a desire for freedom is part of man's makeup. If we pursue physical prosperity, we could lose our spiritual freedom. If we pursue spiritual freedom, we are assured of both spiritual freedom and spiritual prosperity.

July 4

Freedom Is Spiritual

WHILE A LIFE DEDICATED to physical pleasures and pursuits offers spiritual slavery, the Bible promises freedom to the spirit through the means of truth. We are not only bound to this physical plane, but fundamentally bound by sin (Rom 3:23). Jesus said that sin enslaves (John 8:34), but truth liberates: "And you will know the truth, and the truth will set you free" (John 8:32). Freedom is appealing because it is spiritual, because humans are spiritual beings (Gen 1:26), and because the human spirit longs to be free. Spiritual freedom is possible no matter our physical condition; yet freedom is not possible by pursuing it according to physical avenues (1 Tim 5:6). Only in Jesus can the human spirit be free (see John 14:6); but living in a country based on inalienable rights given to us by God, that is, a country that offers political freedom, certainly assists our spiritual freedom. God bless America.

July 5

Keeping Up Our Guard

DANGERS ARE ALL AROUND us, sometimes hidden and sometimes not. We may or may not be able to see a lion walking around our neighborhood; but knowing he is there is the basis of being able to protect ourselves (1 Pet 5:8; there has never been a lion loose in our neighborhood, that I know of). It is important that we, as Christians, keep up our guard (Eph 5:15). One reason we are able to keep up our guard is because we have support. It would be tiring to have to constantly watch and hold up our shield. But, surely, the minute we are spiritually hungry or tired would be an opportunity for evil to move in and possibly harm us (see Matt 4:1–11). Isaiah stated, "The Lord God has given to me [the] tongue of the taught, so I can sustain the weary with a word" (Isa 50:4). Words alone can sustain or deprive us (see tomorrow's "Daily"). God's word offers spiritual sustenance to support us with the strength we need to keep watching. Letting down our guard is one of the surest ways to get caught by lurking sin (Gen 4:7); being supported by God's word is one of the surest ways to keep up our guard. "We should not be like Cain, who was of the evil one and murdered his brother. And why did he murder him? Because his own deeds were evil and his brother's righteous" (1 John 3:12).

July 6

"Worship like David"

WE MAY SAY THAT worship is, by definition, a sacrifice, and sacrifice, by definition, bears a cost. In the OT, sacrifice involved such things as the killing of an animal or offering grain one needed to eat; we today sacrifice our time, money, and some effort spending an hour or so engaging in the acts of worship as specified in the NT. Sacrifice seems to be less meaningful depending on the extent to which we can "afford it" (Mark 12:41–44), or if we part with our offering unwillingly (2 Cor 9:6–7). Thus David, whose life served as the template for the other kings (1 Kgs 15:11; 2 Kgs 14:3, etc.), said, "And I will not offer up to the LORD my God whole burnt offerings which cost [me] nothing" (2 Sam 24:24). David's statement again reinforces what worship is, that God doesn't need what we have to offer (Ps 50:12); and, we may say, if our worship is not at least to some extent a sacrifice, then it isn't worship.

July 7

Sustaining Ourselves with Words

THE FACT THAT GOD's word can sustain us (see "Daily" of July 9) suggests that other words may not. Words themselves are not necessarily good or evil (for example, a dog may not know exactly what the word "hungry" means, but can be conditioned by hearing the word that he will get to eat). Good and evil arise in the heart of man; words convey ideas that can contribute to one or the other. We, therefore, have a need to sustain ourselves with words by choosing what words we hear (Mark 4:24), how we hear them (Luke 8:18), as well as how we dispense them (that is, dispensing the wrong words can affect us negatively). With regard to the proper use of the tongue, James said, "From the same mouth come blessing and cursing. My brothers, these things ought not to be so" (Jas 3:10). Whether it be the sounds one makes with their mouth, or an image on a printed page or a screen, words can affect our psyche and our soul. God's word can only sustain us (Acts 20:32) if we utilize it to be so sustained. If we aren't sustained, we are much more likely to fall.

July 8

"He Must Increase"

OBLIGATIONS OFTEN REQUIRE AN adjustment in attitude away from our will and toward the obligation. Due to the often unpleasant nature of obligations, we might describe this adjustment as a "lowering" of our ambitions. One of the primary purposes of the Christian life is to bring glory to God (Eph 1:12). To do this means the Christian lives their life in such a way as to bring about efforts, accomplishments, and success for a purpose other than such things as pleasure or gaining attention for themselves. John the baptizer said, "He must increase, but I must decrease" (John 3:30; the Greek word translated "must" means that this is obligatory). Our physical life is going to decrease, and our spiritual life should increase (2 Cor 4:16). While there is nothing necessarily wrong with accomplishments or such things as financial success, they should be looked at as rubbish compared to a relationship with Christ (Phil 3:8); and, if the Christian humbles themselves before God, they will be exalted (Luke 14:11). To lower ourselves (as it were) to the obligation of exalting Christ is to provide him the opportunity of exalting us—even though it is not us, but him, we must exalt.

July 9

"By Faith Abel"

ABEL IS HELD UP as an example of faith because he offered acceptable worship: "By faith Abel offered to God a more acceptable sacrifice than Cain, through which he was commended as righteous, God commending him by accepting his gifts. And through his faith, though he died, he still speaks" (Heb 11:4). Genesis 4:4 (as reflected in the Hebrew) states that God looked with favor upon Abel's offering. Abel is a good example because he offered his worship "by faith." The fact that faith comes by hearing the word of God (Rom 10:17) suggests that Abel offered worship in accordance with God's word. Cain did not, and his works were deemed as "evil" (1 John 3:12). We today can know what is acceptable worship before God (John 4:24; reading between the lines, there is no in-between). That is, we are to worship "by faith," or according to his word; lest God not look upon our worship with favor.

July 10

"Because He Cares"

IF WE HAD THE chance to drop off something heavy and unwanted, we might be so glad to get rid of it that it wouldn't matter to us where or to whom we gave it. Jesus taught on why worry is destructive (Matt 6:25–33), and Paul gave a positive alternative to worry (that is, prayer, Phil 4:6). Peter teaches that we have the opportunity (and obligation) to cast our anxieties on God for the spiritual and heart-warming reason that God cares for us: "casting all your anxieties on him, because he cares for you" (1 Pet 5:7). There may be other ways to get worry off of our mind; but we are here given a reason that not only offers the benefit of clearing our mind of that which burdens our thoughts and our soul, but can, in the process, bring us closer to the One upon whom we cast them. Doing this can help us not only to be free of worry but also, after we've dropped our load, to be uplifted by the fact that we have ridden ourselves thereof, and that we have the spiritual benefit of having given them to Someone who cares. By casting our anxieties away upon him, we can thereby draw closer to him.

July 11

When Is Enough Enough?

IF SOMETHING IS LACKING it suggests there's not enough of it. It may be something as unimportant as not having enough ketchup (which may "ruin" a meal), or not having enough money to meet a financial obligation. While the acquisition of knowledge seems to be a never-ending quest, truth can be known (John 8:32; 17:17); and, on the reverse side, a lack thereof could lead to the ultimate ruination of one's soul (see Hos 4:6). Isaiah 59:15 reads, "So the truth was lacking, and the one turning aside from evil was causing himself to be vandalized. And the LORD saw [it], and it was evil in his eyes, because there was no justice." While it may be difficult to know when we have enough truth, Isa 59:15 suggests that it is possible to not have enough, or to be lacking. To continue searching for truth is, therefore, surely necessary, not so much to reach a finite goal but to avoid a lack. Coming up short on ketchup can ruin a meal; coming up short on truth can ruin our soul.

July 12

"A Lack of Knowledge"

JUST AS THE BIBLE speaks of a lack of truth (see yesterday's "Daily"), so it also speaks of a lack of knowledge. Hosea 4:6 reads, "My people are ruined due to [their being] without knowledge." The quest for truth leads to knowledge; yet knowledge and truth are not the same, as one can be "always learning and never able to arrive at a knowledge of the truth" (2 Tim 3:7). In Hosea, God's people are destroyed because they were without not just knowledge but a knowledge of God's law (teaching). It is possible to have knowledge without truth, but it is not possible to have truth without knowledge. It is also possible to lack both. Thus, the Bible teaches Christians to acquire not only knowledge but such things as the "knowledge of Christ" (Phil 3:8; 2 Pet 3:18). Just as with truth, the quest for knowledge may be never-ending; by searching for truth we are likely to find it and thereby acquire proper knowledge. Seemingly more importantly, we also thereby derive the benefit of avoiding a deficit (lack) of both.

July 13

Seek and Read

A RIGHT RELATIONSHIP WITH God is attained by having both a right heart and a right head. Isaiah said, "Seek out from the book of the LORD, and read" (Isa 34:16a). Seeking the Lord begins in the heart and is continued through a knowledge of him by his word (John 8:32). Both seeking and reading are thus necessary to become right with God. Searching the Scriptures, such as to find truth, (Acts 17:11) is necessary, but searching alone is not enough (John 5:39). With a right heart, one who is desirous of knowing God is then driven to study and learn about God; one is then equipped to fulfill obedience (John 1:12; 2 Thess 1:8) to become right with God. Seeking can end with finding (Matt 7:7); yet, since study is a never-ending part of the Christian life (2 Pet 3:18), should not seeking also be? A heart that is seeking combined with a head that is reading leads to a soul being changed into a right relationship with God, and one that continues to seek and to read.

July 14

"The Sacrifice of Praise"

S‍ACRIFICE CAN BE PAINFUL, as, in so doing, one is parting from something they would likely rather keep (otherwise is it really a sacrifice?). There can be different reasons to sacrifice, some of which are unselfish (such as a parent raising a child), and some selfish (such as an investment, wherein one hopes to receive a return). The Hebrews writer thus spoke of the "sacrifice of praise": "Through him then let us continually offer up a sacrifice of praise to God, that is, the fruit of lips that acknowledge his name" (Heb 13:15). The phrase "sacrifice of praise" again illustrates what worship fundamentally is, that is, something offered to please the recipient. To offer praise to God (Pss 145, 146) is for the purpose of glorifying him, not us, and is, therefore, to be a sacrifice. It may be, therefore, that the less it is a sacrifice, the less would be the effect of praise (Mark 12:41–44). God sacrificed for us (John 3:16; Col 1:13), leaving any return on his investment up to our response. He asks us to offer a sacrifice of praise, the return of which will be that which is best for us, that God is thereby pleased (Heb 13:21). How unselfish can we be?

July 15

Something Good

DURING DIFFICULT TIMES WE often say that "something good can come out of this." Evil is evil and good is good (the Bible says "woe" to those who try to redefine them, Isa 5:20). We might wonder why evil is allowed to exist (Matt 5:45). While there may not be an easy answer to that question, we can not only observe that evil exists (Isa 45:7), but also that good may come from the presence of evil. In the Bible yeast is a symbol of evil (Israel was told to eliminate yeast during Passover, Exod 12:15; 13:6–7). Yet the presence of evil, like yeast in dough, can assist the production of good. This idea seems to be illustrated by Paul's teaching that the presence of evil can provide an opportunity for good to be more active. He said, "Do not be overcome by evil, but overcome evil with good" (Rom 12:21). It may be that without the presence of evil the good may not be as active; evil, as it were, provides an opportunity to do good. We don't want evil, because it's bad. But, since it's here, we might as well try to get something good out of it.

July 16

There for You

THE FULFILLMENT OF GOD'S promises seem to depend more on us than on him. That is, God is unable to lie (Heb 6:18), and he is not unable to keep his promises (Matt 19:26). Therefore, for God's promises to have fulfillment depends on our seeking their fulfillment. This can be illustrated by God's promise to be there for us. When we make this promise to our fellows, we are assuring them that we will do all we can to be available and to help, insofar as we are able. God promises to be there for us all (Jer 33:3; Matt 11:28–30), and to be with the Christian especially (Matt 28:18–20). But this promise is also to be understood in view of the fact that God is unchangeable (Mal 3:6; Heb 13:8). For us to benefit from God always being there for us is, therefore, up to us. "Seek the LORD while he may be found; summon him while he is near" (Isa 55:6). Not that he's going anywhere; but to fulfill the promise of his presence, or to find him, depends on us seeking, not on his being found.

July 17

Tired of Trying

It is proper for us to pray so that we may make request of God (Heb 4:16). To receive a positive response to our requests depends, in part, on God's will (1 John 5:14). To become tired of praying because it seems our efforts are not contributing to this end could betray an attitude of selfishness. When, in life, we say that we are tired of trying, it implies that we would only try until we succeed. This, in turn, implies that we would stop if we succeeded. The Christian is not to stop praying (1 Thess 5:17). Rather than only pray so we can get what we want, or engage in prayer as something that we "have" to do, we should look at prayer in part as a means of drawing closer to God. Isaiah 40:31 reads, "But those who wait for the Lord will renew [their] strength; they will raise their pinions like the eagles; they will run and not grow weary; they will walk and not become faint." To wait on the Lord provides physical and, more importantly, spiritual strength. By waiting on the Lord, or giving proper attention to our spiritual life through such things as prayer, we can gain strength to keep on praying because we are not tired of trying.

July 18

A Peace That Guards

Physical violence, which seems to be usually borne of evil, necessitates physical defense (such as a good government defending a country, Rom 13:4). Evil is active (1 Pet 5:8) and does not like to see good (compared to good, which tries to do good, Rom 12:21). Evil also attempts to remove the spiritual blessings that the Christian has been given by God. God offers many reasons that evil will be unsuccessful, including that the spiritual blessings of the Christian life are in heaven (Eph 1:3), that God holds the Christian in his hand (John 10:29), and that God offers something to guard the Christian from evil. Paul thus said, "Do not be anxious about anything, but in everything by prayer and supplication with thanksgiving let your requests be made known to God. And the peace of God, which surpasses all understanding, will guard your hearts and your minds in Christ Jesus" (Phil 4:6–7). While we don't like to think about having to physically defend ourselves, we also, as Christians, don't have to worry about spiritually defending ourselves, because God provides us a peace to guard us.

July 19

"Sing of Covenant Loyalty"

IN SEVERAL VERSES IN the psalms, the writer states that he will sing. One such passage is Ps 101, wherein the psalmist proclaimed, "Let me sing of covenant loyalty and of justice. Let me praise you, O LORD in song" (v. 1). The two things of which the psalmist speaks are surely representative of the many blessings of being a child of God. God's covenant loyalty has to do with his relationship with his people of old. Justice is, of course, that spiritual and legal principle that the right thing will result in the end. It is proper for us to praise God for such things as the house we live in, how much money we make, and when we come through surgery successfully (that is, to sing because we are cheerful, Jas 5:13). When we also concentrate on such spiritual things as justice in our everyday life (Phil 4:8), it will be an easy transition to come to worship and praise him, not just for this one (or two) thing(s), but for all things spiritual and physical. Worshiping in spirit (John 4:24) perhaps begins with concentrating on spiritual things.

July 20

"The Fullness of God"

Some kinds of unhealthy food ("junk food") seem to fill one up, but do not give the body the nutrients it really needs. That is, we might ironically say the body is thereby filled with emptiness. Paul spoke of being filled with the fullness of God: "And to know the love of Christ that surpasses knowledge, that you may be filled with all the fullness of God" (Eph 3:19). While the world offers knowledge, which might even contain some truth, knowledge without God leads one away from truth (2 Tim 3:7), and is, therefore, an empty knowledge. To be filled with the fullness of God is achieved by acquiring knowledge of something Paul said is past knowledge (from the one who called himself "less than the least" of all saints, Eph 3:8). The world offers vast quantities of knowledge that do not offer fulfillment, but rather emptiness. Only God offers the blessing of knowing something that is beyond knowing, something that, by knowing, fills our soul with substance rather than emptiness.

July 21

I Get That

JUST BEFORE SPEAKING OF knowing the love of Christ (see yesterday's "Daily"), Paul spoke of the Christian's being able to apprehend such truth; that is, that his readers "may be strong to apprehend with all the saints what is the breadth and length and height and depth" (Eph 3:18 ASV). The Greek word translated "apprehend" (also translated "comprehend") in this verse has to do with understanding (the word is elsewhere used three times of the darkness not apprehending the light [John 1:5; 12:35; 1 Thess 5:4]). While understanding, in general, may depend on such things as natural talent and applied concentration, Paul speaks of it as something the Christian can seemingly control. Thus, Paul prayed (v. 14) that Christ may dwell in their hearts through faith (v. 17), so that they would apprehend. Faith comes through hearing the word (Rom 10:17). Thus, the way for darkness not to apprehend us, for Christ to dwell in our heart, and for us to apprehend the word of God is by our concentrating on the word of God.

July 22

Heart and Mind

THE HEART (ACTS 2:37; Rom 6:17) as well as the mind (John 8:24) are involved in becoming a Christian, and both the heart (Luke 8:13) and the mind (Rom 12:2) can become corrupted. It is possible to be enthusiastic about something because we like it without putting any thought into it, and it is also possible to do something that we know is right even though our heart is not in it. Inasmuch as evil influences surround (1 Pet 5:8), we can, and are to, do our part to ensure the protection of both (Eph 5:15). Yet God also promises to guard both with a peace that only God can offer: "Do not be anxious about anything, but in everything by prayer and supplication with thanksgiving let your requests be made known to God. And the peace of God, which surpasses all understanding, will guard your hearts and your minds in Christ Jesus" (Phil 4:6–7). We might have to overcome emotions that are unhealthy for our soul; and we may not be able to understand this protection that God offers. Yet, by following Paul's teaching, the result will be the peace of God that guards us in both ways—heart and mind.

July 23

Opening God's Word

BOTH LIGHT AND DARKNESS were created by God (Isa 45:7); both, therefore, surely serve a purpose. There may be times when we might desire physical darkness ("weary with toil I haste me to bed"[5]). There are also those who desire spiritual darkness, inasmuch as error is often easier to accept than truth [John 3:19]). To avail ourselves of spiritual light, however, is necessary for us to overcome spiritual darkness. The psalmist said, "The unfolding of your words enlightens; it gives understanding to the simple" (Ps 119:130; the Hebrew word translated "unfolding" can also be translated "open"). Darkness will not completely overcome light (see John 1:5). Life, and even the Bible (2 Pet 3:16), may be difficult to understand. Some may say they don't open God's word because they don't understand it. Could it be that they don't understand it because they don't open it (see "Daily" of July 25)? Yet to make sense of this world, and to live a life that pleases God, walking in light rather than darkness is necessary (1 John 1:7); and it begins with opening God's word.

---

5. Shakespeare, Sonnet 27.

July 24

Sing One to Another

IF WORSHIP IS FIRST and foremost for God, why does the Bible direct us to sing "one [to] another?" While the Bible does not give a reason therefor, this aspect reminds us both of the fact that worship can benefit us as we worship, as well as the fact that communal worship is to be offered as a gathering of his people. Paul twice said we are to sing "one [to] another": "Addressing one another in psalms and hymns and spiritual songs, singing and making melody to the Lord with your heart" (Eph 5:19; also Col 3:16). Some aspects of worship, such as singing and praying, can be done by the Christian any time, whether alone or not. The fact that the Bible specifies singing "one [to] another" reminds us that, just as with other acts of worship such as communion or preaching, worship is communal as well as individual (1 Cor 16:2). Perhaps it delights God's heart when he hears our voices (and only our voices) praising him in unison (see Ps 133). God is always watching us (see Matt 6:32), and can hear from us at any time; it is only when we gather together that he gets to enjoy, as it were, hearing his people sing to him together as we sing one to another.

July 25

"The Comfort of God"

WHEN WE THINK OF comfort we likely think, for example, of a warm place in winter where we can lie down and sleep undisturbed, an attitude with which there is nothing wrong. The Bible speaks of God comforting us: "Blessed be the God and Father of our Lord Jesus Christ, the Father of mercies and God of all comfort, who comforts us in all our affliction, so that we may be able to comfort those who are in any affliction, with the comfort with which we ourselves are comforted by God" (2 Cor 1:3–4). Paul's description of comfort as coming from God, and as something we can extend to others, is consistent with God's word. We cannot avoid pain in this life, though God will not let the Christian's suffering become unbearable (1 Cor 10:13), and God offers us physical blessings in this life as well (Phil 4:19). God sent to the apostles the "Comforter," the Holy Spirit, who would guide them into all truth (John 14:26; 16:13), even while most of them evidently endured physical persecution. In 2 Cor 12:8, Paul "pleaded with" God to comfort him (the Greek word so translated is from the same Greek word translated "comfort") by relieving him of his "thorn in the flesh." God's denial thereof, led Paul to conclude that it is best for the power of Christ to rest upon him (v. 9; a reference to God's word?). We naturally look for natural comfort. God offers us spiritual comfort through his word, which, by reading, gives us comfort to endure physical discomfort in this life, especially when we know that by enduring, we will one day be comforted for all eternity (Rev 21:4).

July 26

"The Proof of Your Faith"

IT IS SAID THAT conflicts in life serve as the proving ground from which true character emerges (like the saying that winning shows something of one's character, while losing shows all of it). Though it is difficult to know the source of trials, the Bible speaks of a purpose for the trials endured by the Christian, that is, "that the proof of your faith, being more precious than gold that perisheth though it is proved by fire, may be found unto praise and glory and honor at the revelation of Jesus Christ" (1 Pet 1:7 ASV). Trials, which are temporary (1 Pet 1:6), serve the purpose of proving the genuineness of the Christian's faith. Faith is here compared to gold, which also needs to be tested, and yet is eventually going to perish. It is through enduring trials that the Christian can know whether their faith is strong or even genuine. Perhaps if our faith is not proven it will perish?

July 27

Preparing for the Worst

THE BIBLE TEACHES THE importance of being ready, especially in one's mind. Peter said: "Therefore, preparing your minds for action, and being sober-minded, set your hope fully on the grace that will be brought to you at the revelation of Jesus Christ" (1 Pet 1:13). We don't know the future, but we can know some things about the future. The importance of being ready in mind is in achieving a strength necessary to overcome spiritual obstacles (Eph 6:10–20). Faith includes trusting God no matter what is going to happen (Matt 26:42). This can be accomplished by considering what could happen, for example in order to overcome fear (Ps 23:4), or to do the right thing (Dan 3:17–18). To dwell on something we don't know can produce fear; to dwell on what we do know—for the Christian the spiritual assurances regarding God's providence—can produce faith. Though we don't know what will be, we can prepare for what is going to happen (the physical) by concentrating on what we do know (the spiritual, God's word). "And we know that for those who love God all things work together for good, for those who are called according to his purpose" (Rom 8:28).

July 28

Self-Reflection

IT CAN BE BOTH fun and painful to grow. As Christians, we have a need to grow (2 Pet 3:18), which suggests a need to improve. One of the keys to improving is the sometimes painful process of self-reflection. Self-reflection means evaluating ourselves, while realizing that we are not the standard. Proper self-reflection includes a realization of sin (Rom 3:23), of the need to change our heart (Matt 21:28–32), and of the need to imitate Jesus: "Be imitators of me, as I am of Christ" (1 Cor 11:1). Self-reflection is, therefore, for the purpose, not of comparing ourselves with ourselves (2 Cor 10:12), but of comparing ourselves with the standard of God's law (2 Cor 13:5; Jas 1:25). We do this toward the goal of self-improvement, which we achieve by striving to reflect the image of Christ (Col 3:10) for others to see. Self-reflection should be toward the ultimate goal of Christ-reflection.

July 29

"Examine Yourselves"

THE BIBLE SPEAKS OF "the faith" (Jude 3) as well as our own acceptance of, or faith, therein. We may thus say that there is an outside faith which one must accept, or in which one must have an internal personal faith. Again, one's faith is going to be tested from the outside (1 Pet 1:7; Jas 1:3). It is also important for us to see to it that our belief is true according to God's faith, or tested from within. Thus Paul said, "Examine yourselves, to see whether you are in the faith. Test yourselves. Or do you not realize this about yourselves, that Jesus Christ is in you?—unless indeed you fail to meet the test!" (2 Cor 13:5; see yesterday's "Daily"). Many aspects of the Christian life are a do-it-yourself project. To thus examine our faith, using the standard of God's word (Jas 1:25), can help ensure its strength from within. By doing this we can help ensure that it is more likely to withstand pressure from without.

July 30

"Teach Us to Pray"

Two of the clearest expressions of humility are the acts of worshiping someone and of admitting we don't know something. The fact that worship was, at times, rejected by God (Gen 4:5; Mal 1:8) tells us that there is unacceptable as well as acceptable worship. Jesus' teaching on the model prayer is preceded by an unknown disciple asking him how we are to pray: "Now Jesus was praying in a certain place, and when he finished, one of his disciples said to him, 'Lord, teach us to pray, as John taught his disciples'" (Luke 11:1). This disciple's request amounts to an inquiry into the form of acceptable worship. Whether the disciple accepted Jesus' teaching is another question (it is possible to learn something and still not agree with it, John 6:66). Yet, before we worship God, it is good to learn how to worship; both of which require humility.

July 31

"Receive Evil"

JOB SERVES AS A good example because of his enduring evil. After he had lost everything, Job said to his wife: "Would we even receive good from God, but not evil?" (Job 2:10). The tone of Job's question suggests that the action of receiving evil should be understood. Job's "receiving" evil is why James refers to the "steadfastness of Job" (Jas 5:11; the Greek word translated "steadfastness" meaning "to bear up under hardships"). Thus, the Christian today is elsewhere taught to be "steadfast" in the work of the Lord (1 Cor 15:58), to be faithful unto death (Rev 2:10b), and to hold their faith firm to the end (Heb 3:14). The Christian does not give up on God when difficult things happen. Even if we are not able to understand its source or its reason, evil is going to happen to us. Since love does not take account of evil (1 Cor 13:5) one who loves God will bear the trials, temptations, and frustrations of this life—in other words, they will receive evil—like Job.

August 1

Does God Ever Leave Us?

WHY DID THE PSALMIST ask why? "My God, my God, why have you forsaken me [and are] far from helping me, [from] the words of my groaning?" (Ps 22:1). He is surely speaking in a poetic way, out of the anguish of his heart (for example, he uses words to ask why God is far from hearing his words). God promised that he would never leave us (Deut 31:8; Heb 13:5; Matt 28:18–20). The fact that Jesus quoted this psalm on the cross (Matt 27:46; Mark 15:34) is a very difficult question. I personally can't help but notice that one of Jesus' last acts is to quote Scripture. Unpleasant things are going to happen to us in a world that contains evil as well as good. God evidently does not mind our questioning, especially, it seems, when such questions arise from a sincere heart (see Hab 1:2–4). It was evidently not a surprise to Jesus that Peter and others forsook him (that is, he didn't ask "why"; Matt 26:56; Mark 14:50). God understands our anguish, especially when it is caused by the pain we often endure in this life. Like the psalmist, we might be surprised when we don't receive the response we want. But since God promised to not leave us, we can rather look to, and take comfort in, the promise of his word that he will never leave us; why would he?

August 2

Turning to God

THE ENGLISH WORD "CONVERT" has a meaning of "turning to" (literally, "turn with"). We often turn to or from something at pivotal moments in our lives, such as seeking help during time of trouble. "Turning to" also implies that we are turning from. Thus, the Bible speaks of one turning their ears from the truth (2 Tim. 4:4), or turning from God (Heb 12:25), as well as to God from idols (Acts 14:15), and of Jesus' desire to avoid the type of death he suffered, but turning his will over to his Father's (Matt 26:39). Turning to God begins in our head (such as understanding our sin, Acts 2:37), and is dictated by our heart (or repentance, Matt 21:28–31). We can only go on one path at a time, and there will be moments in life when we must direct our heart (back) to God to avoid turning from him. We are going somewhere; when we are faced with a choice, "to whom shall we go?" (John 6:68). Isn't that what turning to God initially (conversion) is all about?

August 3

Good and Pleasant

We often speak of things pleasant (like nice weather) using the word "good," even though something can be good without being pleasant. Like the elements of a recipe or a piece of intricate music, all of the elements of worship work together for good, and are also pleasant. Just as the dynamic of worship is created when Christians assemble, so when we engage in the acts of worship (prayer, singing, the Lord's Supper, communion, and giving), we are offering to God a complete expression of our collective soul. If all of the elements of worship are equally important, it suggests that God will surely notice if we leave one element out, or engage therein improperly (imagine having garlic instead of sugar in a cake). Just as "all things work together for good" in the life of the Christian (Rom 8:28), so, in effect, all of the elements of worship blend together, both for the good of our soul, and to please the One to whom we are offering these things. Worship is therefore both good and pleasant for us and for God: "Praise the Lord! Because it is good to praise our God in song; because it is pleasant, and praise is suitable" (Ps 147:1).

August 4

Rest Assured

IN THIS LIFE IT is inevitable that we are going to labor, while receiving rest for our labor is not. We are going to sleep (1 Thess 5:7), but sleep does not necessarily mean we will become rested. We also sometimes have to take time to rest (Mark 6:31). We labor because we live in a physical world, wherein it is often laborious simply to endure this physical life and its hardships. We are bound to bear the burden of work (Gen 3:17–19); even if one enjoys their job, work is still laborious. Sin is a burden, and bears a price (Rom 3:23) which, though pleasurable (Heb 10:25), is thus laborious (Matt 11:28–30). All of these impose the need for rest. We might say that true rest is spiritual, and, therefore, can only be received from the spiritual source of God. With God we can turn over to him our burden of sin (Heb 12:1–2), we can sleep and become rested (Ps 4:8), and we can labor for him in view of the promise of rest (1 Cor 15:58; 2 Thess 1:7). Though living in this physical world is laborious, God extends spiritual relief—or rest—that is assured.

August 5

How to Read the Bible

THE BIBLE CAN BE read like any other book, but it should not be read like any other book. It can be read like any other because it can withstand the criticisms that are leveled against it (evidence of this may be the fact that the Bible is still here after, likely, being subjected to more criticism than any other book). The Bible should be read differently, because it is different. While the facets of this are many, the bottom line of what makes the Bible different is inspiration. Paul said, "All Scripture is breathed out by God and profitable for teaching, for reproof, for correction, and for training in righteousness" (2 Tim 3:16). The inspiration of the Bible includes such aspects as understanding spiritual things (Eph 3:4), words that affect our soul (Acts 2:37), and words that can change our life (John 6:68; Rom 1:16). Inspiration is a spiritual truth that can't be proven (and can't be disproved), but must be accepted. Maybe the fact that the Bible is able to withstand attempts to disprove it is evidence of the inspiration that can't be proven?

August 6

Enough Is Enough

Talent and ability come from God (Matt 25:14–30), not from ourselves. When we speak of competence to do a job, or talent that amazes everyone else, we often compare whatever ability we have to everyone else's ability. Paul spoke of our sufficiency as coming from God: "Not that we are sufficient in ourselves to claim anything as coming from us, but our sufficiency is from God" (2 Cor 3:5). The Greek word translated "sufficiency" appears only here in the NT, and has a sense of adequacy or competence. God fills our cup (to overflowing, Ps 23:5), and our needs (Phil 4:19), and supplies us with talent and ability to be able to do our part in providing for ourselves (2 Thess 3:10) and others (1 Tim 5:8). To look at such things as a spiritual blessing, that is, as coming from God, can help us not only be satisfied with our sufficiency but also help us to avoid being "puffed up" thereby (see 1 Tim 6:4–10), as well as to use our sufficiency to glorify him for so endowing us. To do so is the right thing to do, and may mean we will be given more to do more with (Matt 25:28; 2 Cor 9:10). We may say that we would thereby be given more sufficiency from the One who supplied it to begin with. It certainly didn't come from us.

August 7

"Test Yourselves"

Depending on our purpose or intention, God invites us to test him (Mal 3:10; Luke 4:12); again, our faith is going to be tested (1 Pet 1:6–7; Jas 1:14). God's system of faith does not change, though our belief therein (our faith) may. Thus, Paul challenged us to make sure of our relationship with God, that is, to test it: "Examine yourselves, to see whether you are in the faith. Test yourselves. Or do you not realize this about yourselves, that Jesus Christ is in you?—unless indeed you fail to meet the test!" (2 Cor 13:5). A saying in medicine is "we are our own worst diagnoser." That is, it is very difficult for one to make an objective assessment of their health compared to a health professional. With regard to spiritual things, we are to assess ourselves according to the standard of God's faith, whereby we can know that we are right with him (1 John 5:13). His faith doesn't change; ours might, and that's why we must test it, in the hope of passing the test.

August 8

"Will-Worship"

IF SOMEONE WANTED TO do something for you to tell you how great you are, how would you want them to do it (social media, a statue in the middle of town, both of these)? What if someone tried to honor you with something you didn't want? All we have to go on to discern God's will is his written word (we may not know, for example, his will regarding events in our lives, Phlm 15). When it comes to worship, God has directed that we sing (Eph 5:19), pray (1 Tim 2:8), give (1 Cor 16:2), participate in communion (1 Cor 11:20), and partake of teaching (1 Tim 4:13). To deviate from his word in this regard, such as changing worship to something we want, is to deviate from his will. Paul said, of false ways and teachings, "Which things have indeed a show of wisdom in will-worship, and humility, and severity to the body; but are not of any value against the indulgence of the flesh" (Col 2:23 ASV). What he calls "will-worship" is surely the opposite of worship of which God would approve; that is, it is worship according to our will versus his. When it comes to worship, a good word to heed are the words of Jesus in the garden, "Not as I will" (Matt 26:39).

August 9

Prepare and Expect

A SAYING IN LIFE is "prepare for the worst, expect the best." These two aspects can both be done properly or improperly. One can, improperly, prepare for the worst out of a heart conditioned by fear, and expect the best out of a heart defined by arrogance. The child of God can prepare for the worst (Ps 23:4; Dan 3:17–18), for the purpose of causing them to rely on God. They can also expect the best (Mark 11:24, whether they wind up receiving it or not) in order to develop faith in God. If both approaches to life are necessary and can be good, what is it that determines them to be acceptable or unacceptable, but one's attitude? The child of God looks at every possibility in life, positive or negative, as a means of gaining spiritual strength (2 Cor 12:9) and of glorifying God (Col 3:17). Thus, whatever they expect, and whatever is to happen, they expect God to take care of it.

August 10

Arrogance Is an Attitude

IT IS SAID THAT arrogance is a disease that makes everybody sick except the one who has it. Arrogance is not a quality that makes one better than others, but, rather, an attitude whereby one thinks they are above (better than) others. Everyone has a talent (Matt 24:14–30), and some certainly have more talents than others. But each Christian is to be a servant of God (Gal 5:13), which means the attitude they are to adopt is that of humility rather than of arrogance. This attitude manifests itself in our treating others better than ourselves, no matter who has more talent. This is the mindset Paul said Christians are to adopt: "Do nothing from selfish ambition or conceit, but in humility count others more significant than yourselves" (Phil 2:3). The physical reality may be that one has more talent than others; the spiritual attitude they are to adopt, however, is that others are better. This is not a denial of truth, but rather the means that God has directed for Christians to properly function as his servants (1 Pet 2:16), and, ultimately, to be exalted (Matt 23:12) for assuming the lower position.

August 11

"The Fragrance of the Knowledge of Him"

THE SMELL OF A fragrance can affect one positively or negatively, since not all fragrances appeal to all people. The smell of food may be very enticing to a hungry person, but not necessarily to one already full. God's word is both powerful (Rom 1:16) and fragrant. Paul said, "But thanks be to God, who in Christ always leads us in triumphal procession, and through us spreads the fragrance of the knowledge of him everywhere" (2 Cor 2:14). The Greek word here translated "fragrance" appears four times in the NT (once of ointment [John 12:3], twice of the fragrance of worship or work offered for God [Eph 5:2; Phil 4:18] and, only here, of the fragrance of the knowledge of him that we can smell). Like our worship and work, the fragrance of which can delight God, so God has offered to us the fragrance of the knowledge of him. It may or may not appeal to everybody (Acts 17:32–34), yet it can affect them positively or negatively depending on whether they are hungry for it (Matt 5:6).

August 12

"All Power"

WE LOSE POWER OR energy as part of living in this physical world. As Christians, we can gain spiritual power through an increased knowledge of God's word (referred to as "the power" in Rom 1:16). In Col 1:11, Paul referred to being strengthened with "all power": "being strengthened with all power, according to his glorious might, for all endurance and patience with joy" (both Greek words translated "strengthened" and "power" come from the same word as in Rom 1:16 translated "power"). The way Paul says "strengthened with power" is almost redundant (like saying "be made wet with water"). The purpose for which Paul speaks of this power is "for all endurance and patience." God offers all the spiritual power we need to be able both to bear up under, as well as to be slow to give in to, life's trials and temptations (1 Cor 10:13). Imagine if it were only a partial power (Matt 17:20).

August 13

Growing Strong in Faith

A FACT OF LIFE is that we, and everything else, again gradually lose energy and strength (see yesterday's "Daily"). Whether physically or spiritually, we can get stronger temporarily, but it does not happen on its own. Becoming physically stronger, for example, begins with going to the gym; but one must also use the machines at the gym to expect a result. The Bible speaks of a Christian's being strong (Eph 6:10) as well as our becoming strong, and that becoming spiritually strong can be attained through faith: "No unbelief made him waver concerning the promise of God, but he grew strong in his faith as he gave glory to God" (Rom 4:20). The Greek word translated "grew strong" (literally "grew more powerful") is related to the Greek word translated "power," used to describe the gospel (Rom 1:16). We are empowered through the power of the gospel. If we hear it (Rom 10:17) and believe it, we can become spiritually stronger. But it won't happen on its own.

August 14

What to Wear

WHAT WE WEAR, BOTH inside and outside, is a choice we make each day. I've heard it said that some (the rich) wear the same type of clothes every day because they don't want to have to make the decision of what to wear every day. How we treat others, how we treat such things as our health, and how (whether) we respond to God is, likewise, a choice. The heart can become hardened (Exod 9:34); but even that may involve a choice (that is, such conditioning may depend on how we react to life's circumstances). Paul wrote to "put on" a certain heart: "Put on therefore, as God's elect, holy and beloved, a heart of compassion, kindness, lowliness, meekness, long-suffering" (Col 3:12). The Greek word translated "put on" appears many times in the NT, including with regard to putting on Christ (Gal 3:27) and the armor of God (Eph 6:11). What we put on in the morning naturally determines how we look, and may affect our attitude toward ourselves as well as others' perception of us (1 Sam 16:7). The kind of heart we put on in the morning spiritually affects the kind of person we are, and determines such things as our actions that others will eventually see (Matt 7:16). How they perceive us is their choice; how we present ourselves to them is our choice, because of what we choose to put on.

August 15

Learning without Truth

FOR TRUTH TO HAVE an effect on the human heart, it must be accepted as well as learned. One can learn all there is to know about the Bible without accepting it as true (see John 5:39). One can also spend their life learning other things without ever coming to the truth. Paul reflected that there are those that are "always learning and never able to arrive at a knowledge of the truth" (2 Tim 3:7). The mind has a great capacity for storing, processing, and, even, distorting information. In (true) science, facts are facts whether we agree with them or not. In the mind, the perception of facts can be distorted so that the same information affects one person differently over the next. That which is being distorted is therefore truth, or facts that do not change. Information, or learning, is important, but truth is more important (if we accept truth we have learned it). To be a disciple is to be a learner (so the Greek word translated "disciple" means). Learning from Jesus means not just learning but accepting truth (John 14:6). And, therefore, accepting him.

August 16

The Time to Worship

Does it matter when we worship? Elijah mocked the prophets of Baal (1 Kgs 18:27), saying that maybe their god was gone on a journey (maybe they needed to try again another time). God is always there for us, and we can call upon God at any time (John 11:42). While there are no time restrictions on some aspects of worship (though see 1 Thess 5:17), other aspects are to be done at a certain time. The Lord's Supper is called a "communion," in part, because we commune with each other while remembering his death (1 Cor 11:20), and Christians are told to sing "one to another" (Eph 5:19). These things, combined with a mention of the "first day of the week" (Acts 20:7; 1 Cor 16:2) point to the worship of Christians as designed to take place at a certain time. There is no magic in simply eating a piece of bread and drinking a spot of grape juice; but, when combined with the other aspects of worship that Christians engage in when they come together, and knowing that Jesus is there as well (Matt 18:20), makes the time and the timing of our worship, special both to us and to God. That time is the first day of the week.

August 17

How Soon We Forget

WHAT WE CHOOSE TO remember is both selective and fickle. When we think, for example, on last year's vacation, we tend to remember the good things. When someone does us a favor, it may not have the same impact as when someone commits an offence against us. While everyone is different, it is generally true that it requires more effort to think on or remember the positive. Jesus directed the apostles to remember in order to get them to understand: "Do you not yet perceive? Do you not remember the five loaves for the five thousand, and how many baskets you gathered?" (Matt 16:9). To both concentrate on and recall evident answers to prayers can give us spiritual strength by drawing us closer to God in a positive way (Rom 2:4). It's a good thing God chooses not to remember the negative things (sin) in the lives of his children (Heb 8:12).

August 18

"Through Him"

Paul's assertion that "I can do all things through him who strengthens me" (Phil 4:13) is a good illustration of understanding the Bible first with a spiritual meaning. Paul elsewhere spoke of the decline of the physical body along with the continued increase of the spirit (2 Cor 4:16). Here he states that his strengthening is "through him" (that is, through Christ, as we have spoken before). Though Paul doesn't state the means of this strengthening, the fact that he states it is through Christ tells us that the strength of which he speaks is a power that affects our soul rather than, for example, our muscles (see also Eph 6:10). This strengthening is the basis for Paul saying he can do "all things"; thus, if the strengthening is spiritual, it follows that the "all things" that Paul can do is fundamentally spiritual as well (in this context, of enduring financial hardship). When we look at the Bible with a spiritual focus, and use it with a spiritual application, it can affect our lives in a physical way (Matt 6:33) but, more importantly, in a spiritual way. Just as we love the Lord with all of our spiritual being (Mark 12:30), which is then manifested in the life we live, so Christ will, in turn, strengthen us spiritually, in order to live the kind of life that pleases him; and do "all things."

August 19

Either/Or

THE CHOICE BETWEEN SEEKING our own things versus seeking the things of Christ is a choice between that which is natural and that which is spiritual. Regarding some who were selfish, Paul said to the Philippians, "For they all seek their own interests, not those of Jesus Christ" (Phil 2:21). While there is a place for having personal desires, the Bible consistently warns against selfishness (Mark 10:17–22) and other natural inclinations. The key to being able to pursue the things that interest us is to turn them from a natural ambition to a spiritual one. We do this by turning our will over to his (Ps 37:4; Matt 26:39), so that our purpose in seeking is unselfish rather than selfish (Jas 4:3; 1 Tim 5:8), and so that we seek spiritual things first (Matt 6:33). In this way, what we seek need not necessarily be an "either/or," but, rather, turning over to God the things that, otherwise, would be ours. By making ours his, what we seek is unselfish, even if it's what we want.

August 20

"The Power of His Resurrection"

IN MY "DAILIES" I am fond of saying that the word "power" in the NT often refers to God's word. In Phil 3 Paul spoke of the power of Christ's resurrection: "That I may know him and the power of his resurrection, and may share his sufferings, becoming like him in his death" (Phil 3:10). While Paul doesn't specify what this is, it nevertheless reminds the Christian of an evident power that is theirs because of Christ's resurrection. Because Christ was raised, the Christian has a hope of also being raised from the dead (1 Cor 15:20), which means that their body, which was "sown in weakness," will be "raised in power" (1 Cor 15:43). The knowledge that we will be raised from the dead provides Christians with hope and confidence that the one enemy we all will face, that is, death, does not hold the power; but, rather, the Christian has power over death (1 Cor 15:54–58) because of resurrection. They have this power because of Christ's resurrection; and, as Paul reflected, this is a truth we can know because we are told in God's word.

August 21

Reasons Not to Worship

THE SAYING IS THAT if we don't want to do something, one excuse is as good as another. If one wanted to, they could come up with many reasons not to worship God. There is a place for reasoning in the Christian life (the Greek word translated "reason" appears about thirteen times in the NT, ten of which are in the book of Acts, usually in a context of Paul reasoning with Jews in the synagogue); yet worship is a spiritual activity that may not always make sense to the reasonable mind (1 Cor 1:18). Jesus taught that we are to worship God "in spirit and truth" (John 4:24); the reason we worship God is therefore spiritual. We might be able to come up with many reasons not to worship God, but there are no good spiritual reasons.

August 22

Now I Get It

WHEN JESUS ASKED THE apostles whether they yet perceived (Matt 16:9 see "Daily" of Aug. 17), he seemed rather surprised. Understanding certain concepts (such as quantum physics) seems largely to depend on natural ability. In the Bible, the Greek word translated "perceive" (also translated "understand" or "think") has to do with grasping a concept in our mind. The English word "perceive" comes from a Latin word meaning "to grasp." While such ability, again, surely includes a natural element, the biblical word is also used of perceiving by such things as observing God's creation (Rom 1:20), of understanding through faith (Heb 11:3), and, therefore, something that can be achieved through reading: "When you read this, you can perceive my insight into the mystery of Christ" (Eph 3:4; see Rom 10:17). Paul even "commanded" Timothy (using this same word) to perceive what he was saying (2 Tim 2:7). Since Jesus seemed surprised that the apostles hadn't grasped his meaning, maybe the kind of perception Jesus would expect is not natural, but spiritual.

August 23

My Way of Thinking

I AM NO PSYCHOLOGIST, but it seems to be a given that everyone's mind works differently. A healthy mind, just like a healthy body, surely begins with a good spiritual life, inasmuch as a Christian is to love themselves (Mark 12:31), and, therefore, do what is best for themselves physically, mentally, and spiritually. How our mind works may be a natural process; for example, the natural reaction to a disagreement may be anger for one person but not another. The Bible offers ways that help both how our mind works (for example, the spiritual quality of love is "patient," or slow to become angry, 1 Cor 13:4) as well as what our mind dwells on. Paul said, "Set your minds on things that are above, not on things that are on earth" (Col 3:2; see also Phil 4:8). If we choose on what our mind dwells, it may contribute to how our mind works. A healthy mind begins with a healthy spiritual life.

August 24

"That You May Be in Good Health"

WITH REGARD TO HEALTH, a saying is that our health will not take care of itself. Like everything else for which we have been given responsibility, our health requires attention and maintenance. Our reasons for taking care of our health are likely all practical (either to avoid pain, financial expense, or to live longer), with which there is nothing necessarily wrong. John wished for his readers to have good health (3 John 2), and Paul stated that our body can be looked at spiritually: "Do you not know that you are God's temple and that God's Spirit dwells in you?" (1 Cor 3:16). The sobering reality is that, even though we do all we can, our health still deteriorates (2 Cor 4:16); yet we still have a need to maintain the one body that we have been given. To look at our health and the maintenance thereof as a scriptural responsibility and a means of glorifying God makes our efforts not practical but spiritual. Even though it will one day come to an end (Heb 9:27), taking care of our health does good, both practically, and, more importantly, spiritually.

August 25

Turn It Around

Momentum can be a good thing if it's going our way. When life seems to be going in a negative direction, however, we need not be bound by its course. Outside events, of course, may be outside of our control (though they are not outside of God's control). But our response to life, whether life be positive or negative, is up to us, and can determine whether we become positive or negative. While the natural inclination may be toward such things as a negative attitude, negative speech, and weakness in the face of negative circumstances, the Bible teaches our need to face difficult times with the opposite. That is, a positive attitude (Mark 11:24), good speech (Jas 3:6–12), and strength (Eph 6:10) are the spiritual forces that can keep negative momentum from affecting us negatively. Perhaps it is that, since these things are not natural, we need to be told in Scripture to do them? By practicing these things we may not change the negative momentum, but we can change ourselves by not letting circumstances change us. We can turn it, I mean ourselves, around.

August 26

Why This Way?

WHY DID GOD DIRECT that certain acts are to be carried out as worship by Christians today? Though we are not given a reason, we can assume that each aspect of worship serves a purpose and that there may be a synergistic purpose to our engaging in all of these acts in one service. Just as Israel of old was directed as to which kinds of sacrifices to offer at certain times, so today, God has directed that Christians sing (Eph 5:19), pray (1 Tim 2:8), participate in communion (1 Cor 11:25–29), give (1 Cor 16:2), and engage in teaching (1 Tim 4:13). One could probably draw many lessons from the various ways our soul can benefit from engaging in these spiritual acts. Perhaps it is not an accident that we are not told why? Regardless, to engage therein reflects faith in God's word, as well as a desire to please the One who so directed us in his word; that is, the One who does not need anything we have to offer.

August 27

"The Pharisees Were Offended"

IN THE BIBLE, THE idea of being offended can have to do with anything from getting one's feelings hurt to being caused to sin (the Greek word can also be translated "stumble," and is from where our English word "scandal" comes). Matthew 15:12 states that the Pharisees were offended by what Jesus said, while in John 16:1 Jesus said that he taught certain things so that the disciples would not be offended: "These things have I spoken unto you, that ye should not be offended" (KJV). Truth does not change, but can change us if we are not offended thereby (or if a negative reaction doesn't keep us from a positive response). The world in which we live demands that we change such things as our speech, depending on whether the hearer is offended thereby. Truth is going to hurt somebody; yet, the hearer can change, even if they are offended. To accept truth is to accept the tool we need to avoid the stumbling of sin (Rom 14:21), or offending, in the future. If we accept truth, it will help us avoid offending God.

August 28

"With All Your Heart"

HAVE YOU EVER FELT the need and, even the desire, to trust someone, but just didn't feel it in your heart? Trust, like other emotions such as love, seems to be more a matter of the head (something we think) rather than the heart (something we feel). This is seemingly reflected by the fact that feelings can come and go, often without a reason. While the heart is part of our makeup, it is the head that influences the heart. Thus, Prov 3:5–6 again reads, "Trust in the LORD with all your heart, and do not lean on your understanding. Know him in all your ways, and he for his part will make your paths straight." The wise man both tells the reader to trust God with their heart, and follows that up with advice that involves the head ("know him"). Based on these verses, the best way to trust God with all of our heart is to use our head.

August 29

Life Is Hard

LIFE IS HARD, IN part because nothing is free (there is no such thing as a "free lunch"). To get things in life costs us either now or later, either in money or in some other aspect, such as our time, our freedom, or our soul. Sin bears a price (Rom 6:23), as does pleasure in general (1 Tim 5:6; Luke 16:19). This is not to say that we can or should avoid all ease and comfort (Mark 6:31). But knowing that there is a cost to life, and that if we don't pay now we are going to pay later, a proper spiritual outlook includes our awareness, as Christians, that, living in a world restricted by time, a sober outlook includes being mindful of life's costs. Fortunately for the Christian Someone paid the price for their sins (1 Pet 1:18–19), which imposes on them the "cost" of Jesus' easy yoke (Matt 11:28–30) and a life of joyous servitude (1 Pet 2:16). It, therefore, seems good to be aware that trying to avoid costs at all costs is something to avoid. If life seems too easy, there is a good chance that it isn't real life.

August 30

"Mindful of God"

THE HARDSHIPS OF LIFE are difficult enough (see yesterday's "Daily") without having to suffer for doing the right thing. We may think that doing the right thing will make our lives better. When one suffers for doing the right thing, therefore, it is doubly painful. Since we are going to have both physical and mental pain in life, it seems evident that we need something to help us endure the pain. Peter expressed it this way, "For this is a gracious thing, when, mindful of God, one endures sorrows while suffering unjustly" (1 Pet 2:19). As Christians, we need to do the right thing. Yet, since it is often difficult to keep going in life anyway, we also need something to help us endure pain. For the Christian, one day there will be no more pain (Rev 21:4). Being mindful of the fact that there are going to be pains in life (including perhaps the injustice for doing the right thing) can help us endure. An even greater strength, however, to endure any pain in this life, can be gained by being mindful of God while we suffer pain.

August 31

"Anywhere with Jesus"

CERTAINLY JESUS IS WITH us, as Christians, wherever we go (Matt 28:18–20; Ps 139:7–10). The world can be a big and lonely place, even when we travel to a big city full of millions of people. When in such places we might wonder as we walk around whether any of these strangers are Christians. Then we can remind ourselves that, as Christians, it would be good to seek out members of a "like precious faith" (2 Pet 1:1), especially so we can worship together on the first day of the week (as did Paul and his companions while traveling, Acts 20:5–7). If we were to find a gathering of God's people in a strange city, we can then know that we have found a venue where Jesus himself would be (Matt 18:20). Again, we, as Christians, are never alone; but how reassuring to know that wherever we go, no matter how lonely we might feel (even though surrounded by people), we can know that there is a way to be with Jesus; that is, by being with his people—in worship.

September 1

"United by Faith"

TRUTH TENDS TO DIVIDE (Matt 10:34–38) while faith tends to unite (many religious groups consist of hundreds of people who believe a false message). Hearing God's word, the Bible (John 17:17), is the means through which one comes to believe in God (Rom 10:17). Yet, hearing alone is insufficient to produce faith therein; many hear the word and do not believe it (Acts 17:32–34). It also seems that some believe it, though it never quite changes their heart. Perhaps a key in this regard lies in the words of Heb 4:2: "For indeed we have had good tidings preached unto us, even as also they: but the word of hearing did not profit them, because it was not united by faith with them that heard" (ASV). After hearing (with our head), the element necessary for God's word to be accepted is faith (with our heart). Acceptance of God's word, therefore, depends not on the word, but on us (Isa 55:11). Faith is the means of unity and of pleasing God (Heb 11:6); imagine if we were all united by faith in the truth.

September 2

Free and Easy

GOD OFFERS FREE SALVATION (Rom 6:23), a life free of sin (John 8:32), and a life with Jesus that is easy (Matt 11:28–30). Life in this physical world is both hard and costly (see "Daily" of Aug. 29) because we live in a world bound by physical limitations and by sin. Being, therefore, prisoners to these things (John 8:34), it is not possible to have complete freedom and an easy life through the physical world. We naturally look for ways to make life in this world easier and less costly. The sad truth is that if we pursue freedom through physical means (such as through such avenues as pleasure or money, 1 Tim 5:6; 6:9), we are likely to invite more pain into our lives. Complete freedom and an easy life in this world can only be gained by pursuing these things not through this world, but through the spiritual means of being a slave to God (1 Pet 2:16), or taking the yoke of Jesus.

September 3

Somewhat Pleasing?

Several verses in the NT (depending on translation), speak of God being "well-pleased" with someone (including Jesus, Matt 3:17; 17:5). The Christian is to walk in the light (1 John 1:7–9) and is not to live a "lukewarm" life (Rev 3:16). Many things, therefore, are either something one is or is not (for example, they either have faith or they do not, Heb 11:6). The Greek word translated "well-pleasing" in other contexts can have a meaning of "approval" or "counting something as good" (Heb 10:6, 8). Not that it is not possible for God to only appreciate the good things one does (Acts 10:4); but why would we want to see only a smile instead of a laugh, or to walk only partially seeing where we are going? Why would we want to be "somewhat pleasing" when we could be "well-pleasing," especially knowing that being well-pleasing means we have God's approval?

September 4

To Have Compassion

THE BIBLE'S DESCRIPTION OF Jesus having compassion reflects the approach he took toward one in need: "And being moved with compassion, he stretched forth his hand, and touched him, and saith unto him, I will; be thou made clean" (Mark 1:41 ASV). The English word "compassion" has to do with feeling with, or taking pity on. The Greek word so translated has the same idea, it appears only in the Gospels, and it is almost always used of Jesus. When someone else has a problem, many times the tendency is for us to think (and say) that it is no big deal. To put ourselves in their place, however, is what Christians are taught (Rom 12:15), and is reflective of such spiritual attitudes as humility and love (1 Cor 13:4–5). While feelings are unpredictable, and, therefore, can come and go, perhaps our feeling compassion is born of a spiritual attitude based on how our heart is affected (such as by someone's unfortunate condition). Isn't compassion what we would want from God?

September 5

Crestfallen Cain

WORSHIP THAT IS BORN of selfishness may or (may not) make us happy, but it certainly will not please God. There were surely many emotions involved when Cain's sacrifice was rejected (including evident envy over his brother's being accepted, Gen 4:3–8). Cain evidently should have known what constitutes an acceptable offering (Gen 4:3; Heb 11:4). Whatever the reason, he was sorely disappointed that his offering was rejected, insomuch that he was downcast over it (Gen 4:5; the Hebrew literally reads "his face fell"). We should want our worship to be accepted by God. Our worship should, therefore, be offered in faith, that is, God's word (Rom 10:17). Unlike Cain, we won't directly know whether God is pleased with it, though by faith we can believe that it is. If our worship is born of selfishness, we may go away happy, and, thus, never do anything as serious as Cain. Unfortunately, worship that is thus offered won't make God happy.

September 6

"Run with Patience"

Running a marathon (so I'm told) and waiting for someone running a marathon (so I'm told) require two different kinds of patience. To run a marathon requires active endurance; to wait for someone to do anything that takes over four hours requires passive endurance. While both may be necessary in life, the Christian is running a race that requires persistent activity: "Therefore, since we are surrounded by so great a cloud of witnesses, let us also lay aside every weight, and sin which clings so closely, and let us run with endurance the race that is set before us" (Heb 12:1). Enduring is necessary in the Christian life (1 Cor 15:58). Both passive and active endurance require a strength to not give up until we reach the goal. By looking to Jesus (Heb 12:2) and waiting on him (Isa 40:31), we can gain the strength we need to endure. The strength God offers to run his race is not physical, but spiritual.

September 7

Never Alone

THE CHRISTIAN LIFE PROVIDES many benefits, both to one's life and to their soul (1 Tim 4:8). One blessing of the Christian life is social. We need other people (Gen 2:18). When one becomes a Christian they are added to a group of spiritually like-minded people (Acts 2:47; Jude 3). We thereby have such things as the promise of family members everywhere in the world (Mark 10:30), a support group to help during difficult times (Gal 6:2), and regular fellowship, which is good for our soul (Heb 10:25). Having a support group is not the goal of being a member of the church; but knowing that we have spiritual friends who are to be there for us is a blessing Christians enjoy while traveling toward heaven. We have this blessing because we are friends with those who are friends with the only Friend (John 15:14), who will be there for us after the end when no one else can. As Christians, we are never alone (Matt 28:18–20).

September 8

"Ignorant and Unstable"

KNOWLEDGE OF SOMETHING THAT is not true can cause instability to the soul. Again, knowledge alone should not be one's goal, but rather a "knowledge of the truth" (1 Tim 2:4; 2 Tim 3:7). To do this requires a heart that is desirous of truth. Peter again referred to the "ignorant and unstable": "Speaking of this as he does in all his letters. There are some things in them hard to understand, which the ignorant and unstable twist to their own destruction, as they do the other Scriptures" (2 Pet 3:16 RSV). The way these two words are combined sounds like they may be understood as a unit (like "cup and saucer"). In other words, perhaps one's instability in their soul contributes to a pursuit of the wrong kind of knowledge, and the acquisition of error contributes to an instability of soul (as those in Acts 17:21, who only wanted to tell or to hear some new thing). Perhaps the answer to overcoming ignorance begins with spiritual stability as provided by God? Perhaps the antidote to overcoming the couplet of "ignorance and instability" is found in Peter's next admonition, to grow, using Peter's next couplet "in the grace and knowledge of our Lord and Savior Jesus Christ" (v. 18)?

September 9

"Autumn Trees"

JUST ABOUT EVERYBODY (IN North America) enjoys the beauty of autumn trees. For people in the ancient world especially, autumn trees meant not only beauty but, more especially, fruit that the people needed in order to live. To not see the fruit in autumn (especially when one waits all year) was, therefore, surely disappointing. Jude spoke of false teachers as disappointing autumn trees: "These are hidden reefs at your love feasts, as they feast with you without fear, shepherds feeding themselves; waterless clouds, swept along by winds; fruitless trees in late autumn, twice dead, uprooted" (Jude 12). Jesus was disappointed both in a teacher (John 3:1–10) and in a tree (Matt 21:18–19), because he expected something from them. God's word won't disappoint him (Isa 55:11), and it won't disappoint us, depending on what we look forward to. Our looking for truth is a key ingredient in our growth (2 Pet 3:18), or in producing fruit, something that surely won't disappoint him.

September 10

Worship and Work

Each aspect of worship offered to God and for God, again, surely does something for the worshiper as well (as all unselfish acts can, Acts 20:35). While such acts as preaching can, among other things, motivate us to carry on in service to God, the act of giving is surely the most practical, as money is necessary for many good works. The occasion which called for Paul's teaching on giving in 1 Cor 16:2 was that the poor Christians in Judea needed help: "On the first day of every week, each of you is to put something aside and store it up, as he may prosper, so that there will be no collecting when I come" (see also v. 3). Paul continued to teach on giving in 2 Cor 8. These, combined with other verses, point to giving as a continued practice in the worship of the early church. Giving is thus an act of worship with a practical result; it is a manifestation of two avenues of glorifying God, his worship, and his work.

September 11

Going Home

GOING HOME CAN BE a pleasant or an unpleasant experience, depending on one's attitude, one's location they are leaving behind, and one's home (I have known people who cry when it's time to go home because they didn't want to leave their "happy place"). In like manner, leaving home can produce certain emotions, whether excitement, fear of the unknown, etc. Paul taught that the Christian is only traveling through this life: "But our citizenship is in heaven, and from it we await a Savior, the Lord Jesus Christ" (Phil 3:20). This life is the only existence we have known; yet, as Christians, it is not "home." It would be natural for us to wonder about, or, even, have a fear of traveling to a place to which we have never been, and of which we have only been told (1 Pet 1:4; Rev 21:4). This negative emotion can be overcome if we concentrate on what we are told about heaven, and if we, like Jesus, look forward to going home to be with our Father (John 17). Heaven is a place prepared for the children of the Father in heaven (John 14:2). One day we will leave this location (Heb 9:27); the attitude we have toward that reality is up to us (1 Thess 4:13). In other words, it can be a joyful thing to go home.

September 12

Complete and Incomplete Knowledge of God

It seems that there are many things about God that we can't know, such as his will with regard to the future (Matt 26:42). It is interesting, therefore, that Paul spoke of knowing God as something that can be both complete and incomplete: "And so, from the day we heard, we have not ceased to pray for you, asking that you may be filled with the knowledge of his will in all spiritual wisdom and understanding, so as to walk in a manner worthy of the Lord, fully pleasing to him: bearing fruit in every good work and increasing in the knowledge of God" (Col 1:9–10). The Greek word translated "knowledge" is the same in both verses, and can have to do with perception as well as acquiring information. If God's will is something we can't always know, maybe when Paul refers to being filled with a knowledge thereof, he is referring to being filled, not with a finite body of knowledge, but rather with an understanding mind that has relinquished our will for God's? Along this line, he said in Eph 5:17, "Therefore do not be foolish, but understand what the will of the Lord is." While a knowledge of God through his word is an ongoing pursuit (2 Pet 3:18), perhaps being filled with the knowledge of his will has to do with emptying our perception, to let it be replaced with the will of God?

September 13

A Return on Our Investment

AN INVESTMENT IS A type of sacrifice, though it is born of self-interest (not that there is anything necessarily wrong therewith). While it can be painful to part, for example, with an investment of money, we do so in the hope of receiving a return thereupon. To wait for a return requires not only sacrifice but other qualities, such as patience. The opposite of this is the pursuit of instant gratification, something that could cost us more later (1 Tim 5:6). The positive things we do, as Christians (a positive attitude, Phil 4:8; good works, Eph 2:10, etc.), are good now, and can be looked at as an investment in a spiritual future. Paul said, "For while bodily training is of some value, godliness is of value in every way, as it holds promise for the present life and also for the life to come" (1 Tim 4:8). Christians look forward to a promised reward of a treasure laid up in heaven (Matt 6:19–20). Jesus invested in the souls of people by his sacrifice on the cross; what can he hope to receive upon his return (Luke 18:8)?

September 14

Ignorance Is No Excuse

COMPLETING AN ESSENTIAL PHYSICAL task, such as replacing a roof, usually requires a knowledge of how to complete the job. It would be unwise to do otherwise, unless we had someone to help us. The Bible teaches that Christians "ought" to pray (Rom 8:26; the Greek word translated "ought" means "it is binding upon us"). Yet Paul also said that being ignorant of what to pray for need not stop us: "Likewise the Spirit helps us in our weakness. For we do not know what to pray for as we ought, but the Spirit himself intercedes for us with groanings too deep for words" (Rom 8:26). While knowledge is essential both to becoming a Christian (Acts 17:30) and to growing in the Christian life (2 Pet 3:18), and a lack of knowledge can be detrimental to our relationship with God (Hos 4:6), not knowing what to pray for is seemingly one of the few times a lack of knowledge will not hurt our spiritual life. Knowing that, in our ignorance, the Holy Spirit is there to help us can help us focus on prayer as a spiritual activity, one we never complete (1 Thess 5:17), and one for which the neglect thereof we have no excuse.

September 15

Worship and Humility

WORSHIP IS FOR THE purpose of praising God, which is an expression of humility. While we all enjoy recognition, we can't both desire praise and offer praise to God; that is, we can't be selfish and unselfish at the same time. Selfish "worship" can be manifested in different ways, including not caring what we offer to God (Mal 1:6-8) or living a hypocritical life while we pretend to offer our best (Matt 23:23-24). Such verses as 1 Cor 14:15 and Mark 12:41-44 remind us that God approves of a heart that desires to please him rather than ourselves (that is, unselfish versus selfish). To bring glory to God, or to exalt him (thereby humbling ourselves), is to receive his approval or glory, and thereby be exalted (Matt 23:12). The opposite is also true as, again, one can't have both: "For they loved the glory that comes from man more than the glory that comes from God" (John 12:43). God, and only God, is entitled to our praise (Mal 1:6) that arises from an unselfish heart. To try to glorify God with a selfish attitude may lead to our humiliation. "Being fond on praise, which makes your praises worse."[6]

---

6. Shakespeare, Sonnet 84.

September 16

"Call to Remembrance"

THERE IS A COST to war, and, therefore, to freedom. For a country to be able to defend itself requires the strength and the means to be able to do so (Luke 14:25–35). One of the lessons from Jesus' temptation in Matt 4 is that he defeated Satan's attacks with the word. Satan threw three flaming darts of temptation at Jesus, and Jesus responded to each one by recalling and using a verse of Scripture (vv. 4, 7, and 10). The one offensive element in the Christian's spiritual armor is, likewise, the word: "And take the helmet of salvation, and the sword of the Spirit, which is the word of God" (Eph 6:17; see also vv. 10–16). Christians are engaged in a spiritual warfare that determines our spiritual freedom both in this world (Gal 5:1) and in the next (Rev 20). Faithful Christians are going to win the battle and the war in which they fight (Rev 2:10b). Our spiritual victory is determined, at least in part, by our ability to use the spiritual weapon of God's word (Heb 5:14), drawn from the arsenal of our mind. The stronger our arsenal, and our ability to use it (that is, to recall Scripture), the more spiritually successful we, as Christians, can fight; just like Jesus.

September 17

United by Righteousness

In 1858, Abraham Lincoln gave the Gettysburg Address, in which he quoted Jesus (Matt 12:25), stating that "a house divided against itself cannot stand." Any group, be it a nation, family, or other, likely cannot stand if the hearts of those who comprise the group are not united in thought and purpose. Disunity is displeasing to God (Prov 6:19), while unity is pleasing to him (1 Cor 1:10). The psalmist compared the beauty of unity to the dew on a mountain: "It is like the dew of Hermon, which falls on the mountain(s) of Zion! (Ps 133:3; see also v. 1). A nation, like a marriage, may become united when the members thereof draw closer to God. The wise man said that "righteousness exalts a nation" (Prov 14:34). When each citizen follows God's standard of righteousness, a nation can thereby be brought upward to God and, in the process, to each other, thereby becoming united. They would then be dwelling in unity, as it were, on a mountain; as it were, closer to God.

September 18

"Fellow Workers for the Truth"

WHILE MANY THINGS CAN draw people together, a spiritual purpose such as righteousness (see yesterday's "Daily") is surely one of the strongest bonds. In life, a common purpose, such as a project, may cause people to come together, even to become personally closer, as long as they have that common goal (reading between the lines, once the project is over, the relationships may or may not endure). John spoke of some of his fellow-Christians as "fellow workers for the truth": "Therefore we ought to support people like these, that we may be fellow workers for the truth" (3 John 8). The Greek word translated "fellow workers" is often used with regard to other spiritual purposes (such as the gospel [1 Thess 3:2] or the kingdom [Col 4:11]). If we, as Christians, are to be united and work together for God, what better bond would serve this purpose than the eternal quality of truth? Just as righteousness and truth are, in Scripture, combined (Ps 119:142), so our following such standards, and having such a goal, can cause us to be joined, to be fellow workers.

September 19

So Much Better

THE WORD "BETTER" IMPLIES that what we already have is good (that is, we speak of "good, better, and best"). In life, this may or may not be the case; for example, to have poor air conditioning is better than no air conditioning when the outside temperature is over one hundred. The book of Hebrews uses the word "better" to describe several blessings in the Christian life (the Greek word so translated appears about fifteen times in the book). Thus, the writer states that we have a better covenant (Heb 7:22; 8:6) that was based on better promises (Heb 8:6), and that Christians can look forward to a better country (Heb 11:16), and to a resurrection (Heb 11:36). Life here may or may not be good, God's old way was good, and in many ways we still live in a good country. Yet what God offers, and what the Christian has awaiting, is so much better. It will be great when we receive it; but knowing that it is coming gives us a better hope (Heb 7:19).

September 20

Prayer as Selfish and Unselfish

WHILE WORSHIP IS FIRST and foremost unselfish, it also benefits the worshiper. This is true because we generally benefit from acting unselfishly when we do so with a right heart (Acts 20:35). Every act of worship, therefore, can bring a spiritual benefit. While some acts of worship carry a promise of benefit to the worship (such as giving, Luke 6:38), one of the few acts of worship in which a worshiper can engage with self-interest is prayer. In the "model prayer," Jesus taught to begin with words of praise to God (Matt 6:9), after which one may use this avenue for personal requests (vv. 11–13; see also Heb 4:16). In prayer, therefore, one is allowed to bring their concerns borne of their own self-interest (or be selfish) in an avenue of worship (which is unselfish), from which they benefit in their relationship with God (which is selfish). This is true because God invites us to selfishly engage in the unselfish act of prayer.

September 21

"Shall We Not Receive Evil?"

GOOD AND BAD THINGS are going to happen to us in life. We may say that receiving good things is physical (it makes us happy), while receiving bad things (that is, with a good attitude) is spiritual. Either way, how we receive them is up to us (a rich person and a poor person may have a completely different reaction to the same good gift). We may not know why anything happens, but we can adopt an attitude by which both good and bad can be received without damage to our soul. Thus, after suffering serious trials without knowing why, Job's wife tried to get him to give up (Job 2:9). Job's rebuke of his wife in reply reflects the kind of attitude we should have: "Would we even receive good from God, but not evil?' In all this Job had not sinned with his lips" (Job 2:10). To receive things we don't want ("evil") is a reflection of humility and trust in God; to not do so is to be foolish. We may not have control over good and bad things happening; we do control how (whether) we receive them.

September 22

"Receive from God"

AFTER JOB AND HIS wife lost their children and everything they had, Job, again, made the statement to his wife, "Would we even receive good from God, but not evil?" (Job 2:10; see yesterday's "Daily"). Job was not aware of the discussion between Satan and God, whereupon God gave Satan permission to afflict Job (Job 1:12). Yet Job acknowledged God for his troubles, even though Satan was the direct agent (God credited Satan for what happened to Job, Job 2:3): "The LORD has given, and the LORD has taken away; blessed be the name of the LORD" (Job 1:21). We may again not know why things happen in life; yet our attitude, and only our attitude, can bring us closer to God (Phil 4:11). Like Job, if we concentrate on God rather than on what we've lost, we can thereby draw closer to him—no matter the reason for our circumstances.

September 23

"See Good Days"

WHETHER ONE HAS A "good life" largely depends upon them. We, again, can't control most of life's events; but we can control our attitude and our actions (response) toward those events. Thus, Peter gave teaching on how to have a good life: "Whoever desires to love life and see good days, let him keep his tongue from evil and his lips from speaking deceit; let him turn away from evil and do good; let him seek peace and pursue it" (1 Pet 3:10–11). Not that this is a recipe for getting life to go our way ("bad" things are likely still to happen). But by following such teaching that begins with our attitude and ends with doing good, we can see good days. Seeing good days depends not on the days but on our seeing.

September 24

Our Renewable Resource

INASMUCH AS OUR MIND is the most powerful instrument in our makeup, the strength and control thereof is of great importance for a good life and, more importantly, for a strong spiritual life (see, for example, Phil 2:5). Based on Paul's wording in Rom 12:2, we may say that the mind is a renewable resource: "Do not be conformed to this world, but be transformed by the renewal of your mind, that by testing you may discern what is the will of God, what is good and acceptable and perfect." I've heard that the brain repairs itself (I'm not a medical doctor); but the brain, like every other part of the body, declines with age. The mind, however, is either a part of, or at least affects, the spiritual part of man (which can grow continually stronger, 2 Cor 4:16). The use of this renewable resource can, therefore, lead to transformation, and is a key to avoiding being conformed to this world. If we are so transformed by the use of our mind, we can be renewed, and look forward to a reality where everything is new (Rev 21:1–4).

September 25

Giving Thanks as Worship

WE USUALLY THINK OF giving thanks as something we do once, in response to something good that has been done for us. The psalmist called on us to give thanks to God as an expression of worship, and, therefore, as something that goes beyond a single act that God has done for us: "Give thanks to the LORD, for [he is] good; for his covenant loyalty is forever" (Ps 107:1). In addition to such things as giving thanks for a meal (Matt 14:19), the Christian is taught to give thanks in everything (1 Thess 5:18). The psalmist calls on us to give thanks not for what God has done for us but because of what God is (good) and because of the enduring love God has for his people (reading between the lines, this is because God is good to us). Worshiping God is good for us; we give thanks because God is good and good to us, qualities that will endure forever.

September 26

Exercising Our Senses

EXERCISE IS GOOD FOR us. While not everyone is able to physically exercise, and not everyone can do the same type of exercise, it is generally good for our body and our brain to do our best to keep physically fit (physical fitness also contributes to mental and spiritual fitness). Keeping spiritually fit is also important. The Hebrews writer spoke of having our senses exercised: "But solid food is for full-grown men, even those who by reason of use have their senses exercised to discern good and evil" (Heb 5:14 ASV). Other verses (using the same Greek word translated "exercised") speak of being trained with regard to chastening (Heb 12:11), in godliness (1 Tim 4:7), and in the negative aspect of covetousness (2 Pet 2:14, illustrating that our soul can be conditioned to anything). A runner who has to switch to walking can feel the difference in the muscles being exercised. So, our spiritual path usually involves an adjustment, likely throughout our lives, that often involves some amount of pain. Yet nothing valuable in life is likely attained without pain; and this pain will be worth the destination, the place to which Christians are running (Heb 12:1), a place where there is no pain (Rev 21:4).

September 27

Handing Down Traditions

To speak of handing something down, such as to the next generation, implies that this is something important to us that we want to see kept (and that we want it to be important to those to whom it is entrusted). Traditions, such as those we enjoy at holiday times, can be joyful (or add joy to) occasions that warm our heart. They are likely kept alive by each generation because of the way they affect the soul; that is, they either warm the heart, or, in such realms as the military, are kept due to their meaning and solemnity. In the NT, the word translated "tradition" has a meaning of "something handed down." It can have to do with man-made traditions (Matt 15:2) that can keep one from following God's word (Matt 15:3), as well as truth. Thus, Paul said, "So then, brothers, stand firm and hold to the traditions that you were taught by us, either by our spoken word or by our letter" (2 Thess 2:15). Scriptural traditions, such as those handed down to us by an apostle (here Paul), ultimately come from God, and are thus the handing down of truth. They are, therefore, such as can also warm our heart, bring us joy, and are something to be passed along to the next generation (2 Tim 2:2)—whether or not it is a holiday.

September 28

Purity in Worship

ONE PURPOSE OF A right relationship with God is spiritual purity; worshiping God is part of that right relationship (1 John 2:3-4). The Christian is to worship God today with purity of heart (Amos 5:21-22), of relationships (Matt 5:23-24), and of intent (Acts 5:1-6). The Lord's Supper, as part of worship today, includes the pure element of unleavened bread (in the Bible leaven is a symbol of evil [Gal 5:9]). We can only do so much in life to have physical purity, inasmuch as our physical world has been tainted by sin (Rom 5:12). Yet God has given us the means of spiritual purity by coming to him therefor (1 Pet 1:22). By worshiping purely, that is, in God's way, we preserve both our spiritual purity and our pure relationship with him.

September 29

What Are You Afraid Of?

FEAR IS AN EMOTION we control, and is, therefore, something that can be overcome. Whether it be by our determination not to be afraid ("I would not fear evil," Ps 23:4), or by following the teaching of God in this regard ("don't ever fear," Ps 91:5), whether it be fear of the darkest imaginable dread ("the valley of the shadow of death," Ps 23:4), or any fear from one end to the other ("the terror of the night, nor the arrow that flies by day," Ps 91:5), fear can be overcome. In these two psalms the fears spoken of are based on something external, yet they are overcome internally. It is the psalmist who has the ability and the motivation to overcome his fears because of spiritual strength provided by God, that is, faith. God's faith today has been provided (Jude 3). We decide what to do with it, including whether to use it to overcome our fears.

September 30

Within or Without?

NOT LONG BEFORE JESUS taught to seek first the kingdom of God (Matt 6:33), he taught for us to have something else first. In Matt 6:1 he used the word "beware." The Greek word (also translated "take heed") has a literal meaning of "have first." It appears several times in Scripture, often with regard to one's being on guard within themselves. An entirely different Greek word, also translated "beware," is used of guarding against outside forces such as false teachers (Phil 3:2). Jesus' word appears elsewhere in Scripture with regard to putting first such things as reading, exhortation, and teaching (1 Tim 4:13), and of not putting false teachings first (Titus 1:14). While outside enemies can surely be a danger, sometimes the greatest threats to our soul lie not on the outside, but on the inside (Acts 20:28). The greatest safeguard against these, therefore, lies within us; or, better, our taking heed, or having first within us, God's admonitions, helps us to be on guard against that which is without.

October 1

Why Else?

PETER'S STATEMENT IN JOHN 6:68 again reminds us of the importance of Jesus' words of life. When Jesus asked whether the disciples would also leave him, "Simon Peter answered him, 'Lord, to whom shall we go? You have the words of eternal life.'" Peter's words suggest several things, including that this is (at least) the main reason to follow Jesus and, perhaps more importantly, that no one else can offer these words of life (John 14:6). So, we today preach Jesus (1 Cor 1:23), and are to speak only where the Bible speaks (1 Pet 4:11). Another important point is that, unlike those who followed Jesus for a physical reason (that is, food, John 6:26), Peter and the disciples followed Jesus for a spiritual reason, his words of life. Why else would they?

October 2

Belief, Faith, and Trust

Is THERE A DIFFERENCE between belief, faith, and trust? While in the Bible one word may be translated in more than one of these ways, these words are also used of such things as acceptance of God's word (Rom 10:17), God's system of faith (Jude 3), and our confident assurance in God (such as with regard to the future) based on his word (Rom 8:28). The Hebrews writer stated, "And without faith it is impossible to please him, for whoever would draw near to God must believe that he exists and that he rewards those who seek him" (Heb 11:6). Faith may be understood and applied in different ways (Rom 1:17); whatever we call it, we can't please God without it.

October 3

"Unleavened Bread"

When Jesus instituted the Lord's Supper, one of the elements he used was bread without leaven or yeast (Matt 26:26). In the Bible leaven, again, represented evil. Israel was told to purge out the leaven during Passover (Exod 13:3–7), and it is referred to as representing evil influence in such verses as Gal 5:9. God, who knows our heart, would have us be sure that our worship and ourselves, when we engage therein, are pure. Worshiping God properly involves purity of heart (Matt 5:23–24), is expressed in purity of action (1 Cor 11:27; 14:15), and is offered to God through purity of elements, such as unleavened bread.

October 4

Making an Impact

It is possible to have an impact in the world for evil or for good. December 7, 1941, and September 11, 2001, made an indelible impact on America. Yet so did the man Jesus, who lived over two thousand years ago, and whose teachings still influence millions today. Regarding Jesus, John said, "The light shines in the darkness, and the darkness has not overcome it" (John 1:5). When we speak of wanting to make an impact (depending on what we mean), this can also be a good thing. Even such things as simply working a job to provide for one's self and one's family can have an impact. That is, one doesn't have to do the extraordinary to bring glory to God. We may even say that the best way to have an impact is by being a Christian. "In the same way, let your light shine before others, so that they may see your good works and give glory to your Father who is in heaven" (Matt 5:16).

October 5

Stumbling at the Word

Rocks are good for many things, but, as a rule, not when one is hiking. That is, they may even serve some purpose on the trail (such as marking a way), but they can also be an obstacle to one's steps (a hiker likely does not want to stumble on a rock). Based on Peter's words, one stumbles spiritually because they choose to: "'A stone of stumbling, and a rock of offense.' They stumble because they disobey the word, as they were destined to do" (1 Pet 2:8). The Greek word translated "stumble" (a different word than that used of the Pharisees in Matt 15:12) literally means "to strike against," as when stubbing one's toe. The picture then is of one confronting the word and, instead of complying with it, of striking it in resistance, just as one would a rock that is in their way. While God is our Rock (Deut 32:4; 1 Cor 10:4), his word is something not to be stumbled upon, but rather complied with. The difference is that the hiker does not mean to stumble.

October 6

How to Lean on the Lord

LIFE IS DIFFICULT ENOUGH that we all, at one time or another, probably need to lean upon someone or something. To lean upon no one, or, on the darker side, to lean upon such things as money or substances, is harmful to one's life and to one's soul. The best thing for us is to lean upon the Lord; yet, even that must be done properly. Isaiah stated, "And it will be in that day, the remnant of Israel and the escaped of the house of Jacob will no longer continue to lean on the one who strikes them, but will lean on the LORD, the Holy One of Israel, in truth" (Isa 10:20). The phrase "in truth" suggests how they leaned on the Lord (as we say "in general," meaning "generally"). The opposite of this, as reflected in the rest of the verse, is either to lean on someone else or to lean on the Lord, but not in truth. Rather than looking to the Lord for a selfish reason, or only when his word suits us (2 Tim 4:3–4), our mind needs to be settled on him (Isa 26:3), so that we lean on nothing else, including ourselves (Prov 3:5–6). All other ground is sinking sand.

October 7

"Without Grumbling"

A LESSON WE LEARN from the book of Habakkuk is that God does not seem to mind the sincere questioner. Sincere questioning is different, however, from grumbling, which God does mind. In Num 11:1, the people complained against God and it made him angry. In the NT, Paul similarly taught us not to complain: "Do all things without grumbling or disputing" (Phil 2:14). Yet, the reason Paul gives is for our spiritual good: "That you may be blameless and innocent, children of God without blemish in the midst of a crooked and twisted generation, among whom you shine as lights in the world" (Phil 2:15). To grumble and complain does spiritual harm, in that it keeps us from being spiritually pure children of God. Words have meaning, and the wrong words (that proceed from wrong thoughts) can do harm to our spiritual life. We often say in life that complaining won't do any good; now we know it does harm, including that it makes God mad.

October 8

The Meaning of Worship

THE REASON THINGS LIKE our favorite coffee cup affect our heart is not so much because of the object, but because of the meaning we attach to those objects. That is, our favorite coffee cup, again, might remind us of happy times with our family or when we were at the pinnacle of our career, but the family dog couldn't care less about it. What we do for an hour on Sunday morning, as Christians, can affect our heart, and thus our soul, because of the meaning we attach to our actions. The reason our singing, praying, engaging in the Lord's Supper, giving, and preaching has meaning is because God assigned meaning to these things. Without meaning (borne of love) our giving is a "clanging symbol" (1 Cor 13:1), our singing might be looked on as ravings (1 Cor 14:15), and our preaching might be looked on as foolishness (1 Cor 1:18). This meaning is what makes worship meaningful; and, being meaningful, makes it mean something to us and to God.

October 9

"Hear and Understand"

When giving direction, one way of emphasizing the desired action is, again, to use two verbs; for example, when we say "go get." This, in effect, emphasizes the action of getting (as it is necessary to go in order to get but it is not necessarily necessary to say the word "go" in order to tell someone to "get"). Jesus spoke in this way in Matt 15:10: "And he called the people to him and said to them, 'Hear and understand.'" It is interesting that he would command his listeners not just to hear, but to understand. For many, even though they have some level of intelligence, it may still be difficult to understand certain concepts (for example, one may have no trouble understanding languages, but have trouble understanding physics). It is possible to hear and not understand, and to understand and not believe, but it is not possible to understand, or to believe, without hearing (Rom 10:17). Jesus wants us to believe (John 8:24) and to understand (Matt 12:7). To believe what we understand, we first need to obey his command to hear.

October 10

"With Regard to the Lord"

Psalm 37:4–5 admonishes the reader to take three actions with regard to the Lord: "and take pleasure in the Lord, so that he would give you your heartfelt requests. Commit your way to the Lord; and trust in him, and he for his part will act." We are here directed to take each action ("delight," "commit," and "trust") with the corresponding words "in" the Lord, "to" the Lord, and "in" him. These last three words are all the same word in Hebrew; it also appears in the rest of the psalm only three other times. The first three actions the psalmist enjoins are important; yet all three actions have meaning because of the One to whom they are directed. One can take delight, commit, and trust, with regard to other things or other people. These things are only of spiritual benefit when they are actions taken with regard to the Lord.

October 11

"The Lord Heard It"

THROUGHOUT THE BIBLE WE read of God's people pleading with him to hear them (Ps 61:1), that God is able to hear us (Isa 59:1), and that false gods are not (1 Kgs 18:27). It is interesting, therefore, when we read in Num 12:2 that "the LORD heard [it]." This verse appears in a context of some complaining about Moses' marriage. There may be a place for a legitimate complaint (such as to solve a problem within an organization). Yet we can say that complaining (or "grumbling") against God is misplaced due to God's infallible nature. That is, if we don't like something, including the way our life is going, the problem lies with us (or a sinful world) rather than God. To complain, therefore, can be a reflection of a bad attitude that is, for example, not willing to accept responsibility or to accept God's will. Knowing that God does not approve of murmuring (Phil 2:14) or speaking evil of a brother (Jas 4:11), and that we will give account of our words (Matt 12:37), Num 12 serves as a good reminder to avoid such speech. When we don't receive what we ask for in prayer, it may seem as if God has not heard us (Ps 22:1); when we grumble and complain, he surely does.

October 12

Truth Is Real

IN LIFE, WE GET cold when the temperature falls, and we can get hurt when we fall down. Such things as gravity and temperature physically affect us, and, therefore, can affect the way we feel, and even the way we think (the temperature can affect our mood). We can say, therefore, that these things are "real." Like gravity, truth is something we can't see, yet it is real. The Bible again speaks of truth being cast to the ground (Dan 8:12), of truth perishing (Jer 7:28), of God's church upholding the truth (1 Tim 3:15), and of others turning from the truth (2 Tim 4:4). The world is constantly trying to remove the concept of truth by saying that there is no truth; or, for example, that everything is a matter of opinion or that we ourselves define truth. God's word is truth (John 17:17), which can be known (John 8:32), and can purify our soul (1 Pet 1:22). We can't see such things as gravity, temperature, or time. Yet they are real. If we ignore such things as gravity, we could be in trouble. How much more if we ignore the truth?

October 13

"Beyond Their Power"

PAUL SOMETIMES PRAISED HIS readers for such things as their faith (1 Thess 1:8) or their giving (Phil 4:15–16), and even praised one church when he was speaking to another. Thus, in 2 Cor 8 he praised the churches of Macedonia while writing to the Corinthians. While the lessons contained in his words of praise are many, the phrase to be singled out here is how, Paul states, they gave: "For they gave according to their means, as I can testify, and beyond their means, of their own accord" (2 Cor 8:3). Whether this means they went into debt, or just gave more than was comfortable, it seems we can say that their giving was certainly sacrificial. Like the widow who gave all that she had (Mark 12:41–44), it shows the kind of attitude God appreciates when participating in the act of giving. If such things as exercise and education come easy to the participant, it could suggest that they don't provide as much benefit as something that requires effort and sacrifice. To give out of our abundance (Mark 12:44) may be easy, but may not help us grow spiritually. If we have the means, we have a God-given responsibility to use it to his glory—perhaps by going beyond our means.

October 14

The Easy Way Out

Is THE CHRISTIAN LIFE easy or hard? On the one hand, Jesus said, "My yoke is easy" (Matt 11:30). On the other hand, some verses of Scripture tell us that the Christian life is one of discipline, which suggests that the standards of the Christian life may, at times, be challenging. Thus the Bible teaches us to "strive" (Luke 13:24; the Greek word therefor is literally "to agonize"), to work (1 Thess 4:11), and Paul said he "disciplined" his body daily (1 Cor 9:27). To not live a life according to discipline or standards usually means we (or someone else) is going to pay a higher price later. The Christian life can be both easy and hard, in that what makes the Christian life easy is the fact that we want to do it (see Ps 37:4). Sin may seem easy or seem to make life easier (Heb 11:25), but it actually enslaves (John 8:34) and is a burden (Heb 12:1). The easy way out is Jesus' yoke.

October 15

Don't Run

I HAVE READ THAT if one is confronted by certain animals (such as a dog or a bear), one action not to take is that of running, as it ignites within the animal the instinct to chase. When confronted by a spiritual enemy, it is equally important that we "stand" (Eph 6:14), as well as fight (1 Tim 6:12). James thus said, "Submit yourselves therefore to God. Resist the devil, and he will flee from you" (Jas 4:7). Whether we stand and fight in a physical confrontation may depend on several things. Spiritually, what more important thing could there be to defend than our soul? If we run our enemy may chase us (see 1 Pet 5:8), in which case we are more likely to lose. For these reasons we stand and fight, so that Satan, not us, will flee.

October 16

It Doesn't Hurt to Ask

It seems that when we use the phrase "it doesn't hurt to ask," what we mean is that asking is worth the risk, in that it doesn't cost any money or cause other physical harm. To make repeated requests of people can cost, however, in spiritual terms. In Luke 18 the judge finally gave in and granted the lady's request because she was wearing him out with her requests (the lesson being that we "ought always to pray," v. 1). God wants us to ask (Heb 4:16), and his ear does not grow heavy with our petitions (Isa 59:1). In the physical realm (with people) it could hurt to ask, such as if we ask too often, ask for too much (see Prov 18:19), or ask for things which we ourselves can provide. In the spiritual realm of asking God in prayer, we may or may not receive what we ask for (see 1 John 5:14), but we benefit spiritually by the process of asking. With prayer, it doesn't hurt to ask; it rather hurts not to.

October 17

"He Is a Good Man"

When we refer to something as "good," it likely means that it suits us in some fashion. Our use of this word, therefore, often depends on us, rather than a standard such as truth. The Bible warns of the possibility of our calling evil "good" and good "evil" (Isa 5:20). Along these lines, the people were divided in opinion regarding Jesus: "And there was much muttering about him among the people. While some said, 'He is a good man,' others said, 'No, he is leading the people astray'" (John 7:12). Jesus said he came not to bring peace, but a sword (Matt 10:34). He also came to bring truth (inasmuch as he is truth, John 14:6), and truth divides (Heb 4:12); hence the multitude was divided in opinion over Jesus because their opinions were not based on truth. There may be times when we are divided over what course to take or what to believe. Truth is the standard upon which such decisions should be based. To not choose truth may seem "good," but will surely divide us from the Lord.

October 18

You Won't Be Disappointed

THE PHYSICAL LIFE WHICH the Christian lives contains many, often seemingly, unbearable pressures, from which most people would like to escape. We often point out that the biblical meaning of "hope" is a more positive concept than is usually meant. In Rom 5:3–5, Paul gives a series of spiritual blessings for the Christian, beginning with the physical hardship of tribulation, and ending in hope: "Not only that, but we rejoice in our sufferings, knowing that suffering produces endurance, and endurance produces character, and character produces hope, and hope does not put us to shame, because God's love has been poured into our hearts through the Holy Spirit who has been given to us." The Greek word translated "tribulation" contains a notion of something pressing down upon one. Paul's description of hope here includes that hope does not put to shame, or disappoint, again emphasizing the positive nature of biblical hope. While we wait for hope to be realized, God gives us the spiritual stability to endure, a quality of which God approves. The Christian's life can end with his or her being released from this life because of a hope that not only helps us expect but in which we won't be disappointed, an end result that began with our being physically pressed down. Until then we endure.

October 19

Exchanging the Truth

BESIDES CALLING EVIL "GOOD" and good "evil" (Isa 5:20), the world also likes to try to incorporate errant beliefs and lifestyles along with their belief in Christianity. While there are legitimate matters of opinion, many things are incompatible with Christianity (as taught in the Bible). Thus, Paul spoke of those who exchange the truth for a lie: "Because they exchanged the truth about God for a lie and worshiped and served the creature rather than the Creator, who is blessed forever! Amen" (Rom 1:25). The phrase "exchanged the truth" suggests several things, including that the subjects once had the truth, that they willingly gave it up for something else, and that they could not possess both simultaneously. Jesus is the truth, meaning there is no other (John 14:6; Acts 4:12). While many turn their ears from the truth (2 Tim 4:4), many know its appeal, and, therefore, try to keep it along with other beliefs that also appeal to them. The trouble is that lies are often more appealing than truth. By trying to keep both error and truth in possession, those who do so have actually exchanged the truth for a lie.

October 20

Our Little Secret

PAUL'S DESCRIPTION OF CONTENTMENT in Phil 4:12 is that of a knowledge only God provides: "I know how to be brought low, and I know how to abound. In any and every circumstance, I have learned the secret of facing plenty and hunger, abundance and need." The phrase "I have learned the secret" is a translation of one word in the original Greek. It has to do with being instructed with special knowledge from God, and appears only here in the Bible. The reverse of contentment is to always be wanting more or wanting something else, the attainment of which does not bring lasting fulfillment anyway. God offers a spiritual life consisting of joy (Gal 5:22), contentment (Heb 13:5), and a love for life (1 Pet 3:10–12), through the knowledge that only he offers. While one can evidently find a form of contentment and happiness in life on their own, godliness with contentment (1 Tim 6:6) can only be found with God. It's our little secret that God wants everyone in on.

October 21

"All Things New"

WHILE BOTH THINGS OLD and things new have an appeal (Matt 13:52), all of us in some way appreciate things that are new. Revelation 21:5 reads "And he who was seated on the throne said, 'Behold, I am making all things new.' Also, he said, 'Write this down, for these words are trustworthy and true.'" The physical world is winding down (and, therefore, we ourselves are winding down, no matter our age). God makes things new, the only one who can. He makes us spiritually new (2 Cor 5:17), a condition in which we not only remain but which continues as we live the Christian life (2 Cor 4:16). This newness is possible through the gospel (see 1 Pet 1:22), the good news that never grows old. While we, as Christians, are to walk, as it were, on the old paths (Jer 6:16), a spiritual life with God is new. Just wait until we leave this old world behind to go to the place where everything is new (Rev 21:1–4), and nothing ever grows old.

October 22

The Real Enemy

IF WE BELIEVE THE truth, we are going to have enemies (2 Tim 3:12). Inasmuch as truth divides (Heb 4:12), and is a light that shines on every way of life (John 3:19–21), it is, therefore, the standard by which everything is defined, by which we can know who is a friend (John 15:14) and who is an enemy. To blur the distinction between friend and enemy seems to be a result of straying away from truth (Gal 4:16). It is easy to believe in a false enemy (as much as a false friend, 2 Cor 11:14–15), and the more the Christian blends in with the world (Rom 12:2), the more we lose sight of who the enemy is (Luke 6:26). We avoid this by believing the truth. We need to know who the enemy is so that we may engage in the spiritual warfare before us (1 Tim 6:12), to ensure victory (Rev 2:10b) and, following Jesus' teaching, so we can know whom we are to love and pray for (Matt 5:44).

October 23

"The Lord Has Sent Me"

Moses' words in Num 16:28 remind us that Christians today also have a commission from the Lord: "Then Moses said, 'Hereby you will know that the Lord has sent me to do all of these works, that it has not been of my own mind'" (Moses then gives them a means by which his works can be tested in vv. 28–30). Christians today can know that they are similarly to do service to God, in such things as evangelism (Matt 28:18–20), benevolence (Gal 6:10), and other good works (Eph 2:10). While we may have ideas on how to carry out God's work, the instructions ultimately come from his word, not our heart (the phrase in Num 16:28 translated "of my own mind" is literally in Hebrew "of my heart"). God's work is defined by God's word (see John 9:4), and is fulfilled through following his will (John 6:38), not ours (Matt 26:39). It is, however, by means of our heart that the essential ingredient of love (1 Cor 13:3) gives meaning to those works.

October 24

"Buy Truth"

TRUTH IS UNIVERSAL. NOT everyone has it, yet everyone needs it (John 8:32). Thus Prov 23:23 reads: "Buy truth, and don't sell [it]; wisdom, discipline, and understanding." The book of Proverbs is written in poetic language. The phrase "buy truth" is here understood to be an emphatic statement of the need to seek, and thus attain, truth. Possessing truth does not change what it is (as when one buys a product becomes their possession, though the product doesn't change), though truth changes the person (1 Pet 1:22). The action of getting (the Hebrew word translated "buy" can also be translated "acquire") suggests the value of truth and the desire of one making the necessary sacrifice in order to acquire it (see Matt 13:44–45). Truth is important enough that not only should one be willing to sacrifice to acquire it but, once they do, to not let it go; this is true for everybody.

October 25

In Denial

JESUS TAUGHT THAT TO be his disciple it is necessary to "deny" oneself: "Then Jesus told his disciples, 'If anyone would come after me, let him deny himself and take up his cross and follow me'" (Matt 16:24). The Greek word translated "deny" can also have a meaning of "disown." This word appears in this verse, in Mark 8:34, and in Luke 9:23, where Jesus adds the word "daily" (in context of Peter denying the Lord during his trial and crucifixion (Matt 14:30, 72), and of one denying Jesus before others (thus he said, "But the one who denies me before men will be denied before the angels of God" Luke 12:9). It is as if we can only recognize one at a time. Denial of self-ownership is the key to being properly owned by the Lord (Acts 27:23). Only one person can sit on the throne of our heart at a time. If we refuse to recognize ourselves, and that on a daily basis, we are assured of seeing Jesus' face light up when he sees us in the end; that is, he will recognize us.

October 26

The Privilege of Worship

Worshiping God is a privilege, and should be counted as such. Everyone is invited to come into the spiritual presence of God to praise him through the designated avenues of worship (see 1 Cor 14:23). To be privileged in life is to have a position (that is, it is physical [see 1 Sam 16:6–12]); to count something a privilege is to adopt a certain attitude toward the activity in which we are engaged (the only verse I could find with the word "privilege" is the NIV of 2 Cor 8:4, which is a translation of the Greek word meaning "grace"). To adopt this attitude reflects the humility of an obedient servant (Luke 17:10), an attitude which God will reward with exaltation (Matt 23:12). We can count worship as a privilege because we have been graced with the opportunity to be with God in worship for a short time (Matt 18:20). By availing ourselves thereof, we can have the privilege of praising him for all eternity (see Rev 4:10).

October 27

Wavering through Unbelief

To NOT BELIEVE IN God or his promises is never a good idea. To believe in him requires a type of strength, in that it requires our mustering up an unwavering faith in our heart. The faith God would have is that which is pure or total. With regard to Abraham, Paul said, "No unbelief made him waver concerning the promise of God, but he grew strong in his faith as he gave glory to God" (Rom 4:20). To not believe in God's promises is to "waver," and contributes to our spiritual weakness (see tomorrow's "Daily"). The Greek word translated "waver" also appears in Matt 21:21 (Jesus' teaching on having faith as a grain of mustard seed), and Jas 1:6, where James said to "ask in faith, with no doubting." When we make a promise we are to do our best to keep it; when God makes a promise there is no question as to its truthfulness, and there is to be no middle ground with regard to our believing it. It is up to us whether to believe it. If we choose not to, our unbelief causes us to waver.

October 28

On the Other Hand

Paul's teaching on Abraham's faith (see yesterday's "Daily") includes not only Abraham's unwavering belief but his growing stronger as well: "No unbelief made him waver concerning the promise of God, but he grew strong in his faith as he gave glory to God" (Rom 4:20). The Greek word translated "but" in the second part of the sentence has a meaning of "on the other hand." Just as we either believe or don't believe, so there also exists a choice of becoming spiritually weak or strong. The means of gaining strength, both here and (similarly) in 2 Cor 12:9, is through giving glory to God. There are pivotal moments in life when we can choose to believe or not, to focus upon ourselves and our problems or to focus upon bringing glory to God through our troubles. There are moments wherein we can choose to become weaker or stronger; we can't choose both.

October 29

"Have Salt"

I'M NOT A MEDICAL doctor, but I've heard my whole life that too much salt is not a good dietary habit. Physical salt has many good qualities, including that it can add flavor to food (unless one is eating strawberry pie). Jesus taught that Christians are the salt of the earth (Matt 5:13), and also that having "salt" as a spiritual quality is something to which we must give attention: "Have salt in yourselves" (Mark 9:50; also, Paul said to let our speech be seasoned with salt, Col 4:6). Knowing that food without salt can be bland (Job 6:6), and that Jesus won't tolerate a lukewarm Christian (Rev 3:16), imagine how he feels about a bland (saltless) Christian. One may have only one talent (Matt 25:14), or have a bland personality; but by adding the salt of spiritual qualities (derived from God's word) we can make our lives palatable to others (though not all) and, more importantly, to Jesus. Please pass the "salt."

October 30

"Led to Repentance"

IT HAS BEEN SAID that success inflates the natural person, and humbles the spiritual person. Along these lines, Paul said, "Or do you presume on the riches of his kindness and forbearance and patience, not knowing that God's kindness is meant to lead you to repentance?" (Rom 2:4). Sometimes things happen in life which we can't explain. Again, if we realize them as "good" (Jas 1:17), the spiritual benefit can be that these things help us to look to God. Being "led" to something (like Jesus being led to an unjust trial [John 18:13], or the Christian being led by the Spirit [Gal 5:18], all of which have the same Greek word translated "led") suggests a humility that is the basis of repentance. Life's "good" events can lead us to God if our heart is able and willing to recognize God's goodness—that is, if our heart is spiritual.

October 31

A Matter of Balance

To worship God properly requires that we bring a certain life to his presence (for example, Matt 5:23–24), so that the "how" of our worship balances the "what." Thus, Paul so taught with regard to the Lord's Supper: "Whoever, therefore, eats the bread or drinks the cup of the Lord in an unworthy manner will be guilty concerning the body and blood of the Lord" (1 Cor 11:27). The Greek word translated "unworthy manner" has to do with something that is not fitting or does not bring honor, as it doesn't match (like unbalanced scales). The opposite of this is a life that is "worthy," in that it is balanced by proper repentance (Matt 3:8), as exemplified by one's living the Christian life (Eph 4:1). We can't be worthy by ourselves (such as by earning salvation, Eph 2:9); but by living the Christian life, God has promised us glory which is not worthy to be compared to (is not balanced by) the sufferings we endure in this life (Rom 8:18). In worship, God doesn't ask for the extraordinary, just a life and worship that are in balance with him—that is, that we worship in a worthy manner.

November 1

You Mean You Haven't?

JESUS SEEMED TO HAVE expectations with regard to certain things such as faith (Luke 8:25) and thanksgiving (Luke 17:17). More than once he asked a question which contains an element of negative surprise, as if to say "you mean you haven't . . .?" He thus asked the chief priests and scribes (those who worked with the law), "Have you not read this Scripture?" (Mark 12:10); Nicodemus, "Are you the teacher of Israel and yet you do not understand these things?" (John 3:10); and the disciples, "Are you also still without understanding?" (Matt 15:16). We read so that we can know, and knowledge is for the ultimate purpose of understanding. Just as the blessed man avoids a progression that takes him away from God (that is, he does not "walk . . . nor stand . . . nor sit" with the ungodly, Ps 1:1), so intellectual development can be spiritual, beginning with reading and ending with understanding God's will or truth. We should much rather hear Jesus say, "Well done," (Matt 25:23) than, "You mean you haven't?"

November 2

Spiritual Diversion

WE ALL NEED TIMES of diversion, whether it be regular (sleep) or occasional (such as hiking). Our bodies usually tell us when it's time to physically shut down and spend time away from the world to recharge, that is, to sleep (Mark 14:34). We also have a need to reinvigorate our spirit, though our soul may not alert us as clearly to this need. The Bible therefore tells us to keep up our prayer life (1 Thess 5:17), to study God's word (2 Pet 3:18), and to fellowship with God's people (Acts 2:46), all of which have the added benefit of reinvigorating our spirit by providing a distraction from this world. There were times when Jesus sacrificed the physical rejuvenation his body needed in order to spend an entire night in the spiritual rejuvenation of prayer (Luke 6:12). Not that we are necessarily required to do the same (though he is our example, 1 Pet 2:21); but, just as he told the disciples to come apart and rest (Mark 6:31), so our spirit needs to have moments away from the burdens of this physical life. God has alerted us to this need in his word. By taking heed to God's word, our soul can find reinvigoration in a moment of diversion.

November 3

Diversion or Distraction?

INASMUCH AS GOD'S WORD is a sword that divides (Heb 4:12), it is often difficult to remain neutral upon its hearing (though some may put it off, Acts 17:32). Depending on one's interest in truth, the word can be a diversion (see yesterday's "Daily") or a distraction. The psalmist said, "I will never forget your precepts, for by them you have given me life" (Ps 119:93). To the worldly minded, however, the word is often a distraction they don't want to hear (I have seen people grimace at the very mention of the Bible). Just like droning words that put one to sleep (Esth 6:1), or a stinging message that hurts the ears (Acts 7:57), truth is painful to many. Thus, many turn their ears from it (2 Tim 4:4) or turn and walk away from Jesus because of his words (John 6:66). God's word can be a diversion from the cares of this life (that is, toward God), or a distraction from one's worldly pursuits. In which direction we are pulled doesn't depend on unchanging truth, but on the response of our heart.

November 4

Whence Cometh Meaning?

WE ASSIGN MEANING TO things, and even to words. One of my favorite possessions is a coffee cup we bought while on a family vacation to Colonial Williamsburg, Virginia, in 1987. This item has meaning for me; not just because it holds coffee, but because it reminds me of a happy time and place of our past. Words also have meaning, and we may even assign a different meaning to words (during World War II my father would write letters to my mother in code while he was away in the Navy). God's word, however, is not assigned a meaning, but rather contains a meaning (Matt 12:7) that God placed therein (John 17:17). The psalmist said, "Make me understand the way of your precepts, so that I may converse on your wondrous works" (Ps 119:27). We like to keep happy memories alive; hence, treasured possessions lift our spirit because of the meaning we assign. God's word can change our spirit because of the meaning he assigned.

November 5

Regular Worship

MANY PEOPLE UNDERSTAND THAT work is part of life in this world (Gen 3:17–19). Worship, as presented in the Bible, is an event (Acts 8:27) in which Christians are to regularly engage (see Heb 10:25; 1 Cor 16:2). Some things are regular but pleasant (like a meal). With other things (like cutting the grass) we might be glad when they are over, and dread having to do them again (though we know, with the grass, we will have to do it again). The psalmist said, "I will exalt you, my God, O King, and I will bless your name forever and ever" (Ps 145:1). An attitude of heart that helps us plan on the event of worship can help us look forward, rather than dread, this spiritual event as a regular part of the Christian life. Unlike work, to which we may not look forward, and from which we will one day rest, our worship of God will not end, but will last for all eternity (Rev 4:8)—if we do it regularly.

November 6

The Reason Why

PAUL AGAIN EVIDENTLY HAD some kind of physical trouble which he could not escape (2 Cor 12:7), but from which pain he would like to have been relieved. We don't know what Paul's "thorn in the flesh" was, though he does say why he had it. Paul tells us of his response to this evident condition: "But he said to me, 'My grace is sufficient for you, for my power is made perfect in weakness.' Therefore I will boast all the more gladly of my weaknesses, so that the power of Christ may rest upon me" (2 Cor 12:9). When we have trouble in life we may not know the reason why it is happening. Rather than relief from the pain, God assured Paul of his grace, and assures us as well that he won't let our trials be too much to bear (1 Cor 10:13; reading in between the lines, we can know by faith that our burden is just right). While it is natural to want relief from our trouble, and to know a reason why we have it, both of these are born of self-concern and probably have to do with the physical. Paul chose rather to concentrate on the spiritual, that is, the power of Christ resting on him. What if we asked the reason for our troubles and we didn't like the answer?

November 7

Daily Renewal

Our body, brain, mind, and spirit need to be refreshed. Yet, the only one of these that is truly renewed is our spirit. Paul taught that while our physical life deteriorates, our spiritual life does not: "Wherefore we faint not; but though our outward man is decaying, yet our inward man is renewed day by day" (2 Cor 4:16). The body and brain reset themselves in sleep; the mind, which I'm told is always active, can evidently be renewed somewhat through sleep (depending on what's on our mind) or by getting away from distractions (such as by hiking). As Christians, we can assist our spiritual renewal by not being "conformed to this world" (Rom 12:2), and by putting on the new man (Col 3:10, and see Titus 3:10). Our physical life can be somewhat refreshed through the natural process of sleep, yet our physical life nevertheless naturally continues to deteriorate. By giving attention to our spiritual life, God provides a continuous renewal of our spirit that grows ever stronger while the body grows weaker.

November 8

"Words of Grace" (No Wonder)

More than once God's word is described as a word of grace, including Luke 4:22: "And all bare him witness, and wondered at the words of grace which proceeded out of his mouth: and they said, 'Is not this Joseph's son?'" (also Acts 20:32). We aren't told why the hearers wondered at Jesus' words. After his explanation of the Scripture that he had read, they became angry to the point of wanting to kill him (vv. 28–29). It could be because they had never heard such a message (see Matt 9:33, wherein appears the same Greek word), or perhaps they were expecting something else (it didn't match their preconceived ideas). Whatever the reason, their rejection of Jesus' words of grace is a reflection of their heart, more so than the unchanging message of God's truth (John 17:17). Grace can change one's soul (Eph 2:8) if the heart is receptive to the change imposed by the words of grace. No wonder.

November 9

"What to Do First?"

THERE ARE NO SPECIFIC rules in the Bible (that I know of) regarding our daily priorities. What each of us does first after waking surely depends on the individual. Our priorities can, however, be governed by the spiritual direction of our thoughts as defined by Jesus' teaching in Matt 6:33: "But seek first the kingdom of God and his righteousness, and all these things will be added to you." This being a seemingly general rule, it therefore doesn't tell us what to do, or necessarily in what order to do it; but it does suggest the attitude we are to have both in the actions we take and the general order into which we place those actions. Everyone likely has a routine, and we often pick up habits to help us have a "good day." Knowing that our physical actions are a reflection of our spiritual priorities (Matt 7:16; Eph 2:10), we should ask whether our physical actions, and the priority we place on them, are contributing to a strong spiritual life. We likely can't know the last thing we'll do in this life; but actions based on seeking first his kingdom can contribute to an eternal existence, rather than only a memory of a physical life (Luke 16:25)—if we put spiritual things first.

November 10

Service in Worship

SERVING THE LORD IS different from worshiping the Lord, yet we can think of worship as service (again, we often called it a "worship service"). The psalmist stated, "Serve the LORD with gladness! Come before him with a joyful cry!" (Psalm 100:2). The first word in Hebrew is simply "serve" (there are other Hebrew words for "worship"). Yet the context is describing worship (some English versions translate this word "worship"). It is good to be reminded that in worship we serve God, rather than ourselves. Certainly those up front are assisting the worshiper, and, therefore, serving them in one sense. Yet worship being an unselfish act(s), we, as worshipers, are to properly engage therein with a right heart. This means that, rather than expecting something in return, we engage in service, which requires humility (Luke 17:10), but which, in turn, brings a reward of exaltation (Matt 23:12). This is because in worship we exalt God (1 Sam 2:1) by serving him, rather than ourselves, and that in humility.

November 11

Wait for Strength

Hope is powerful because it is positive, and that which is positive gives energy. We gain physical strength by such things as physical activity, including challenging ourselves (that is, increasing our exercise), and also by rest. With God, our strength comes through waiting on him: "But those who wait for the Lord will renew [their] strength; they will raise their pinions like the eagles, they will run and not grow weary, they will walk and not become faint" (Isa 40:31). The idea of "waiting" in this verse has to do with hope, and, therefore, contains the many positive elements that accompany hope (anticipating reward [1 Cor 9:10]; overcoming such things as no hope, or a life without God [Eph 2:12], and overcoming grief [1 Thess 4:13]). Just as God tells us, as Christians, to be strong (Eph 6:10), so Isaiah states that our strength can be renewed; not through physical means, but through spiritual, through waiting on the Lord.

November 12

Having Our Heart Set

LIVING IN A TEMPORAL world filled with evil and pain means that we are going to suffer disappointment. Though it is not necessarily wrong, to have our "heart set" on something can therefore be a way to set ourselves up for disappointment. One way to avoid this is to set our heart on something that is not physical, but spiritual. The wise man, again, said, "Trust in the LORD with all your heart, and do not lean on your understanding" (Prov 3:5). To set our heart wholly on temporal things is often to prepare ourselves for disappointment. A way to avoid this is by letting our heart lean on something else by tempering our will with God's will (Ps 37:4; 1 John 5:14; Matt 26:42). Even the "fulfillment" we experience in this life is often either not fulfilling enough, not fulfilling at all, or it is, at least, temporary. If we set our heart on God's will we will never be disappointed; unless God's will is not our will.

November 13

What Went Wrong?

WHEN SOMETHING "GOES WRONG" in life we often seek an explanation therefor. If we lose money, or the meal doesn't turn out right (perhaps we forgot to add salt), etc. we often try to come up with a reason, perhaps, in part, to justify ourselves. Such a desire can be good, for example, to help us avoid a mistake the next time. When seeking to explain all of life's events, however, we may not always be able to determine a reason. In Acts 21:14, those trying to persuade Paul as to his course of action resigned themselves to God's will: "And since he would not be persuaded, we ceased and said, 'Let the will of the Lord be done.'" While there may be a physical explanation from which we can learn, sometimes an answer can only be found by looking to the spiritual (such as Christians being the "salt of the earth" [Matt 5:1] in an earth containing evil), ultimately, to God's will (Matt 26:42). When something goes "wrong," and it is God's will, can we really say it went wrong?

November 14

React or Respond?

IF WE ARE PRESCRIBED a new medicine, it is possible that our body will react, which is negative, or respond, which is positive, to the medicine. While truth by definition does not change, the human heart can and does change (such as seen in repentance). The Scriptures provide us with many examples of those who rejected the truth, including the violent reaction to Stephen's speech in Acts 7: 54: "Now when they heard these things they were enraged, and they ground their teeth at him." It has also been said that the further one strays from the truth, the more angry they become when their beliefs are challenged. If upon hearing truth our heart has a reaction thereto, one can also look at that as an opportunity to learn more (such as the true meaning of Scripture). In other words, we might respond (Mark 12:37), react and reject (Luke 4:28–29), or have a reaction (Acts 2:37) that causes us to respond.

November 15

Rejoice and Weep

PAUL'S TEACHING TO "REJOICE with those who rejoice, weep with those who weep" (Rom 12:15) is a reminder to look at life, in this case in our dealings with others, spiritually. If someone is crying due to a problem, our tendency might be to look at the problem in order to evaluate it. Being an outsider (that is, it not being our problem), we might be tempted to say something like "it can't be that bad" (or if the person had good news, to say "it can't be that good"). Based on this verse, God would have us look not at the physical (the problem or the blessing), but rather at the person's heart from whence the tears or the joy are springing. Thus, if they are crying, we are to cry with them. On the occasion of Lazarus's death Jesus cried with his family (John 11:35), even though he was just about to raise him from the dead (wouldn't this be the best time for someone to say "it can't be that bad?"). Unlike animals, man has tears and a smile that are reflections of the soul given to them by God (Gen 1:26). To look at the tears or the smile is, in effect, to look at the person's soul in order to help them; it is to look at their circumstances spiritually.

November 16

Christians Do Good

IT SEEMS THAT THE nature of evil is that it can't keep still (1 Pet 5:8). Assuming this to be true, in an age when evil is constantly portrayed as good and good as evil (Isa 5:20), one can know which is which by looking at their resulting actions. Thus Jesus said, "You will recognize them by their fruits" (Matt 7:16). Truth, and a lack of desire therefor, is seemingly becoming such a scarce commodity in the present age that, in many ways, one can often identify evil and good by assuming the opposite of what we are told (this point presented with just a bit of humor). Doing good alone doesn't make one right with God (Matt 7:21–23); but Christians are to do good (Eph 2:10). Though in the world we are often presented a picture of a pretty white outside (Matt 23:27), the evil contained within is not content to stay there. It will likely eventually show itself, and thereby we can know it for what it is (2 Cor 2:11). Can the same be said of goodness?

November 17

"Buy Truth and Don't Sell It"

WE CAN BUY IDEAS just as we buy groceries or clothes, as when someone says, referring to a new idea, "I don't buy it." The wise man again said, "Buy truth, and don't sell [it]; wisdom, discipline, and understanding" (Prov 23:23). Proverbs is written in poetic language; and this verse reminds us that truth is not a commodity to be bought, but rather an idea to be accepted. The two main points of this proverb are to do all we can (including make sacrifices), to get truth and, once we do, to keep it for the rest of our lives. Unlike a commodity, truth is not something we buy once, but can be a perpetual goal, and is something everyone is to acquire. If we value something enough we will make every effort to acquire it (Matt 13:44). I don't know why anyone would want to sell truth; but if it's for sale, buy it. And don't let it go.

November 18

The Trouble with Lies

MOST PEOPLE KNOW THAT lying is wrong, but how many people do it? What makes a lie a lie is the intent to deceive. Sarah was Abraham's half-sister, but Abraham told Abimelech she was his sister to avoid the truth that she was his wife (Gen 20:12). Avoiding the truth anytime may provide a quick fix (such as sparing someone's feelings), but we often ultimately pay a price for any temporary pleasure. Not that this will always happen, but such an end result can be illustrated by the lies of Nazi Germany or the Jonestown cult. One of the worst forms of deception is when we lie to ourselves, such as when the Jews told Jesus that they "have never been enslaved" (John 8:33). We may say that true or ultimate good can only come from following the truth. Lying or believing a lie may provide a quick fix, but no good will ultimately come therefrom, either for the liar (Rev 21:8) or for the follower thereof (2 Tim 4:4). Besides being wrong, the trouble with lies is that people believe them.

November 19

"Learned and Received"

To ARRIVE HOME AND see a notice that a first attempt was made to deliver a package is to learn that we have a package coming, though we haven't yet taken receipt thereof. It seems that one can acquire knowledge without learning (see Matt 17:13), and to have knowledge alone is not necessarily the goal (John 13:17; 2 Tim 3:7), among other things because one can learn the wrong thing (see yesterday's "Daily"). Learning is the first step toward understanding, and is the basis of being a disciple of Jesus (Matt 28:18–20). A follow-up step to learning is to "take receipt" of the things we've learned. Paul said this is what the Philippians did in this regard: "What you have learned and received and heard and seen in me—practice these things, and the God of peace will be with you" (Phil 4:9). The Greek word translated "receive" again has to do with a kind of official action, such as receiving a body of teaching (1 Cor 11:23). To believe that the Bible is God's word is to learn of the "delivery." To understand what it says is to comprehend its meaning. To receive it is to take delivery of God's will into our home, that is, into our heart, and thereby to ensure that God is with us.

November 20

To Wait on the Lord

To return to a familiar passage, Isa 40:31 again reads, "But those who wait for the Lord will renew [their] strength; they will raise their pinions like the eagles, they will run and not grow weary; they will walk and not become faint." We may raise the question of what it is to wait on the Lord. Among other things, Isaiah's wording generally teaches us to look at life spiritually. To wait on something in life (such as the delivery of a package or an important event) is tedious, because we are thereby focusing on that which we don't have. It also surely takes energy. We wait on the Lord by such things as concentrating on him and things spiritual (such as seeking first the kingdom, Matt 6:33, the result of which will be that God will take care of the physical things that we don't have), and doing his will (in the Akkadian language [a sister language to Hebrew], the corresponding word has a meaning of "serve," such as a server in a restaurant). To wait on things physical takes energy. To concentrate on things spiritual, or wait on the Lord, gives energy.

November 21

A Day to Be Thankful

SO MUCH ABOUT THANKSGIVING seems like a contradiction. On this holiday we take one day to give thanks while Christians are taught "in everything give thanks" (1 Thess 5:18). On Thanksgiving we engage in a physical pleasure (eating) on a day set aside for spiritual contemplation (giving thanks). Eating is also selfish (not that it's wrong), while giving thanks is basically unselfish. All of this reminds us that when God directs us to do something such as give thanks, it is for our spiritual good. Just as with faith (Luke 18:8), Jesus expects us to be thankful (Luke 17:15–17). In a world where it is easy to become preoccupied with the things of this life (2 Tim 2:4), and, as a result, lose sight of spiritual things such as thankfulness, surely that is one of the main blessings of taking a day to be thankful.

November 22

To Know Love

LIKE TRUTH, LOVE SEEMS to be a concept that we like to define ourselves (hence, many have an experience where they wonder whether they are "in love"). While love can be a complicated emotion (the ancient Greeks had four words for it), it is yet a fundamental aspect of our being as humans made in the image of God, who is love (1 John 4:8). Paul described it in several lines thus: "Love is patient and kind; love does not envy or boast; it is not arrogant or rude. It does not insist on its own way; it is not irritable or resentful; it does not rejoice at wrongdoing, but rejoices with the truth. Love bears all things, believes all things, hopes all things, endures all things. Love never ends" (1 Cor 13:4-8). God has both defined as well as demonstrated truth (John 14:6; 17:17) and love (John 3:16; Col 1:13). We can, therefore, see love in action by looking at God (1 John 4:8) as well as his Son (John 15:13). We can know what love is, not by looking to ourselves (Jer 10:23), but to the truth of God's word—and thereby know how to love.

November 23

Just Right

WHEN WE HAVE A problem or a need in life, the solutions we come up with may be extreme, compared to the way of God, who knows what is best for us. That is, God offers several assurances that what he offers will be just right. This can be because God knows better than we what is best for us. The Bible assures us that God will not let the fire of trial get too hot (Mal 3:3), that there is no trial one can't bear (1 Cor 10:13, which includes a way of escape), that God will provide for our needs (Phil 4:19), and that his grace is sufficient (spoken to Paul, 2 Cor 12:9). When life is difficult, or something seems to be lacking in our lives (Ps 23:1), it may be that God is meeting another need. If this is the case, it seems that the only way to make sense thereof is to look at life, and these circumstances, from the perspective in which God directs us; that is, spiritually. The solutions God offers are just right.

November 24

Permanent Unity

UNITY IS A GREAT thing because it is desired of God (Ps 133). One of the surest ways for a group to no longer be a group is to think of themselves in categories rather than as a unit. A people within a country, for example, that thinks of themselves primarily as part of a smaller group, rather than part of the larger political unit (in our case, America), contributes to the fracturing of the country. Not that we can't think of ourselves as individuals (see Gal 2:20); but Paul taught the Corinthians not to think of themselves as following Paul, Apollos, Cephas, or Christ (1 Cor 1:12), but rather to be united: "I appeal to you, brothers, by the name of our Lord Jesus Christ, that all of you agree, and that there be no divisions among you, but that you be united in the same mind and the same judgment" (1 Cor 1:10). The best way for America to be united is for us to accept the ideals set forth at her beginning, based on her founding documents (the Declaration of Independence and the Constitution). The best way for Christians to be united is to accept the principles upon which Christianity is based, that is, the NT (inasmuch as it is God's truth; John 17:17; 1 Cor 1:10–17). Other things (such as a disaster that befalls our country or fun times of fellowship in church) might help us become closer; but any cohesion will last only when it is based on something permanent. The most permanent thing that can unite a people before God is that which doesn't change, the truth (Matt 24:35).

November 25

Familiar Worship

WHILE THAT WHICH IS new can be exciting, that which is familiar can be comforting (such as coming home after a trip). Worship, as taught in the Bible, is to be consistent (such as giving, 1 Cor 16:2). This is logical, inasmuch as if we are allowed to change the avenues of worship, there would be no end to what it would become. Some examples of those who (evidently) only wanted something new include Nadab and Abihu, who offered "forbidden fire" (Lev 10:1-2); the philosophers on Mars Hill who only wanted to tell or to hear some "new thing" (Acts 17:21); and perhaps those who are "always learning and never able to arrive at a knowledge of the truth" (2 Tim 3:7). God, who doesn't change (Mal 3:6), but rather makes all things new (Rev 21:5), expects to be able to recognize certain things, including the worship that he desires (Amos 5:21-24). Knowing this, worship may not be exciting to some because of its familiarity; but by following God's word, these familiar avenues of expression can be comforting to us and pleasing to God, as this is what he is looking for. What did you expect?

November 26

Birds Don't Worry

JESUS TAUGHT THAT BIRDS, in effect, don't worry (Matt 6:26). Unlike humans, birds are not spiritual beings, and, therefore, seem to not have the capacity for worry. Man can worry; but with the ability to worry, comes also the ability to overcome it. Jesus' approach to helping us not worry included getting us to look at life spiritually ("consider," Matt 6:28; "look at," v. 26; both of which contain a meaning of contemplation) by appealing to us that worry does no practical good (v. 27), that life is more important than worry (v. 25; reading between the lines, worry is destructive of life), and by using logic (v. 30). Jesus' teaching is reinforced by the teaching of Paul in Phil 4:6, whereas Jesus simply tells us three times not to worry (Matt 6:25, 31, and 34). Instead of worry, birds have an instinctual means of self-preservation, as reflected, for example, in migration. Man, again, not only has the ability to worry but, more importantly, the means to overcome it. To exercise the ability to worry is destructive. To exercise the ability to overcome worry is spiritually productive. In other words, dealt with properly, worry can help us fly to heaven.

November 27

Opportunities to Not Sin

A PHYSICAL PROBLEM, SUCH as repair work on a house, provides an opportunity for such positive things as adding a new tool to one's collection and learning how to fix a new problem. It is best for our well being if we don't worry, become angry, or harbor other destructive emotions. Anger affects judgment and can lead us to sin; worry seemingly is a sin (Matt 6:25–34), and is detrimental both to our physical and spiritual health (see yesterday's "Daily"). Yet it seems that most of these emotions are natural, as reflected in Paul's words in Eph 4:26: "Be angry and do not sin; do not let the sun go down on your anger." Circumstances that give birth to anger, worry, etc. provide an opportunity not only for these emotions to come alive, but also for us to overcome them, and thereby to become spiritually stronger in the process. One day Christians will have an existence without anything to make us angry or worry (see Rev 21:4). It can be good in this physical world to have something to make us angry or worry about; as long as we don't worry or sin through anger. That's something else.

November 28

"Much Conflict"

CONFLICTS CAN BE GOOD, in that they are a moment of proving. Times of conflict in life are inevitable, and are usually not enjoyable. But conflicts can be the moment our true character is both revealed and developed. It is revealed because conflicts are difficult; it is developed because difficult times are how we grow (an African proverb states that "smooth seas do not make skillful sailors"). Some sources of conflict in the Bible include disagreements (John 6:66), the challenges of the Christian life (1 Tim 6:12, wherein the Greek word translated "fight" is elsewhere translated "conflict"), and the gospel: "But though we had already suffered and been shamefully treated at Philippi, as you know, we had boldness in our God to declare to you the gospel of God in the midst of much conflict" (1 Thess 2:2). The common denominator of all of these is truth. We can't change the inevitability of truth or of conflict; but conflict brought about by truth can show, or change, who we are.

November 29

"In Which He Trusted"

THE ONLY ONE IN whom we can ultimately trust is God. We can trust our neighbors for some things but, again, even the best of friends can't attend one another's funerals. God desires that we trust him rather than (entirely) ourselves (Prov 3:5–6; Heb 11:6). This includes not putting our faith in physical things, such as barns (Luke 12:18) or armor: "But when one stronger than he attacks him and overcomes him, he takes away his armor in which he trusted and divides his spoil" (Luke 11:22). Before David slew Goliath he expressed his faith not in his weapons but in God: "Then David said to the Philistine, 'You come to me with a sword and with a spear and with a javelin, but I come to you in the name of the LORD of hosts, the God of the armies of Israel, whom you have defied'" (1 Sam 17:45). Faith in God, which is spiritual, can help us overcome life's obstacles and trials, which are physical, including the final "obstacle" of death (1 Cor 15:55). The ultimate victory belongs to God (Rev 2:10; 1 Sam 17:47). Like David, we need physical things to help us through this life. But like David, our trust is not in physical armor that can fail but in God, in whom is our trust, and, therefore, our victory (1 Cor 15:57).

November 30

"Holy Hands"

THE INSECT KNOWN AS the praying mantis brings glory to God because he is part of God's creation (Ps 104:24), one with hands folded as if in prayer. Unlike him, we choose the type of hands we offer in prayer. Praying, as an act of worship, is a reflection of a relationship with God, one that requires that we be holy (1 Pet 1:16). While the act of praying is necessary (Luke 18:1–8) and can be spiritually beneficial (Heb 4:16), the mechanical action of praying alone is not all that God wants (he already knows what we need, Matt 6:32). Paul said, "I desire then that in every place the men should pray, lifting holy hands without anger or quarreling" (1 Tim 2:8). The phrase "lifting holy hands" I understand to be an emphasis on the type of hands, more so than the action of lifting hands (similarly to the teaching on the holy kiss [1 Pet 5:14], more so than the cultural mode of greeting). Holy hands, like proper words (Matt 12:37) and benevolent actions (1 Cor 13:3) are to flow from a holy life, one which follows God's word. To lift improper hands, that is, from an unholy life (Prov 6:17) is to offer improper worship. Like the mantis, we can lift our hands to God, but it will only draw us closer to him if those hands are holy.

December 1

Our Father Knows Best

God ultimately controls our circumstances (1 Cor 10:13), while we, again, control our attitude. The Bible teaches that God won't let the fire (in life) get too hot: "So he will sit [as] a smelter and purifier of silver; and he will purify the sons of Levi and refine them like gold and silver, and they will be the Lord's, those who bring offerings in righteousness" (Mal 3:3). The Bible also teaches that we are to have a certain attitude toward our circumstances (1 Tim 6:8). We can therefore say that we may, at times, want something different—we may want our circumstances to be different, while God wants our heart to be centered on him (Prov 3:5–6). This means that the important thing is not whether the fire is too hot or that we have what we need (or even how we evaluate life) but, rather, the extent to which we trust God. Faith may or may not change our circumstances (1 John 5:14); but knowing that "all things are possible" (Mark 9:23) to the one who has but faith as small as a grain of mustard seed (Matt 17:20), perhaps the answer lies not in whether the fire is too hot, or whether we think the fire is too hot but that we trust him that it isn't.

December 2

Working Power

MOST ACCOMPLISHMENTS ARE ATTAINED through such positive qualities as work and persistence. We often point out that the Greek word translated "power" in Rom 1:16 (referring to the gospel) is the word from which we derive our English word "dynamite." Unlike dynamite, the gospel is a spiritual power that can be productive as well as destructive. Thus Paul referred to a power that "works" in the Christian: "Now to him who is able to do far more abundantly than all that we ask or think, according to the power at work within us" (Eph 3:20). The same word translated "work" is used with regard to other positive spiritual forces such as God (Phil 2:13), faith (Gal 5:6), prayer (Jas 5:16), and life (2 Cor 4:12), as well as negative spiritual things such as the spirit of disobedience (Eph 2:2), death (2 Cor 4:12), and sinful passions (Rom 7:5). It seems as if something is going to work in us; and surely that which is good for us, like exercise, won't happen on its own. Rather than letting worry or other destructive forces work in us (or, as we say, work on us), how much more productive to let God's spiritual qualities, including the power of the gospel, work in us.

December 3

Lifting Our Spirit

WE OFTEN NEED SOMETHING, such as colorful flowers, pleasant weather, or someone to smile at us, to "lift our spirits." There is nothing necessarily wrong with seeking to change our mood with music or colors. But these things are physical, and, therefore, temporary. That which ultimately lifts our spirit comes from the One who gave us a spirit, and provides an elevation to our life, rather than to our humor only: "Besides this, we have had earthly fathers who disciplined us and we respected them. Shall we not much more be subject to the Father of spirits and live?" (Heb 12:9). The spiritual life God provides, which is fulfilled by attention to his word, to prayer, and to the church, helps our spirit carry on in life (Ps 121:1–2), and, eventually, to be lifted to heaven (1 Cor 15:24). Our spirit can only be truly lifted with a spiritual life with God.

December 4

"The Lord Takes Pleasure"

IT IS COMFORTING TO know that when we worship God in spirit and truth (John 4:24), God can be pleased with what we have to offer. The reverse is also likewise true (in Amos 5:21, God said he "hated" their feasts. The word "hate" in the Bible often means "to reject"). The psalmist said, "For the Lord takes pleasure in his people" (Ps 149:4). These words are offered in a context of worship, though the means of expression then is different from today (v. 3). Still, this verse reminds us again of the choice we have in coming to worship, whether to engage therein for God or for ourselves. We today strive to please God with songs from the heart (Eph 5:19), prayers (1 Cor 14:15), sincere communion (1 Cor 11:20–29), preaching, (Matt 15:9), and cheerful giving (2 Cor 9:7). By offering these things to please to God, it can, in turn, leave us pleased (1 Cor 13:5) unless our worship was not for him to begin with. It can't be both; or can it (Ps 37:4)?

December 5

"The Spirit Gives Life"

SINCE THE SPIRIT COMES from God (Eccl 12:7), it follows that only God can truly lift our spirit. We, again, may be able to change our mood (see yesterday's "Daily") with positive external circumstances that give us a good humor. It is generally good to give attention to the flesh, for example, seeing to our own good health (1 Thess 5:23). But to have our spirit lifted, we look to the Father of spirits to lift us from this realm to the heavenly, where our spirit can be truly free. Jesus said, "It is the Spirit who gives life; the flesh is no help at all. The words that I have spoken to you are spirit and life" (John 6:63). Our favorite song, food, or person can help us through today. It is in Jesus' word that our spirit has life, and is lifted to live beyond today. Only God gives life (Gen 2:7), and only God can truly lift our spirit.

December 6

Determining Truth

OUR FINDING TRUTH, AGAIN, does not depend on what we think of it, but does depend (to some extent) on our desire for it. We, therefore, don't define truth, but we do determine it. What is it that keeps us looking for answers in life (for example, do we stop only when we've found a satisfactory answer)? Just as something can't be simultaneously both true and not true, so man's will is usually at odds with God's will (John 1:13). With regard to truth, Jesus said, "If anyone's will is to do God's will, he will know whether the teaching is from God or whether I am speaking on my own authority" (John 7:17; see also v. 18). We can thus use our will to direct our ears toward, rather than away from, truth (2 Tim 4:4), and to cause us to ever seek it as we would for gold or silver (see Matt 13:44; Prov 2:4). If we desire truth, a solid beginning point is not an attempt to change it to conform to our will, but to change our will to God's, for the purpose of finding truth.

December 7

Learning in Our Situation

A SAYING IN EDUCATION is that students learn to do what they do. The Christian life, or piety, is also practical (Heb 5:14). Regarding his personal growth, Paul said, "Not that I am speaking of being in need, for I have learned in whatever situation I am to be content" (Phil 4:11). Our situation in life surely is not static. That is, it will change over the course of our life; and the state in which we find ourselves may not always be agreeable. There surely will be times when we would like life to be different. We can only control so much about our circumstances. More important than changing our situation, however, is changing our attitude toward it. We do this by concentrating on learning with God. Learning has to do with growth (2 Pet 3:18) and with doing (in Phil 4:11, by learning to adapt to our circumstances). It is possible to never be content where we are (to always wish our situation were different), to be content where we are, or, seemingly the most important, to learn to be content where we are. We do this by applying ourselves to learning in whatever situation we are. Let's do this!

December 8

Growing Weary (or Not)

IN MAL 2:17, THE Lord again replied that his people had "wearied" him "with words." The picture of God being weary is, of course, a figure of speech in which God is described in human terms to help us understand his dealings with us. That is, God does not really become weary (Isa 40:28). On the other hand, Isaiah also stated, "But those who wait for the Lord will renew [their] strength; they will raise their pinions like the eagles; they will run and not grow weary; they will walk and not become faint" (Isa 40:31). This description of God presents a challenge to his children, of our being persistent in our spiritual lives to the point that God is pictured as being worn out with hearing our tiresome words, as well as being worn out with listening to our prayers (Luke 18:1–8). Surely, a reason God would welcome this is because this is good for us spiritually. That is, by our giving consistent attention to our spiritual life, we will become spiritually stronger, and thus never grow (spiritually) weary; though he will (but not really).

December 9

"Good" Worship

WORSHIP CAN BE EITHER good or bad. This is because God defines what is good and bad (for example, Gen 1:10), and God decides what he "loves" (accepts) or "hates" (rejects; Rom 9:13). Amos 5:21, again, reads, "I hate, I despise your feasts, and I take no delight in your sacred assemblies." We naturally may evaluate worship as we do a music concert or a meal, depending on how it satisfies us (especially in things we pay for). Yet God sees things differently than we (Isa 55:8–9). While worship is a sacrifice (Mark 12:41–44; Heb 13:15), it cost God much more than we have to offer for him to have a relationship with us. Worship is, again, a spiritual exercise, which God evaluates based on his parameters (John 4:24). If we concentrate on the spiritual, it can help us offer worship in spirit that is then acceptable to God, with our opinion being secondary. Being natural beings, it is natural for us to enjoy (or not) certain aspects of worship. But what is more important is that, when we leave worship, God has "enjoyed it." If we offer worship according to God's standard (his word), it is surely good.

December 10

Setting Our Hope

HOPE IS AN ATTITUDE that often can make the difference in our struggle to get through even one day of this life. That is, knowing that something positive awaits us tomorrow gives us a strength to overcome the pain of today. Hope is a gift from God (1 Pet 1:3); yet, there can be a false (Jer 6:14) or misplaced hope (see John 5:45). It, therefore, is an attitude that the Christian must not only adopt, but do so properly. Peter taught not only to set our hope but how: "Therefore, preparing your minds for action, and being sober-minded, set your hope fully on the grace that will be brought to you at the revelation of Jesus Christ" (1 Pet 1:13; the Greek word translated "fully" comes from the word that has to do with both perfection and with having a goal. The ASV translates as "set your hope perfectly"). Christians can survive today because of hope for tomorrow, if we adopt it properly. God not only tells us in what to hope, but how.

December 11

The Step of Belief

BELIEF MAY BE DESCRIBED as a type of mental acceptance that has found its way into one's heart (to illustrate with the contrary, one may accept, but still disagree with, another's belief). We often believe in things that aren't true, and sometimes have to force ourselves to believe something that is obviously true. With regard to Scripture, we can hear Scripture (John 5:39), (mis)place our hope therein (John 5:45), and even learn Scripture (2 Tim 3:7). But unless we choose to believe what we read, it may not have the same effectiveness for us. Thus, Jesus said that with belief "all things are possible" (Mark 9:23), which would mean that "all things work together for good" ("for those who love God" Rom 8:28) because love believes all things (1 Cor 13:7). One may have verses memorized; but, until they accept them in their heart as true, including putting their belief into practice (Heb 5:14), this word could be a power that lies dormant (they must accept the light that is shining all around them, John 12:36). Belief is then seemingly one of the last steps to God's word having an effect in our lives. When it comes to salvation, it is one of the first steps (John 1:12).

December 12

Choosing to Believe

WE CHOOSE WHAT WE believe. Belief should be based on evidence (Rom 10:17; Heb 11:6), though we often believe things based on the direction of our heart (see yesterday's "Daily"). To become and remain a Christian requires that we believe God's word (John 8:32; Rom 1:16). There may be times when what we are told or what we would like to believe may conflict with God's word, which imposes upon us a choice. Thus the man told Jesus "I believe; help my unbelief!" (Mark 9:24). We choose to believe such truths that God created the world in six days, according to Gen 1 (Heb 11:3); that even though life be in turmoil, somehow this can result in good if we love God (Rom 8:28); and that there is a place Christians will go after death, even though we can't see it (Heb 11:1; 1 Pet 1:4). Love, again, believes all things (1 Cor 13:7), and love is a choice (Deut 7:7–8). To believe otherwise when we are confronted with a choice is to reject the evidence of God's word. It's your choice.

December 13

Believe to Overcome Fear

Like belief (see yesterday's "Daily"), fear is also a choice. Whether due to an external force (1 Pet 3:14), or something we harbor, fear is natural and can trouble our heart. Jesus' words to the apostles in John 14:1, however, tell us that the natural emotion of fear is to be overcome with the spiritual element of faith: "Let not your hearts be troubled. Believe in God; believe also in me" (John 14:1; see also v. 27). Just as taking a deep breath can help calm down our physical heart, so taking a deep breath of God's word (John 20:22; Heb 3:7) can infuse us with faith to calm down our troubled heart. Better to be one of the faithful than one of the fearful (Rev 21:4).

December 14

Consistent Worship

MANY BENEFITS IN LIFE (medicine, exercise, education) come from consistency rather than singularity or a onetime effort. God is faithful to his children (1 John 1:9), in part because that's who he is (Mal 3:6), but also surely because it's what we need. God does not need such things as our offerings (Ps 50:12), nor to have his mood brightened by our singing. Yet he desires, and we need, a relationship with him; and, relationships require consistency. With God this includes consistency in worship. Jesus is again our example in this regard: "And he came to Nazareth, where he had been brought up. And as was his custom, he went to the synagogue on the Sabbath day, and he stood up to read" (Luke 4:16). Neither we nor God keep score of our good works, but we, rather, give attention to a proper relationship with God (Matt 7:22–23). Since we look forward to praising God for all eternity (see Rev 4:8), how good it is to praise him for a short time, and that regularly, while we wait.

December 15

If You Love Something

THE CONTEMPORARY PROVERB STATES, "If you love something, let it go." God wants everybody to be saved (2 Pet 3:9). He, therefore, doesn't want any follower to leave him (2 Pet 2:22). The rejection of an idea often produces a strong reaction, seemingly more often from the side of non-truth (Luke 4:16–30; Acts 7:54–60). The Lord also wants willing followers (Rom 6:17). There are several scriptural examples of those who left the Lord and he simply let them go: "After this many of his disciples turned back and no longer walked with him. So Jesus said to the twelve, "Do you want to go away as well?'" (John 6:66–67; see 1 Tim 1:20). While error can be appealing (2 Cor 11:14), it enslaves, while truth sets free (John 8:31–36). Perhaps a reason truth is not forced upon the will of man is because God's will is not only that man be saved, but that man be saved according to his will as well as His will. If a child of God leaves him, it will surely break his heart (see Eph 4:30). But he would let us go, even if it means into the slavery of error, because he loves us and wants us to be free.

December 16

That's What You Think

ONE OF THE BEST uses we can make of our thoughts is to use them to change our mind. It is fine to have an opinion in matters of opinion (strawberry ice cream is not morally superior to vanilla). Yet, such scriptural truths that God's thoughts are higher than ours (Isa 55:8–9), and that we need to conform to the mind of Christ (Phil 2:5–8) tells us that truth, not ourselves, is the standard. To conform to Jesus is to conform to truth (John 14:6). This requires changing our mind (the Greek word translated "repent" literally means an "after-mind"). It is often not easy for us to change our mind, as it could amount to an admission that we are wrong (could this be why [it seems] most of us, in conversation and in class, make statements rather than ask questions?). There is a standard to which our mind must conform, and it is not our thoughts—unless they conform to the standard of truth.

December 17

We Have Come to Worship

THE VISIT OF THE wise men after the birth of the Christ child is a touching and romantic element in the birth account of Jesus (Matt 2:1–2). While there are many interesting aspects of their visit, their statement "we . . . have come to worship him" naturally provides a lesson for us today. There are many differences between worship then and worship now, including that we don't need to be in one particular physical location (John 4:21), and that Christians today worship God through Jesus (Rev 19:10; 1 Tim 2:5). One similarity, however, is that worship is still something we go and do (Acts 8:27). Christians today, therefore, on the first day of the week go to worship. We might go to a building on Sunday morning for many other understandable reasons (including to see others or out of a sense of obligation, Heb 10:25). The main reason we should go is to worship.

December 18

Truth First

TO BE EQUIPPED IN the battle for our soul, God has given the Christian spiritual implements that help us both externally (Eph 6:10–18) and internally (Phil 4:8–9). In these two lists Paul includes truth (or "true") as the first element thereof. His teaching on the Christian armor begins with "stand therefore, having fastened on the belt of truth" (Eph 6:14), and his teaching on what to take account of in our mind begins with "finally, brothers, whatever is true" (Phil 4:8). Though Paul doesn't tell us why, could it be that truth is the necessary foundation upon which these spiritual principles will work? A house built upon a weak foundation is liable to not stand (Matt 7:26–27), and the truth itself needs to be upheld (1 Tim 3:15). If we adorn equipment based on something other than truth, or our minds dwell on everything good except truth, our lives, and especially our spiritual lives, might not withstand in the evil day. Even if that's not what Paul intended, it still seems like a good idea.

December 19

Belief Means Obedience

BELIEF IS THE BASIS of obedience; and, to believe that the answer is spiritual can result in a better physical life. The Christian is to spend time in such spiritual activities as prayer (1 Thess 5:17), Bible study (2 Pet 3:18), and spiritual application of their mind (Rom 12:2; Phil 4:8). Such spiritual conditioning is the basis for the Christian working (1 Thess 4:11 and being a good employee, Col 3:22–24), doing good works (Eph 2:10), and living a physically pure life (1 Cor 6:19–20). Jesus' words in John 3:36 show the parallel of belief with obedience: "Whoever believes in the Son has eternal life; whoever does not obey the Son shall not see life, but the wrath of God remains on him." To only do "good things" will not necessarily please God (Matt 7:22–23). To obey him will, because true obedience, or a proper physical life before God, is the result of belief, or a proper spiritual life.

December 20

"Pleasant and Suitable"

ONE OF THE PRIMARY purposes of worship is to glorify God. Yet, as we often point out, worship spiritually benefits the worshiper (by drawing them closer to God), and can influence the non-worshiper as well. Just as partaking of the Lord's Supper involves looking inward (1 Cor 11:25) as well as outward (1 Cor 11:26), so the psalmist's words in Ps 147:1 reflect a similar twofold benefit: "Because [it is] pleasant, [and] praise is suitable." The words "pleasant" and "suitable" are, in Hebrew, a couplet, like the phrase "fender bender." The word "pleasant" is internal, reflecting that worship can affect our heart in a positive way. The word "fitting" is external (like clothes that fit properly), reflecting that, in worship, others can perhaps be influenced by the Christian's devotion. Just as love for each other can benefit us (see 1 Cor 13:1) and is something the world can see (John 13:34–35), so the different avenues of worship provide many blessings—not just to the worshiper, but possibly to the world. It could be that when we worship the one true God according to his multifaceted mode of worship, everybody benefits.

December 21

Understanding Worship

LIKE ANY SPIRITUAL EXERCISE, worship involves the use of the mind (or heart; 1 Cor 14:15; 2 Cor 9:7; Matt 15:9; 1 Cor 11:24). God's creation praises him (Ps 19:1–6), but it does not worship him from the heart as humans do. In the context of the use of tongues in worship (a gift that modern-day Christians do not have), Paul included other aspects of worship, such as singing and praying (something modern-day Christians do engage in), in terms of the mind: "What am I to do? I will pray with my spirit, but I will pray with my mind also; I will sing praise with my spirit, but I will sing with my mind also" (1 Cor 14:15; the Greek word translated "mind" again is in some other translations "understanding"). While worship is not a scholarly conference, such teachings remind us of the importance of the use of our mind in the spiritual exercise of worship. While emotions are also certainly involved in worship (Col 3:16), worship can serve to bring us closer to God, not only because of what we have felt in our heart, but because of what we have understood in our mind.

December 22

Be Angry, But

God permits many natural acts and emotions, as long as they don't corrupt us spiritually. This includes desires within marriage (1 Cor 7:5), other appetites such as hunger (1 Tim 4:3), and emotions such as anger. Thus, Paul stated, "Be angry and do not sin; do not let the sun go down on your anger" (Eph 4:26). This is not a green light for the destructive emotion of anger, but rather a reminder to choose the spiritual over the physical (Paul taught to put anger away, Eph 4:31). Some emotions and desires, such as worry and lust (Phil 4:6; Matt 5:28), again, are not permitted of the Christian (a guy once said to me that his wife actually told him "you don't worry enough"). An emotion like anger is going to happen; that is, it is natural. How it causes us to speak, act, or, otherwise, what it does to our health or, more importantly to our soul, is spiritual. And that's something else.

December 23

No Bitterness

MY LATE FATHER-IN-LAW USED to say that the trouble with being a sweet old man is that one first has to be a sweet young man. While some bitter flavors (such as lemon) can be pleasurable, the Christian is not to have a bitter disposition. Thus, Paul taught that the problem of bitterness, along with anger and other destructive emotions (see yesterday's "Daily"), is to be solved by putting it away: "Let all bitterness and wrath and anger and clamor and slander be put away from you, along with all malice" (Eph 4:31). Some things are incompatible in the heart and life of the Christian (such as falsehood and truth [Eph 4:25], and cursing and blessing [Jas 3:10]). The answer to the problem of bitterness is not, for example, to try to overcome it or ignore it; the goal for the heart of the Christian should rather be to eliminate it, like removing yeast from a household (Exod 12:15). By concentrating on our spiritual lives (Gal 5:22, including the sweet honeycomb of God's word, Ps 119:103) we can thereby produce the fruit of the Spirit, and remove the harsh taste of bitterness. We can't have it both ways.

December 24

Be Sure to Do

Usually in life we do things to get things done. One might also look at activity and physical accomplishments as a measure of a "successful" spiritual life, even though the outer display of our physical life is not always an indicator thereof (John 9:2–3). There are certain things we are obligated to do in the Christian life. While we need help with such things as carrying in the groceries, the One who created everything we can see and everything we can't see, does not need our help (Ps 50:12–13). Thus, when God calls on us to do something, there is surely a spiritual element to accompany the physical act; that is, such actions are intended for our spiritual good. Deuteronomy 8:1 reads, "All of the commandments which I am commanding you this day you are to be sure to do" (the phrase translated "be sure to do" is in Hebrew literally "keep to do"). To think of our tasks with a spiritual element could emphasize that they are not just for accomplishment, but to reinforce such spiritual qualities as motivation, determination, and commitment. To not only obey but to obey from the heart (Rom 6:17) will surely draw our heart closer to God's. Not just because we were active but because our heart made sure of it.

December 25

The Gift of God's Son

IT HAS BEEN OBSERVED many times that the celebration of Christmas today revolves around commercial activity. Not that this is necessarily wrong; and, I don't believe that recognizing the birth of Jesus is necessarily wrong. But it is important to remember why this Child was born. While Jesus went about doing good (Acts 10:38), including teaching (Matt 9:35) and miracles (Acts 2:22), the purpose of his life was the spiritual impact of his death on the cross. Thus, Paul said, "The saying is trustworthy and deserving of full acceptance, that Christ Jesus came into the world to save sinners, of whom I am the foremost" (1 Tim 1:15). Jesus' life and death was a manifestation of God's grace (Heb 2:9), inasmuch as the act of giving is a grace (2 Cor 8:1–6); and it is by grace that we have been saved (Eph 2:8–9). What more ultimate gift could one give than their only Son (John 3:16), and what more ultimate gift could one give than their life (John 15:13)? Jesus' life and death exemplified giving; and, it is by the gift of his death that we are blessed by the gift of his birth.

December 26

"The Knowledge of His Will"

IT IS HARD TO imagine being filled with any kind of knowledge (that is, it seems as if there is always more to learn). Yet Paul spoke of our being filled with the knowledge of the will of God: "And so, from the day we heard, we have not ceased to pray for you, asking that you may be filled with the knowledge of his will in all spiritual wisdom and understanding" (Col 1:9). While much of God's will can't be known (Matt 26:42; Acts 21:14), that which God would have us know of his will has been revealed to us through his word (1 Thess 4:3; Eph 5:17). To be filled with the knowledge of his will, therefore, would seem to be done by filling our head with his word. Surely if we do this we will, likewise, fill our heart with his will (John 7:17). Maybe if we so fill our head, the blessings of God will fill, even overflow, our heart (Ps 23:5).

December 27

Not You, But Me

MORE THAN ONCE JESUS said that what he came to do and say originated with his Father. For example, he said, "My teaching is not mine, but his who sent me" (John 7:16; also Matt 26:42). He also told the apostles that when they continue with his work, the reactions of the world will be a reflection of their attitude toward him, rather than them. Thus, he said that the world will hate them (John 15:18), and may or may not receive them (Matt 10:40) because they are working on behalf of him. Just as Jesus' ultimate purpose was to bring glory to God (John 17:4), so it can be comforting to know that when we live to bring glory to God (Eph 1:12), our "success" and "failure" in his work is a reflection not necessarily on us, but on the hearer's attitude toward his message (1 Cor 1:18). "For it is not you they have rejected, but me" (1 Sam 8:7).

December 28

Making Room for the Word

FREEDOM, AT LEAST IN one sense, is the result of something allowed as well as restricted (as seemingly embodied in the words of the American Constitution, "congress shall make no law..."). Physical freedom includes physical mobility. Spiritual freedom means one is not bound by the shackles of sin (Heb 12:1). That which provides spiritual freedom is the word of God (John 8:32), by its having a place in our heart. Jesus said to those who wanted to kill him, "I know that you are offspring of Abraham; yet you seek to kill me because my word finds no place in you" (John 8:37). The phrase "finds no place in you" is translated from one word in Greek, and contains a notion of having room, such as when things are not too crowded (Mark 2:2; John 21:25). In John 8, some Jews had believed him (v. 31); but their evident lack of completely accepting his teaching (a lack of truth) led to their wanting to kill Jesus. God does not impose his word or his will (Rom 10:21). But by our allowing God's word a place in our heart, so that it is not bound (2 Tim 2:9), we would then use it wherever we go (Deut 6:4–9), and not let other things crowd it out of our heart (Phil 4:6–8). We will thereby find ourselves free to move about—not necessarily physically, but spiritually.

December 29

The Best Use of Time

TIME IS ONE COST we can never replace. Life includes pleasurable things such as rest (Mark 6:31) and eating (1 Tim 4:4), as well as work (that is, it is not necessary that we work constantly). Yet, we have only one life; hence, it is wise to make the most of the time we have. Paul said, "Making the best use of the time, because the days are evil" (Eph 5:16). The Greek word translated "making the best use of" only appears here and in Gal 3:13 and 4:5 (both referring to Christ redeeming us from the law). In Eph 5:16, the word has to do with making the most of an opportunity. God gave us the gift of time (Gen 1:1), and invested in our redemption. We can't redeem ourselves, and we can't buy back, or store up, time (it is time that devours us[7]). One of the best uses to make of something as elusive as time is to make the most of it. It is going to slip away, and we may not get to do everything we would like in the time we are given. But, we can use every opportunity to bring glory to God (Eph 1:12).

---

7. Shakespeare, Sonnet 60.

December 30

Time Is Running Out

ONE OF MY LATE family members used to say, "If you're going to do it in [2024], you'd better hurry." When we speak of deadlines, we usually do so from the point of view of completing tasks, for such legitimate purposes as statistics or taxes. Paul again encouraged Christians to make the most of their time for a spiritual reason: "Making the best use of the time, because the days are evil" (Eph 5:16). The reason Paul gives for making the most of our time is because "the days are evil." We might know that the current year is about to come to an end, but even that is conditioned upon time continuing for the next day (we actually have no idea how much time we have). We do know that evil is persistent (1 Pet 5:8), that it can grow, but that it can be overcome (Rom 12:21). For these reasons we do good (Eph 2:10), and that with urgency. Not because the year is about to come to an end, but because it's good to.

December 31

Facing the Future

Facing the future is easier when we recall the promises of God. Times of transition, such as the New Year, can evoke positive feelings because they represent a blank slate, and, therefore, give us positive feelings with regard to what may be. The physical things that may happen to us in the coming year are, of course, yet to be seen. Yet God promises many spiritual things which can offer the Christian hope. Thus, Peter said God "will himself restore, confirm, strengthen, and establish you" (1 Pet 5:10). While the lessons contained herein are no doubt many, they include that God will make our spiritual life right in view of the past ("restore") as well as the future ("strengthen"). Like taking care of a tree by cleaning it, shoring up its base, and providing proper sustenance, by following God the Christian can be assured that God will help them in their spiritual life. Based on this promise the Christian will then, like a plant, have a future in which they flourish and grow (Ps 1:3; Gal 5:22–23), and can, therefore, face the future today with the hope God provides for the coming year.

Afterword

RECEIVING ANSWERS IN LIFE can be gratifying, especially when certain difficult questions arise. This means that it can, therefore, be good for questions to arise. It can be difficult, and at times seemingly impossible, to understand life. The pursuit of answers can, however, be an important part of a spiritual journey, possibly more so than arriving at the answer itself. Being given an answer is not the same as receiving an answer. That is, as many teachers know, simply giving someone an answer is no guarantee that the recipient is going to accept it or learn it. The Bible provides answers, yet its message needs to be received in order to do any good in the heart of the hearer (Paul commended the Thessalonians for receiving the message they heard, 1 Thess 2:13).

The written word is still important, even in today's digital age. God used to communicate in different ways (Heb 1:1–2), but his message today has been communicated through his Son. The natural world nonverbally testifies to God's existence (Rom 1:20), but his written word instructs us regarding his will. It is hoped that the present collection of written words is, in that regard, appropriate, to ultimately serve to point us to God's written word.

I have appreciated another opportunity to share a collection of biblical thoughts with you. As with my first book, *The Answer Is Spiritual*, this collection is presented with a similar purpose, that of motivating us to draw closer to God through a better knowledge of his word. Answers can be gratifying; questions can prompt us to look for answers which, if we embark upon a pursuit thereof, can take us on a spiritual journey through a process by which we grow spiritually by growing scripturally.

Index of Scripture

Genesis

1	69
1:1	364
1:4	111
1:10	344
1:26	175, 186, 320
2:2	162
2:7	340
2:16–17	180
2:18	168, 251
2:18–20	175
3	88
3:1–8	61
3:9–12	159
3:10	99
3:11	99
3:16	105
3:17–19	217, 310
4:3	249
4:3–8	249
4:4	191
4:5	212, 249
4:7	187
4:13	159
13:13b	156
18:22–33	156
20:12	323
21:11–12a	12
22:1–8	14
24:21	18
50:20	91

Exodus

8:10	81
9:34	227
12:15	35, 197, 358
13:3–7	277
13:6–7	197
20:6	125
20:7	125

Leviticus

10:1–2	330

Numbers

11:1	281
12	285
12:2	285
16:28	297
16:28–30	297
32:23	159

Index of Scripture

Deuteronomy

4:7	48
6:4–9	363
7:7–8	347
8:1	359
15:15	65
31:8	214
32:4	279

Ruth

2:5	173

1 Samuel

2:1	315
3:19	58, 122
8:7	362
15:22	111
16:6–12	300
16:7	12, 82, 227
17:26	95
17:45	334
17:47	334
21:10–15	52

2 Samuel

12:13	159
24:24	188

1 Kings

11:4	62
11:4–5	118
15:11	188
18:27	229, 285

2 Kings

4:9	101
14:3	188
18:21	144

Esther

4:14	23
6:1	308

Job

1–2	83
1:12	266
1:21	50, 59, 266
2:3	266
2:9	265
2:10	213, 265, 266
6:6	303

Psalms

1	120
1:1	51, 73, 306
1:2	51, 60
1:3	136, 366
1:4	60
1:6	56
2:1	60
4:8	52, 100, 217
6:5	68
9:1	72, 103
14:1	92
19:1–6	356
19:14	72
22:1	214, 285
23:1	328
23:4	114, 163, 209, 222, 273
23:5	219, 361
25:1	125
34:1	170
37:3	58, 86

Index of Scripture

37:4	61, 76, 90, 147, 152, 232, 288, 317, 339	119:105	73, 169, 171
		119:130	169, 171, 205
37:4–5	384	119:136	44
37:25	153	119:142	262
37:27	120	121:1–2	338
45:1	70	122:1	112
46:1	164	126:1	32
46:2	164	127:1	86
46:10	164	133	206, 329
50:11–13	93	133:1	261
50:12	16, 179, 188, 349	133:3	261
50:12–13	359	138:2	48, 119
54:6	111	139:7	99
61:1	285	139:7–10	244
63:4	155	139:10	99
73:28	130	139:11–12	69
78:13	173	142:1	67
91:5	273	142:2	67
96:9	82	142:5–6	67
100:2	315	145	196
101:1	201	145:1	11, 310
103:1	6	145:2	11
104:24	335	145:14–20	11
105:3b	53	146	196
107:1	269	147:1	82, 216, 355
108:1	20	149:3	339
115:17	155	149:4	339
117:1	30		
117:2	30	## Proverbs	
119:11	44	1:10–19	21
119:27	309	2:4	341
119:71	122	2:4–6	113
119:89	173	3:5	76, 317
119:93	308	3:5–6	18, 86, 142, 144, 241, 280, 334, 336
119:98	169		
119:99	169	3:5a–6b	123
119:100	169	3:6	73
119:103	358	6:17	72, 335

Psalms *(continued)*

6:19	261
14:12	61
14:34	156, 261
18:19	102, 290
22:6	5
23:23	298, 322

Ecclesiastes

1:14	28
9:10	64, 123
12:7	340

Song of Solomon

2:14	82

Isaiah

1:18	34, 96, 132
1:18 ASV	181
2:5	132
5:13	138
5:20	21, 23, 111, 124, 197, 291, 293, 321
7:9b	136
10:20	280
14:24	143
18:4	164
18:5	164
18:6	164
26:3	75, 128, 136, 172, 280
30:1	162
31:3	144
34:16a	195
40:28	343
40:31	84, 199, 250, 316, 325, 343
45:6	111, 124
45:7	8, 21, 69, 197, 205

50:4	187
53:5	127
53:6	183
55:6	53, 198
55:8	142
55:8–9	12, 139, 344, 351
55:11	173, 245, 253
59:1	97, 285, 290
59:15	193
64:6	82

Jeremiah

1:6	61
1:12	44, 95, 104
2:8	53
3:11	55
3:15	43
5:8	118
5:19	62
6:10	55, 58, 95
6:14	345
6:16	295
7:28	58, 286
8:8	70
8:11	128
9:2	86
9:3	74
10:23	61, 142, 327
16:12	81
17:1	70
17:5	76
17:14	77, 127
20:9	78, 180
25:9	144
29:11	60, 93
29:13	53
31:23	100
31:25	100

31:26	100	**Habakkuk**	
31:34	4	1:2–4	214
33:3	67, 80, 198	3:18	83
35:17	111		
36:23	108	**Malachi**	
36:24	108		
36:32	108	1	179
42:6	111	1:6	259
		1:6–8	259
Lamentations		1:8	35, 179, 212
3:41	125	2:17	343
		3:3	328, 336
Ezekiel		3:6	48, 198, 330, 349
3:1	104	3:10	220
3:3	104	**Matthew**	
29:6–7	76	2:1–2	352
		3:3	135
Daniel		3:8	117, 305
1:8	174	3:17	247
3:17–18	209, 222	4	260
3:18	114	4:1	113
8:12	58, 122, 286	4:1–11	41, 120, 187
		4:16	26, 88, 108
Hosea		5:1	318
4:6	193, 194, 258	5:6	160, 224
6:6	137, 138	5:11	52
13:6	47	5:13	156, 303
		5:14	156
Amos		5:16	33, 101, 148, 278
5:21	140, 339, 344	5:23–24	20, 77, 140, 272, 277, 305
5:21–22	272	5:28	357
5:21–24	330	5:44	296
8:11	43	5:45	121, 197
		6:1	274
Joel		6:9	116, 264
2:13	108	6:11–13	264

Index of Scripture

Matthew *(continued)*

Reference	Pages
6:19–20	98, 257
6:21	129
6:24	87
6:25	331
6:25–33	192
6:25–34	3, 73, 332
6:26	331
6:27	331
6:28	331
6:28–30	41
6:30	331
6:31	331
6:32	206, 335
6:33	94, 231, 232, 274, 314, 325
6:34	331
7:1	151
7:7	15, 113, 195
7:8	53
7:13–14	18
7:16	227, 314, 321
7:21	117, 118
7:21–23	321
7:22–23	111, 349, 354
7:24–27	74, 86, 91
7:26–27	353
9:4	8, 21
9:12	xi
9:13	137
9:28	80
9:29	80
9:33	313
9:35	360
10:28	133
10:34	128, 291
10:34–38	245
10:40	362
11:28–30	106, 132, 198, 217, 242, 246
11:30	84, 141, 288
12	138
12:7	39, 40, 43, 138, 158, 283, 309
12:25	261
12:30	124
12:36	148
12:37	158, 285, 335
13:30	139
13:44	171, 322, 341
13:44–45	298
13:52	295
14:19	269
14:28	13, 61
14:30	299
14:72	299
15:2	271
15:3	271
15:8–9	130, 131
15:9	62, 72, 339, 356
15:10	283
15:12	240, 279
15:16	306
16:8	96
16:9	230, 235
16:24	299
17:5	247
17:13	324
17:20	85, 225, 336
18:20	25, 92, 112, 168, 229, 244, 300
19:4	39, 90
19:26	198
20:1–16	141
21:16	90
21:18–19	253

Index of Scripture

21:18–22	90	9:23	336, 346
21:19	54	9:24	347
21:21	301	9:50	303
21:25	96	10:17–22	232
21:28–31	215	10:30	251
21:28–32	210	11:13–14	37
23:12	135, 223, 259, 300, 315	11:24	157, 222, 238
23:23–24	259	12:10	306
23:27	321	12:30	231
24:14–30	223	12:31	161, 236
24:35	17, 55, 58, 162, 172, 329	12:37	319
25:1–13	91	12:41–44	188, 196, 259, 287, 344
25:9	149	12:44	287
25:14	303	14:34	307
25:14–30	38, 161, 219	14:50	214
25:23	306	15:34	214
25:28	38, 219		
26:26	277		
26:39	14, 215, 221, 232, 297		
26:42	61, 143, 147, 157, 209, 256, 317, 318, 361, 362		

Luke

2:49	63
2:52	135
3:14	149
4:12	220
4:16	349
4:16–30	350
4:22	313
4:28–29	313, 319
5:21	96
6:12	307
6:20	52
6:26	296
6:38	80, 264
8:4–15	40, 55, 66
8:11	58
8:13	204
8:15	71
8:18	95, 158, 189
8:25	115, 306

26:56	214
27:46	214
27:50	67
28:18–20	168, 198, 214, 244, 251, 297, 324
28:20	99

Mark

1:7	117
1:41 ASV	248
2:2	363
2:8	96
4:24	95, 158, 189
6:31	33, 123, 168, 217, 242, 307, 364
8:21	90
8:34	299

Index of Scripture

Luke (continued)

9:23	299
10:26	40
10:27	40
10:28	40
11	126
11:1	212
11:8	126
11:22	334
11:24	81
11:25	81
11:26	81
12:9	299
12:15	56
12:18	135, 334
12:32	150
13:24	288
14:4	260
14:7	260
14:10	260
14:11	135, 142, 190
14:25–35	260
15:7	112
16:19	242
16:19–31	ix
16:25	314
16:29–31	ix
17:5	9
17:6	9
17:10	300, 315
17:11–19	19, 42
17:15	50
17:15–17	326
17:17	306
18	131, 290
18:1	290
18:1–8	109, 116, 335, 343
18:5 ASV	97, 126
18:8	39, 90, 257, 326
18:9–12	131
18:13–14	131
22:14–23	150

John

1:1	148, 172
1:5	17, 26, 203, 205, 278
1:11	165
1:12	195, 346
1:13	341
1:14	148, 172
2	178
2:15	178
3:1–10	253
3:10	39, 90, 306
3:16	83, 165, 196, 327, 360
3:19	205
3:19–21	296
3:20	101
3:20–21	88, 99
3:30	135, 190
3:36	354
4:21	112, 352
4:24	93, 103, 167, 174, 179, 181, 184, 191, 201, 234, 339, 344
4:35	1
5:28–29	163
5:39	195, 228, 346
5:45	345, 346
6	166
6:7	149
6:26	275
6:38	297
6:63	340
6:66–67	212, 308, 333, 350
6:68	51, 162, 166, 177, 215, 218, 275

Index of Scripture

7:12	291	15:13	327, 360
7:16	362	15:14	124, 251, 296
7:17	341, 361	15:18	362
7:18	341	16:1	240
7:24	37	16:13	7, 207
8	363	16:24	157
8:24	204, 283	17	255
8:31	363	17:4	362

8:31–36   350
8:32   26, 47, 106, 141, 142, 175, 180, 186, 193, 195, 246, 286, 298, 347, 363

17:17   xi, 17, 70, 119, 137, 162, 173, 193, 245, 286, 309, 313, 327, 329

8:33	323	17:20–21	28
8:34	106, 141, 186, 246, 288	18:13	304
8:37	363	19:11	133
9:2–3	359	20:22	348
9:4	297	20:29	157
10:10	123, 135, 153	21:25	363

Acts

10:28	33	1:25	34
10:28–29	172	2:22	360
10:29	49, 200	2:36–37	159
11:35	176, 320	2:37	108, 181, 204, 215, 218, 319
11:42	148, 229	2:38	181
12:3	224	2:40	66
12:32	150	2:46	307
12:35	203	2:47	251
12:36	346	4:12	293
12:43	101, 259	4:13	169
13:17	4, 68, 152, 324	5:1–6	272
13:34–35	355	5:1–11	103
14:1	12, 348	5:38–39	143
14:2	255	7:54	319
14:3	91	7:54–59	108
14:6	115, 119, 162, 186, 228, 275, 291, 293, 327, 351	7:54–60	350
14:15	121	7:57	308
14:26	7, 28, 207	8:27	310, 352
14:27	348		

Index of Scripture

John *(continued)*

8:30	39, 174
8:30–31	43
10:4	166, 247
10:15	110
10:38	21, 42, 360
13:15	57
14:15	215
15:39	182
17:2	96
17:11	83, 195
17:18	252
17:21	252, 330
17:27	53
17:30	258
17:32	308
17:32–34	40, 55, 224, 245
18:5	180
19:8	96, 181
20:5–7	244
20:6–7	150
20:7	229
20:28	274
20:32	60, 177, 189, 313
20:35	6, 16, 24, 170, 254, 264
21:13	114
21:14	61, 157, 318, 361
23:1	5
24:25	34, 108
26:18	26
26:28	181
27:23	299
28:26–27	41, 43

Romans

1:16	17, 37, 38, 70, 71, 113, 133, 152, 156, 171, 172, 173, 218, 224, 225, 226, 337, 347
1:17	276
1:20	235, 367
1:25	293
2:4	42, 80, 230, 304
2:4 ASV	23
2:5	98
3:23	34, 115, 141, 186, 210, 217
4:3	14
4:18	10
4:18–19	85
4:19	10
4:20	10, 226, 301, 302
5:1	52
5:3–4	133
5:3–5	292
5:4	176
5:10	124
5:12	272
6:1–2	19
6:2	163
6:17	37, 204, 350, 359
6:23	47, 242, 246
7:5	337
7:15	79
8:18	305
8:26	258
8:28	4, 12, 56, 73, 80, 121, 209, 216, 276, 346, 347
9:13	344
10:10	67
10:15	160
10:17	9, 10, 34, 39, 44, 47, 85, 191, 203, 226, 235, 245, 249, 276, 283, 347
10:21	363

Index of Scripture

12:2	180, 204, 268, 296, 312, 354
12:9	79
12:11	54
12:15	31, 176, 248, 320
12:19	183
12:21	1, 21, 22, 27, 42, 81, 120, 164, 183, 197, 200, 365
13:4	200
13:5	5, 211
14:21	240
15:4	104
16:25	29

1 Corinthians

1:2	25
1:3–4	177
1:10	261, 329
1:10–17	329
1:12	329
1:18	234, 282, 362
1:23	275
2:9	36
2:13	x, 148
2:14–15	51, 94
3:6	54
3:16	185, 237
4:2	38
5:9–10	40
6:7	183
6:19	33
6:19–20	354
7:5	357
9:10	316
9:27	288
10:4	279
10:12	49
10:13	58, 78, 207, 225, 311, 328, 336
11:1	210
11:17–21	20
11:20	92, 140, 221, 229
11:20–29	339
11:21–22	140
11:23	165, 324
11:23–29	30, 150
11:24	145, 179, 356
11:25	145, 355
11:25–29	239
11:26	355
11:27	57, 62, 77, 87, 117, 277, 305
11:28	145
13:1	72, 282, 355
13:2	71
13:3	24, 170, 297, 335
13:4	236
13:4–5	78, 248
13:4–8	327
13:5	6, 93, 151, 170, 213, 339
13:7	346, 347
14:15	72, 103, 174, 179, 259, 277, 282, 339, 356
14:23	300
15:1	165
15:20	163, 233
15:24	338
15:33	42
15:34a ASV	32
15:43	233
15:54–58	233
15:55	334
15:57	334
15:58	1, 66, 123, 146, 164, 213, 217, 250

Index of Scripture

1 Corinthians (continued)

16:2	38, 77, 170, 206, 221, 229, 239, 254, 310, 330
16:3	254
16:10	57

2 Corinthians

1:3–4	7, 207
2:11	321
2:14	224
3:5	219
3:14	57
4:12	337
4:13	148
4:14	19
4:15	19
4:16	10, 85, 190, 231, 237, 268, 295, 312
5:1	4
5:9	13
5:10	8
5:17	295
6:2	81
8	16, 254, 287
8:1–6	360
8:3	287
8:4	300
8:4 ASV	16
8:7	24, 54
9:6–7	188
9:7	179, 184, 339, 356
9:10	38, 219
9:15	165
10:12	210
11:14	350
11:14–15	296
12:7	149, 311
12:8	149, 207
12:9	149, 207, 222, 302, 311, 328
12:10	3, 122
13:5	210, 211, 220
13:8 ASV	17

Galatians

1:6–10	40
1:10	64
2:20	33, 329
2:20b ASV	77
3:13	364
3:27	82, 227
4:5	364
4:16	296
5:1	185, 260
5:6	337
5:9	35, 42, 81, 182, 272, 277
5:13	223
5:17	52, 56, 94
5:18	304
5:22	176, 294, 358
5:22–23	37, 56, 86, 89, 366
6:2	75, 251
6:5	75
6:9	42
6:10	63, 297

Ephesians

1:3	185, 200
1:12	42, 59, 101, 121, 155, 190, 362, 364
2:1	69, 163
2:2	337
2:8	47, 313
2:8–9	44, 86, 102, 360
2:9	305

Index of Scripture

2:10	63, 257, 297, 314, 321, 354, 365
2:12	316
3:4	218, 235
3:8	185, 202
3:14	203
3:17	203
3:18 ASV	203
3:19	202
3:20	9, 37, 38, 71, 80, 133, 167, 337
3:20–21	46
4:1	18, 73, 305
4:3	146
4:15	160
4:25	358
4:26	178, 332, 357
4:29	125
4:30	350
4:31	357, 358
5:2	224
5:11	26
5:14	32
5:15	187, 204
5:16	364, 365
5:17	181, 256, 361
5:19	67, 77, 206, 221, 229. 239, 339
5:22–6:4	161
6:10	1, 84, 226, 231, 238, 316
6:10–16	260
6:10–18	353
6:10–20	161, 209
6:11	49, 227
6:12	21, 94
6:14	289, 353
6:14–15	32
6:17	113, 260

Philippians

1:15	xii
2:3	223
2:5	31, 37, 175, 268
2:5–8	351
2:7–8	135
2:8	31
2:9	135
2:13	337
2:14	281, 285
2:15	281
2:21	232
3	233
3:2	274
3:3	135
3:8	190, 194
3:10	233
3:13	65
3:20	255
4:4	89
4:6	19, 153, 192, 331, 357
4:6–7	200, 204
4:6–8	363
4:7	107, 172
4:8	21, 41, 59, 60, 107, 114, 134, 154, 201, 236, 257, 353, 354
4:8–9	353
4:9	107, 154, 324
4:11	266, 342
4:11–12	19
4:12	294
4:13	2, 231
4:15–16	287
4:18	224
4:19	2, 56, 121, 149, 153, 185, 207, 219, 328

Colossians

1:9	361
1:9–10	256
1:11	225
1:13	196, 327
1:23	117
2:1	28
2:2	28
2:6	120
2:12	9
2:23 ASV	221
3:2	12, 33, 90, 106, 163, 236
3:3	33, 163
3:10	210, 312
3:12	227
3:16	206, 356
3:17	13, 64, 135, 222
3:18–4:1	161
3:22–23	160
3:22–24	354
3:23	64
3:24	64
4:5	18
4:6	148, 303
4:11	262

1 Thessalonians

1:8	25, 287
2:2	333
2:13	367
3:2	262
4:3	361
4:11	64, 288, 354
4:12	64
4:13	255, 316
4:18	7
5:4	203
5:7	217
5:7–8	69
5:11	151
5:17	25, 97, 109, 199, 229, 258, 307, 354
5:18	19, 269, 326
5:23	161, 340

2 Thessalonians

1:7	84, 217
1:8	195
2:14	121
2:15	271
3:2	96
3:2 ASV	34
3:10	219
3:15	41, 78

1 Timothy

1:15	360
1:20	350
2:4	252
2:5	352
2:8	125, 221, 239, 335
2:8 ASV	25
3:7	37
3:15	63, 286, 353
4:2	5
4:3	357
4:4	364
4:7	270
4:8	85, 251, 257
4:13	57, 221, 239, 274
4:16	66
5:6	186, 242, 246, 257
5:8	219, 232
5:25	101
6:4–10	219

Index of Scripture

6:6	294
6:8	149, 336
6:9	185, 246
6:10	64
6:12	289, 296, 333
6:17	153, 185
6:19	91

2 Timothy

1:9	121
1:10	155
2:2	271
2:4	326
2:7	235
2:9	108, 363
2:15	104, 160
2:22	120
3:2–4	37
3:5 ASV	37
3:7	83, 194, 202, 228, 252, 324, 330, 346
3:11	50
3:12	296
3:16	218
4:2	151
4:3	128
4:3–4	280
4:4	17, 26, 95, 215, 286, 293, 308, 323, 341

Titus

1:14	274
3:10	312

Philemon

15	137, 221
16	23

Hebrews

1:1–2	367
1:2	162
1:3	172, 173
2:9	360
3:7	162, 348
3:14	213
3:19	118, 146, 154
4:2	245
4:4	162
4:6	146
4:11 ASV	146
4:12	291, 296, 308
4:16	97, 116, 126, 157, 199, 264, 290, 335
5:7	167
5:8	152
5:11	95, 158, 160
5:12–14	39
5:14	260, 342, 346
5:14 ASV	270
6:11	54
6:12	158
6:18	198
6:19	91, 136
7:19	263
7:22	263
8:6	263
8:12	102, 230
9:27	61, 145, 163, 172, 237, 255
10:6	247
10:8	247
10:24 ASV	182
10:24–25	140
10:25	182, 217, 251, 310, 352
11:1	347
11:3	235, 347
11:4	191, 249

Hebrews (continued)

11:6	245, 247, 276, 334, 347
11:16	263
11:19	14
11:25	79, 288
11:36	263
12:1	250, 270, 288, 363
12:1–2	141, 217
12:2	166, 250
12:9	338
12:11	270
12:25	215
13:5	99, 149, 214, 294
13:5–6	48
13:6	170
13:8	48, 168, 198
13:9	44
13:9a ASV	47
13:15	67, 196, 344
13:21	196

James

1:3	211
1:6	47, 134, 136, 301
1:14	220
1:17	23, 304
1:25	210, 211
2:24–26	9, 15, 71, 94, 161
2:26	118
3:2–12	158
3:5–12	7
3:6–12	151, 238
3:10	189, 358
4:3	50, 59, 90, 109, 126, 232
4:7	120, 289
4:8	130
4:11	285
4:13–15	56
4:14	123
4:15	46, 90, 143, 147, 164
5:3	98
5:11	213
5:13	201
5:16	337
5:17	157
5:17–18	157

1 Peter

1:3	345
1:3–14	44
1:4	36, 102, 255, 347
1:6	208
1:6–7	220
1:7	211
1:7 ASV	208
1:13	91, 209, 345
1:16	335
1:18–19	35, 242
1:22	17, 89, 119, 272, 286, 295, 298
2:8	279
2:16	106, 223, 242, 246
2:19	243
2:21	307
2:24	159
3:10	123
3:10–11	267
3:10–12	294
3:11	27
3:14	348
4:1	91
4:11	275
5:6	135
5:7	3, 192

Index of Scripture

5:8	1, 22, 27, 164, 182, 187, 200, 204, 289, 321, 365
5:10	366
5:12	49
5:14	335

2 Peter

1	54
1:1	244
1:3	177
1:5	54, 154
1:5–9	68
1:8	54
1:10	146
1:11	154
1:12	65, 134
1:13	65, 68
2:14	270
2:22	350
3:8	69
3:9	148, 168, 350
3:10	64
3:11	61
3:14	146
3:16	40, 110, 158, 205
3:16 RSV	252
3:18	5, 29, 39, 60, 68, 84, 110, 152, 175, 181, 194, 195, 210, 253, 256, 258, 307, 342, 354

1 John

1:7	26, 168, 171, 205
7–9	247
1:9	58, 349
2:3 ASV	4
2:3–4	272
2:5	44
3:2–3	69
3:12	62, 187, 191
3:18	84
4:8	16, 93, 327
4:21	45
5:2	45
5:13	4, 43, 74, 220
5:14	73, 97, 147, 157, 199, 290, 317, 336

3 John

2	237
8	262
9	86

Jude

3	100, 162, 251, 273, 276
12	37, 43, 253
17	134
24	167

Revelation

1–2	28
1:16	142
2:10	22, 123, 334
2:10b	182, 213, 260, 296
3:16	247, 303
4:8	179, 310, 349
4:10	300
5:13	155
9:9–10	104
14:1	101
19:10	6, 93, 352
20	260
20:11–15	156
20:14	182
21:1–4	268, 295

Index of Scripture

Revelation *(continued)*

21:4	78, 102, 105, 207, 243, 255, 270, 332, 348	21:8	323
		21:10–21	36
		22:14	82
21:5	295, 330	22:18–19	44, 100

www.ingramcontent.com/pod-product-compliance
Lightning Source LLC
Chambersburg PA
CBHW071224230426
43668CB00011B/1299